A Death-Dealing Famine

The Great Hunger in Ireland

Christine Kinealy

Pluto  Press

LONDON · CHICAGO, IL.

First published 1997 by Pluto Press
345 Archway Road, London N6 5AA
and 1436 West Randolph, Chicago, Illinois 60607, USA

British Library Cataloguing in Publication Data
A catalogue record for this book is available from the British Library

Library of Congress Cataloging in Publication Data
Kinealy, Christine.
  A death-dealing famine: the great hunger
in Ireland/Christine Kinealy
    p. cm.
  Includes bibliographical references and index.
  ISBN 0-7453-1075-3 (hc)
    1. Famines—Ireland—History—19th century.   2. Ireland–
–History—1837–1901.   I. Title.   II. Title: Gorta mór.
DA950.7.K56   1997
941.508—dc21   96–49017
                                                        CIP

Impression: 99 98 97 5 4 3 2

Designed and produced for Pluto Press by
Chase Production Services, Chadlington, OX7 3LN
Typeset from disk by Stanford DTP Services, Milton Keynes
Printed in Great Britain

A Death-Dealing Famine

Contents

For Kieran, Siobhán and Arthur

Acknowledgements

The research and writing of this book has been made easier and more stimulating thanks to the support and encouragement of a number of people.

I am particularly grateful to Eileen Black, Seán Egan and Diana Newton for reading the text and offering valuable insights. Opinions, interpretations and mistakes are, however, my own.

Special mention is due to Don Mullan of *Cait*, whose knowledge and experience of contemporary famines has offered a special insight into Ireland's Great Hunger. Thanks are owed also to Gary White Deer of the Choctaw Nation and Gabriel Byrne for their creative inspiration and their company and sensitivity during the annual AFRI Famine 'walk' in Louisburgh.

I have benefited from discussions regarding the Famine with Patricia Brandwood, James Donnelly, Peter Gray, Patrick Hickey, Eamon Kirwan, Brian Lacey, Gerard MacAtasney, Frank Neal, Cormac Ó Gráda, Sean Sexton, Patrick O'Sullivan, Trevor Parkhill, David Sheehy and Roger van Zwanenberg.

The staff and archivists of the various record offices and libraries in Ireland, England and America have shown unfailing courtesy. The staff of the Maritime Archive in Liverpool and the National Library in Dublin deserve special mention.

Hugo Flinn kindly financed part of the research for this book. I am also grateful to the current Earl of Clarendon for permission to cite from the papers of his ancestor.

A number of close friends have played a valuable role in bullying, cajoling and encouraging me. They are Bernadette Barrington, Angela Farrell, Rita Rhodes, Rita Egan, Linda Christiansen and Val Smith. Additional support has come from John Archer, Cormac Behan, John Brandwood, Jenny Buelvas, Morag Egan, Laurie Feehan, Richie Gentry, Tina Hadlow, Bev Harrison, Jo Jones, Pat Jones, Geoffrey Keating, James Kelly, Noel Kissane, Stephen Lalor, Josie McCann, Chris Parker, Jean Parker, Ruth Peel, Christine Tant and Christine Yates.

My research has also brought me into contact with a number of of 'faminists' in America and I have been encouraged and enthused by Angela Power, Owen Rodgers, Eileen Crimmins, Aine Grealy, David Burke, James Gallagher, Patrick Campbell, James Mullin, Charlie Laverty, Stuart Healy, Rita Mullan and Father Sean McManus.

To my family a special debt is owed: to my Irish grandparents who never had a chance to be buried in the country of their birth, and to my parents, Andrew and Mabel, who first taught me to love Ireland. Thanks also to Patricia, Bob, Jane, John, Margaret, Carol and Michael.

Finally, but most importantly, I wish to acknowledge my gratitude to those who have lived with me during the writing of this book. My beloved Wicklow collie, Trot, has been my constant companion, listened to all my concerns, and agreed with all my conclusions. Siobhán and Kieran continue to make everything worthwhile. And Arthur, as ever, for his encouragement, insights and Belfast wit.

CHAPTER 1

The Great Hunger in Ireland.
Ideologies and Interpretations

The Irish Famine of 1845–52 was a defining event in the history
of modern Ireland. Yet until recently it has been the subject of
relatively little scholarly research, despite a rich resource of
contemporary evidence. Documentary evidence relating to the
Famine years is abundant and this has led some historians to
identify a historiographical silence from the 1930s to the 1970s.[1]
It is only in recent years that researchers have started to access these
sources and, as a consequence, more has been written to
commemorate the 150th anniversary of the Great Famine than was
written in the whole period since 1850. Despite this, the folk
memory of the Famine and popular interest have remained strong.

The relative absence of academic research arose partly from
ideological struggles concerning the nature and purpose of Irish
historical research during the period from 1845 to the present. Even
the designation of the Famine has been an area of debate. In
popular understanding 'The Great Famine' has become the most
common sobriquet for the years of devastation and destruction in
Ireland. Yet, 'The Great Hunger', 'The Great Starvation', 'The
Bad Times', 'God's Visitation', 'The Great Calamity', 'The Irish
Holocaust' and the Irish phrases 'An Gorta Mór', 'An Droch-
Shaoghal' and 'Bliain an Ghorta' are all ways of describing the same
event, and indicate differences of interpretation and emphasis.
Canon O'Rourke, in his early account of the Famine published in
1874, noted that during the course of the Famine, relief committees
and government officials avoided using the term 'famine',
substituting instead 'distress', 'destitution', 'dearth of provisions,
'severe destitution', 'calamity', 'extreme misery', and so on.[2] The
Irish phrase 'An Gorta Mór', meaning 'The Great Hunger', is
regarded by some as being an accurate description of years of
hunger, which were not simply caused by food shortages. For the
same reason, the use of the term 'famine' is disliked by a number
of nationalist commentators on the grounds that between 1845 and
1852, large volumes of food were exported from Ireland as thousands
died of starvation. For others, the word 'holocaust ' is too emotive
and ascribes too much culpability to the British government. The
word is also closely associated with the extermination of the Jews

1

by the Nazis in the twentieth century, although it was used by a number of nineteenth-century commentators when describing the Famine – Michael Davitt, for example, refers to it as 'the holocaust of humanity'.[3]

The historiographical silence and the language of denial employed both during and after the Famine are remarkable in view of the scale of losses suffered by the Irish people during the Famine years. Between 1846 and 1851, at least one million people died out of a base population of over eight million people. To this can be added the high mortality amongst emigrants, which may have accounted for a further 100,000 deaths. Furthermore, many of the survivors of the Famine years experienced shortened lifespans as a consequence of successive years of privation. Overall, the high population losses make the Irish Famine one of the most lethal in modern world history.[4] Even 150 years later, Ireland has not recovered demographically from the consequences of the Famine, and within Europe, Ireland is the only country to have a smaller population than it had in 1840. Psychologically, it is only beginning to be recognised that the scars left by this tragedy have been deep. It is only now, as Ireland emerges with a distinctive and positive identity within Europe, that Irish people throughout the world have been able to come to terms with the impact of these years and define what it means for their culture and history.[5]

In view of the enormity of the Famine and the significance of its legacy, the dearth of research until recently is even more surprising. Moreover, since the 1930s, and more overtly since the 1960s, scholarly research has been dominated by what is collectively referred to as a 'revisionist' interpretation of Irish history. At its heart this reinterpretation of Irish history aimed at being totally research-driven, objective and value-free. In regard to the Famine though, revisionism explicitly set itself in contrast to a 'nationalist' interpretation, which it viewed as politically inspired or judgemental, the antithesis of what the revisionists were trying to achieve.[6] In its more extreme form revisionism has gone down an overtly anti-nationalist path in its own values. These claims in regard to revisionist interpretations of the Famine have in turn been challenged.[7] Fundamentally, the concept of a value-free history, whilst noble in its intentions, is flawed in its execution. In striving for objectivity, that very purpose itself violates the concept, as the quest reflects the writer's own value-system and is set in the context within which the historian is writing. Hence, 'revisionism' in its attempts to demythologise Irish history in the middle years of the nineteenth century, and its conscious debunking of 'nationalist myths', imbued Irish Famine revisionists with a particular set of alternative values, which coloured their judgement on the sources and material. As Dr Malcy observed in relation to the revisionist debate, 'The "objective" historian sees identity as something that everyone else has too much of.'[8]

From the 1930s to the 1980s, when the revisionist approach was in the ascendant, only two major books were produced on the Famine. Yet whilst little original research was carried out during this period, a number of influential orthodoxies emerged. These shaped scholarly research on the nineteenth century, in which the Famine was given no special significance. At the core of the revisionist view of the Famine lay three main assertions: first, that the Famine was not a watershed in modern Irish history but merely an accelerator of existing trends; second, that in view of Ireland's large population and underdeveloped agricultural sector, a subsistence crisis was inevitable; and third, that, judged by the standards of the 1840s, the British government did all that reasonably could have been expected of it. Within this interpretation, suffering, mortality and blame were minimised, and the legacy of colonialism and the role of cultural stereotyping and racist attitudes were marginalised.[9]

The Irish Famine did not occur in a vacuum and it is better understood within the continuum of Anglo–Irish relations. Yet within revisionist interpretations, the political relationship between England and Ireland has been downplayed. In its more extreme form, this has resulted in an 'exculpation of imperialism' which has attempted to prove that there was 'no real design or evil intent' behind England's 'conquest, dispossession and cultural extirpation' of the native Irish.[10] The Act of Union of 1800 altered the political relationship between England and Ireland. At its core, however, the Union was essentially a device for controlling and regulating Ireland. Whilst the Union may have created a unified political machine based in London, the underlying colonial relationship between the two countries was still evident. The Famine provides compelling evidence of this inequality, for after 1847, the British government decided to throw the financial burden for Famine relief exclusively on Irish, not British, taxpayers.

Dr Brendan Bradshaw, in a controversial and debate-provoking article published in 1989, identified a gulf that had emerged between the revisionist interpretation of the Famine and the traditional nationalist understanding of this event.[11] Bradshaw may have overstated the polarities of this divide, and, since this article was published, much of the writing by historians has been clearly within the post-revisionist camp. Recent research is challenging not only the dominant revisionist viewpoint, but also a number of accepted canons of the nationalist interpretation. However, a number of key issues are still apparent within the revisionist/post-revisionist divide, although the most bitter disputes appear to be between non-historians.[12]

More recently, Bradshaw has refined his position. He continues to believe that as a consequence of their commitment to so-called value-free history, revisionists 'have not succeeded in recovering the actuality of the Irish historical experience' and thus 'have not been able to convince the Irish public at large about the authenticity of their depiction of the Irish past'. Bradshaw argues for a new way forward, based on rigorous research and a determination to revise myths or 'bad' history, but in which the historian is at the same time 'both committed and objective ... sympathetic and critical'.[13]

The origins of the revisionist/nationalist interpretations date from the Famine period itself, although the nationalist construction was given a sharper political focus in the latter decades of the nineteenth century. An early interpretation of the Famine, which many revisionists were later to restate, was provided by a key player in the British government's relief operations, Sir Charles Trevelyan, Permanent Secretary at the Treasury and commander-in-chief of Famine relief. At the end of 1847, Trevelyan declared the Famine to be over, despite the fact that 1.5 million people were still dependent on a minimal and punitive form of state assistance. As thousands of people continued to die in Ireland and evictions and emigration increased, a myth was simultaneously being created concerning the causes, impact and duration of the Famine.

In 1848, Trevelyan published his own account of Famine relief. This was the only written account of the Famine produced by a senior relief official. He employed a moral and providential framework in which to place the Famine, which he described as 'the judgement of God on an indolent and unself-reliant people', a people, moreover, who liked to 'make a poor mouth'. He further asserted that no government had ever done more to alleviate the suffering of its people.

In an effort to suggest empathy with the suffering Irish, Trevelyan, whose family came from Cornwall, described himself as a 'reformed Celt', which he contrasted with the 'unreformed' Celts in Ireland.[14] But Trevelyan's interpretation was scorned by many relief officials, including Clarendon, the Lord Lieutenant in Ireland.[15] A pointed criticism was made by George Poulett Scrope MP, who had opposed many of the government's policies in Ireland. He said of Trevelyan's book:

> A stranger to the real events of the last two hundred years might read through the whole hundred pages without ever finding out that during the 'Irish Crisis' several hundred thousand souls perished in Ireland of want, through the inefficiency of those 'colossal' relief measures.[16]

Trevelyan's interpretation, nevertheless, has been influential. A number of English and Irish historians have echoed some of his assertions regarding the causes of the Famine. For example, the English social historian G. M. Trevelyan stated that:

In Eighteenth Century Ireland the population rose even faster, from about one and a half millions to four millions. But social and racial characteristics were not favourable to economic change, and instead of industrial or agricultural revolution, there was chronic starvation and frequent famine among the potato-fed population, culminating in the disaster of 1847.[17]

A number of contemporary historians have viewed the Irish Famine as the realisation of a Malthusian prophecy or, in the words of the economic historian Peter Mathias, 'the fate predicted for it by Malthus'.[18] The eminent Irish historian Roy Foster described the Famine as a 'Malthusian apocalypse'.[19] Malthus himself showed little interest in the affairs of Ireland (until commissioned by the *Edinburgh Review* to do so) and was far more interested in the demography of Sweden and Norway.[20] As the Famine raged in Ireland, leading political economists and their disciples carried out ideological battles in the lecture theatres, journals and even pulpits and schoolrooms (political economy was part of the national school curriculum in nineteenth-century Ireland) of the United Kingdom.[21] Archbishop Whately, W.E. Hearn and William Neilson Hancock, amongst others, argued that the economic development of Ireland required a reduction in population and an increase in capital investment. Despite mass mortality, they also doggedly argued for less government intervention and more free trade. Overall, 'the Famine crisis made it all the more important that the principles of political economy should be applied to Ireland. Any relaxation, however nobly motivated was a "killing kindness" ... for protectionism.'[22] The relationship between population, poverty and potatoes superficially was an attractive one, but was greatly overstated. However, one consequence of the high dependence on the potato of a large section of the Irish people was that on the eve of the Famine, Ireland had one of the tallest, healthiest and most fertile populations in Europe. At the same time, and in contrast to popular perception, alongside the potato economy a large commercial corn sector existed, which on the eve of the Famine was exporting sufficient corn to England to feed 2 million people, thereby earning Ireland the title of 'the granary of Britain', whilst it was being simultaneously depicted as a peasant economy.

The scale of the tragedy of the Famine makes it difficult to depict or understand on either a national or an individual level. Writers who have attempted to convey this horror have been criticised for not being sufficiently clinical and detached in their approach. Hence, Cecil Woodham-Smith's popular interpretation *The Great Hunger. Ireland 1845–49* (first published in 1962) was dismissed by one of the doyens of Irish history, F.S.L. Lyons, as being too 'emotive'.[23] Woodham-Smith's work was further marginalised and ridiculed by the academic community in Ireland: in 1963 a university undergraduate examination paper asked students to discuss the proposition: *The Great Hunger* is a great novel'.[24] A number of years later, in a provocative, if ironic, essay entitled *We are all Revisionists Now*, Roy Foster categorised Woodham-Smith as a 'zealous convert'.[25] These comments set the tone for the teaching of the Famine to a generation of undergraduates. However, they did not deter the general public from reading Woodham-Smith's publication, which ensured that *The Great Hunger* became one of the best-selling history books of all time. And today scholars are more willing to acknowledge the contribution of Woodham-Smith to the historiography of the Famine.

In contrast, the various revisionist interpretations have, in general, avoided the central issues of responsibility, culpability and blame. Within this context, the involvement of the British government is pivotal, although the roles played by landlords, merchants, local shopkeepers, public opinion, the press, the Catholic Church, the Irish nationalists and Irish taxpayers are also important. As more research is carried out on these groups, a more textured and nuanced view of the Famine will emerge, although a number of core questions (and possibly answers) will remain.

The issue of responsibility is perhaps the most clear-cut. One consequence of the Act of Union of 1800, was that Ireland lost its own parliament in Dublin and thereafter sent 100 MPs to the Parliament in Westminster. The Irish MPs, even following Catholic Emancipation in 1829, were predominantly Protestant and landlords who did not pursue an obvious 'Irish' interest, but followed the traditional Whig/Tory division of British politics. Daniel O'Connell and his supporters were an exception, although traditionally they allied themselves with the Whig Party. However, when the potato blight first appeared in Ireland, O'Connell was already old and weak. He died in 1847 en route to Rome, having left Ireland at the height of the distress. An uprising by a group of radical nationalist known as Young Ireland early in 1848 (which can be viewed as a part of the European-wide 'year of revolutions'), found little support within Ireland. However, their rebellion served to harden attitudes within the British Parliament and press towards the protracted Famine in Ireland. Although insignificant at the time, Young Ireland's uprising left a legacy of nationalist writings, including John Mitchel's oft-quoted accusation that 'the Almighty, indeed, sent the potato blight but the English created the Famine'.[26]

Throughout the course of the Famine, all legislation and policy formulations emanated from Westminister. Advice from the relief commissioners in Dublin, and the increasingly sympathetic interventions of Lord Clarendon, the Lord Lieutenant of Ireland after 1847, were ignored. The British government in the 1840s was by modern standards an undemocratic and unaccountable institution. Although the Reform Act of 1832 had extended the franchise, it was only to the propertied upper middle classes, whose main concerns in the 1840s were ending trade protection, cutting taxes (especially the hated income tax, from which Ireland was exempt) and achieving a return to cheap government. Their opinions found both an outlet and a coherence in the columns of the influential *The Times*, which argued that money spent on Irish relief was money wasted. The rest of the population – the majority – remained outside these debates. For the most part, they were disenfranchised and, given the high rate of illiteracy, probably uninformed about the situation in Ireland. The draconian 'new' Poor Law of 1834 had demonstrated the anti-poor attitude of the ruling classes. The pitilessness of life in England was apparent from the contemporary writings of Charles Dickens, Frederich Engels and Elizabeth Gaskell, amongst others, and the short life expectancy in the major industrial towns. However, as the Irish Poor Law of 1838 (and its amendment in 1847) demonstrated, there were a number of important differences regarding the treatment of pauperism in England and in Ireland, the Irish Poor Law being more inflexible and parsimonious than its English counterpart. These differences were exacerbated during the Famine crisis, begging the question whether such scenes of suffering and such mortality would have been tolerated in England. The duality of approach was clear to a Committee of Inquiry appointed in inquire into the continuation of high levels of mortality in County Clare. They concluded that:

> Whether as regards the plain principles of humanity, or the literal text and admitted principle of the Poor Law of 1847, a neglect of public duty has occurred and has occasioned a state of things disgraceful to a civilised age and country, for which some authority ought to be held responsible, and would long since have been held responsible had these things occurred in any union in England.[27]

The ability of the British government to alleviate the impact of six successive years of potato blight – including the total harvest destructions in 1846 and 1848 – has also been questioned. There is no doubt that the scale of the shortages that confronted the government and private relief agencies was unprecedented. For this reason a number of historians have suggested that the role of the government should be viewed in a 'sympathetic light'.[28] At the same time, it is suggested, the government was itself constrained by various ideological and economic doctrines, most significantly its reluctance to interfere with the sanctity of the marketplace. In this context, the decision of the British government not to import or distribute food after 1846 becomes more understandable. Intervention, they argued, would have upset the corn merchants and the equilibrium of the market. Thus, the historian Mary Daly is able to argue that:

> Criticism is frequently voiced of the failure of the British government to directly intervene in the food market that year [1846], but the sheer size of the task and the fact that it would undoubtedly have led to a boycott of the food trade by private traders made such an action of limited effectiveness.[29]

There is no doubt that after the potato failure in 1846 a high level of intervention would have been necessary to compensate for the food shortages. However, the resources available to the British Empire were massive. Furthermore, ports in Ireland were highly accessible thanks to developments in steam shipping, road and rail transport. Although the corn harvest throughout Europe had been poor in 1846, the United States had enjoyed a bumper harvest and was only too happy to export its surplus to Europe. Nevertheless, high freight charges and legislation, which stated that goods coming to the United Kingdom had to be carried in British vessels, restricted the amount of food that was available to Ireland and directly constrained the free movement of food supplies.[30]

Britain's willingness to intervene in the marketplace when it chose to do so, unhampered by ideological or moral constrictions, is also apparent. For example, Britain went to war with China (1839–42) to force it to accept Britain's trading policies, including the sale of opium to the Chinese population. Within Ireland, in the decades following the Union, the British government intervened on many occasions to import food during periods of shortages, including in 1817–18, 1822, 1830 and, most successfully of all, in 1845. Although the writings of Adam Smith and Edmund Burke were selectively quoted to justify the policy of non-intervention, especially after 1846, the authors' acknowledgement that economic principles were secondary to the moral imperatives of governments to alleviate the suffering of their people in periods of famine was generally overlooked. Moreover, the flexibility which the British government demonstrated in dealing with distress in England (for example, the Outdoor Relief Act in 1842) was not extended to Ireland. Finally, there is no evidence or precedent to suggest that Irish corn merchants would have boycotted the trade if the government had intervened in 1846, although there is no doubt that they preferred to have a monopoly of the corn trade. Again, there was a precedent for such intervention. During the food shortages of 1782–84, the Irish government intervened to restrict exports of food by closing the ports. They simultaneously offered merchants a bounty for importing additional foodstuffs into the country. Whilst the corn merchants did not like this intervention, they did not boycott the trade, nor did they suffer significant financial losses. More importantly, this policy minimised the impact of the food shortages and the consequent suffering in Ireland.[31] Even by the standards of the eighteenth century, the actions of the British government in the 1840s could be seen as short-sighted and ineffective.

After 1846, the decision by the government not to close the ports to export of food allowed Irish merchants to seek markets where prices were highest; this inevitably meant those outside of Ireland. This led to Mitchel's claim that more food was continuing to leave Ireland than was coming into the country. By the spring of 1847, as a number of historians have been keen to point out, more food was coming into Ireland than was being exported, although given the climate and trade cycle of Ireland such an imbalance is hardly unexpected. Moreover, this assertion overlooks the fact that during the winter months of 1846–47 there was a starvation gap in Ireland which the British government failed to address.[32]

During the winter of 1846–47, the rise in mortality was not just the result of the scarcity and high price of food. During these months, relief was dependent on undertaking hard, physical labour on public works schemes. Wages were paid according to the amount of labour performed, which put those who were already weak or debilitated at a disadvantage. When this combined with numerous bureaucratic controls, dishonesty, incompetence, low wages and unusually cold weather conditions, the outcome was disastrous. Overall, the public works were intended to be punitive, reflecting the ideological concerns of the ruling classes, rather than meet the needs of a starving and debilitated people.

Ironically, the public works were the single most expensive item of Famine expenditure by the British government, and their expense and unmanageability resulted in a further change of policy in the summer of 1847. Soup kitchens were opened throughout Ireland to distribute free food. This development was important for two reasons. For the first and only time during these years, the government tackled the problem of hunger directly, without imposing a test of destitution on the people, thus giving practical considerations priority over ideological ones. Second, at the peak of this scheme, over 3 million people were receiving free rations of food every day (even if it was of low nutritional value) demonstrating the logistical and administrative capability of the government to provide relief on a massive and unprecedented scale. This brief episode singularly undermines the notion that the British government did not possess the ability to relieve such a mass of destitution.

If the British government had the capability to intervene in this Famine, why did they not do so? Was the starvation of Ireland's masses a wilful act, a neglectful one or a careless one? It was, in fact, probably none of these. The British government had identified a number of critical and seemingly intractable problems with the Irish economy in the previous two decades. The population was immense and vast numbers were poor and dependent upon a single crop, the potato. The potato enabled them to maintain (allegedly) a lazy and indolent lifestyle: there was no incentive for the Irish people to modernise their agriculture or their economy. For government officials and political economists, who believed in the sanctity of the free market, this was a hard pill to swallow. Intervention in the Irish economy seemed to be the only way to change this state of affairs. When the Famine did come, many members of the ruling elite saw it as a chance for the economy (belatedly) to achieve its natural balance: to do any more than the minimum to alleviate the starvation would deprive Ireland of the opportunity to achieve the right balance and to modernise.

In reaching an understanding of how the government and its officials reacted to the Famine it is essential to appreciate that this whole approach and ideology informed the judgements and choices of these people. This was simultaneously reinforced by class and cultural analyses of the Irish 'problem', which suggested that peasant and landlord alike needed to be reconstituted. Further subtleties and nuances of understanding are reached in the context of the ruling elite's prevailing and variable religious and racial prejudices. At the same time, the human suffering caused by the Famine resulted in quite different reactions from people from the same background – for example, Edward Twistleton resigned from his post as Chief Poor Law Commissioner in protest at how little was being done, whilst Charles Trevelyan, Secretary at the Treasury, increasingly supported a *laissez-faire* approach as the best course for Ireland (and, of course, for Britain also).

The question of culpability remains the most controversial aspect of the Irish Famine. In a number of early accounts of the Famine, including Edwards' and Williams' publication, the central issues of mortality and culpability were avoided, yet this publication won far more academic plaudits than Woodham-Smith's book. The recent willingness to tackle these issues again has received most impetus from non-historians, or historians from outside Ireland.[33] Furthermore, the issue of blame, especially in regard to the role of the British government, has been increasingly politicised since the late 1960s, coinciding with the latest rounds of 'Troubles' in the north of Ireland. Historians who have been critical of the British government have been accused of having a 'nationalist' agenda or, more damningly, of giving 'ideological bullets' to the Irish Republican

Army.[34] Within this context, the Famine has become an intellectual minefield and this has resulted in a form of self-imposed censorship by Irish historians. Thus the significance of the Famine in the development of modern Ireland has been frequently suppressed.[35] The revisionist interpretation, by 'playing down' the Famine in all its aspects, led the way to an accommodation with Britain and a simultaneous softening of the colonial relationship (which was frequently brutal) between the two countries. Moreover, a number of non-historians have cited anecdotal evidence or used emotive arguments to suggest that any debate on the Famine is furthering the cause of Irish Republicanism.[36] Within this highly charged political climate current ideological concerns were given priority over informed historical debate.

A further myth about the Famine, and one that again has its roots in the event itself, is the widespread belief that there was no Famine in Ulster.[37] Ulster, unlike the rest of Ireland, contained many Protestants. Moreover, Belfast and its hinterland was regarded as the industrial heartland of the country. The impact of the potato blight on this province has largely been ignored by historians, and for Unionists this has contributed to a reaffirmation of the existence of 'two Irelands'. However, rural poverty in Ulster had many parallels with poverty elsewhere. There was also high dependence on the potato, the population growth was rapid and competition for land was intense. By the 1840s, in fact, County Armagh was the most densely populated county in Ireland and many of the poor landless labourers were Presbyterians or members of the Church of Ireland. The potato blight first appeared in Ulster in September 1845 and it reappeared in an even more virulent form in 1846. In 1846–47, the blight coincided with a bad oats harvest and a recession in the linen industry. The resulting destitution in parts of Ulster, even in Belfast itself, was as harrowing as in the west of the country.

During the Famine years, mortality in Ulster doubled and the population dropped by an average of almost 20 per cent. The number of evictions quadrupled. These events cut across religious divides, and local research has revealed that in some areas mortality was highest amongst non-Catholics.[38] In many ways, therefore, the Famine was a major blow to the Act of Union, even for those people who had hoped to gain most from it. Furthermore, after 1847, the issue of imperial responsibility for financing relief was abandoned when the tax burden was placed exclusively on Ireland. This distancing was more apparent after 1849 when a new tax was imposed on the east of Ireland to subsidise areas in the west. The Protestant taxpayers in the north responded, not by questioning the purpose of the Union, but by attacking the poor in the west of the country for making such an imposition necessary. This was evident in the objections to the new taxation on the grounds that the northern taxpayers would be 'keeping up an army of beggars, fed out of the industry of Ulster'.[39] Religious, economic and cultural superiority fused as the Famine provided an opportunity for increased sectarianism and polarisation within Ireland rather than political unity.

The centenary of the Great Famine did not pass unnoticed, despite coinciding with the end of the Second World War in Europe. It resulted in a 'false start' in reassessing the Famine years. First, the Irish Folklore Commission circulated a questionnaire on the Famine which was preserved and provides a rich if underused source of Famine memories. Second, Eamonn de Valera, who was then Taoiseach, was instrumental in commissioning a comprehensive academic publication on the Famine. Despite providing a generous grant for the research and publication of this work, the Famine book took almost twelve years to appear and was far less substantial than what had been commissioned. Instead of being a comprehensive overview of the Famine, it was reduced to a fragmented collection of essays, titled *The Great Famine. Studies in Irish History*.[40] De Valera, and even the editors themselves, were disappointed with the final outcome.[41] More significantly, a number of key issues were avoided, notably the questions of mortality and culpability, whilst the human dimension of the tragedy was minimised. One chapter which had been written on 'English Public Opinion' was dropped as it was disliked by one of the early editors. The time lag also contributed to an uneven approach and layout. For example, Sir William MacArthur's excellent chapter on the medical aspects of the Famine was published without comprehensive footnotes – one of the editors apparently having lost them in a London taxi.[42] Overall, the failure of professional historians in the 1940s to confront the great tragedy of modern Irish history in the writing of *The Great Famine* meant that an opportunity was lost, and remained lost for a further generation. Overall, the publication was, in the words of one its editors, 'dehydrated history'.[43] It was left to Woodham-Smith to fill part of the vacuum, although the international popular success that she enjoyed may have contributed to her marginalisation by many academic historians.

The 150th anniversary of the first appearance of potato blight in 1845 has created a renewed popular and academic interest in this topic and has prompted a reassessment of the key issues. Recently, a multidisciplinary approach has emerged in relation to the Famine and it has started to attract the international attention of folklorists, geographers, demographers, linguists and political activists, together with specialists in nutrition, disease, gender issues, colonial histories, emigration and Third World studies. The wide geographic spread of this interest reflects in part the Irish diaspora, but has also captured a more general attention to the history and culture of Ireland.

Whilst there is no doubt that the 'silence' about the Famine has been broken, already the new research has demonstrated that there is still much to learn about the Famine, especially at the local community level. Historians are beginning to look at the impact of the Famine on the 'winners' – the small minority of people who benefited from the dislocation. These included the merchants who obtained high profit margins in 1846–47, mostly by seeking markets outside of Ireland, and farmers who benefited from the exodus from the land and the availability of cheap property. A long-term impact of the Famine was that it contributed to the creation of a large-farmer/grazier class. These new agricultural masters proved to be no more sympathetic than the landlord class which they replaced.

The re-emergence of interest in the Famine is also forcing a re-evaluation of the nationalist version of the Famine. The traditional and popularly accepted interpretation of the Famine was shaped in the second half of the nineteenth century and was constructed largely by Irish nationalists who were living outside Ireland.[44] During the course of the Famine Irish nationalists paid relatively little attention to the suffering of the poor Irish, but focused instead on the ideological battles within the different factions of the movement. Thus, in 1847, 'the participants and the issues remained almost entirely divorced from the realities of the starvation and the death'.[45] The Young Ireland uprising of 1848 was primarily a middle-class patriotic struggle, which lacked popular support. Mitchel gave it a wider justification by arguing, 'better that men should perish by the bayonets of our enemy than by their laws'.[46] Subsequent writings and interpretations also gave it a greater political significance than it enjoyed at the time within Ireland. Within Britain, its impact was important as it shaped both political and popular discourse and ensured that British intervention was viewed against a backdrop of Irish ingratitude and rebellion.

Many of the leading post-Famine writers had experience of personal suffering during the Famine years. John Mitchel was imprisoned then transported for his part in the 1848 uprising; Michael Davitt's family were evicted from their home in Mayo in 1850; and O'Donovan Rossa's father died whilst employed on the public works and he himself was a survivor of Famine fever. These experiences would have found resonance with many of their readership, especially those amongst the Irish diaspora whose recollections of Ireland had left tragic and bitter memories. Consequently, they would have been receptive to this type of interpretation.

Within the nationalist sphere, there are a number of differences in perceptions and emphases. The concept of blame – the *bête noir* of the revisionist camp – is readily and variously attributed to the

British government, the 'English' Queen Victoria and the Irish landlords. Such easy and obvious targets of opprobrium were challenged by revisionist historians. Postrevisionist writing has tended to seek out the nuances of response within these groups. In the nineteenth century, a number of radical Irish nationalists, including Mitchel and Davitt, identified other targets of blame, the constitutional nationalists (especially Daniel O'Connell) and the Catholic Church, both of whom undermined the resistance of the Irish people and urged them to accept the status quo.[47] However, the criticism of the Catholic Church and the constitutional nationalists did not linger in the public consciousness and, as the nineteenth century progressed, the British government and Irish landlords, aided and abetted by Queen Victoria, were identified in the nationalist memory as the real villains of the Famine years.

An integral component of the nationalist interpretation has been the continuing controversy over the issue of the export of food. The images provided by John Mitchel of this trade have been both enduring and moving; and he repeatedly made the point in his post-Famine writings that 'a government ship sailing into any [Irish] port with Indian corn was sure to meet half a dozen sailing out with Irish wheat and cattle'.[48] Although the statistics used by Mitchel and many other nationalist writers vary greatly and tend to oversimplify the quantities involved, the underlying principle is correct – the demands of the commercial sector were given priority over the needs of a starving people. Economic imperatives triumphed over humanitarian concerns, regardless of the cost in human lives. The fact that contemporary politicians and political economists saw this suffering as part of the price to be paid for Ireland's economic regeneration may have made this pill more unpalatable. Throughout the course of the Famine an intellectual elite viewed Ireland as 'a diseased body, in need of the strong, even harsh medicine of political economy, which was seen as all the more effective for being unpalatable'.[49] The passionate rhetoric of the nationalist writers may have provided a timely juxtaposition to overt indifference to the unfolding of such an immense human tragedy.

The writings of the Irish nationalists were further reinforced as they closely complemented the oral folklore of the Famine. Until recently historians, especially revisionist historians, have been wary about using written or oral memories of the Famine, believing that they would be too personal and too subjective. In the introduction to the Edwards and Williams volume, they state that they were going to avoid relying on 'the political commentator, the ballad singer, and the unknown maker of folk-tales'. However, as recent research has demonstrated, the folk history of the Famine can sharpen and give depth to both nationalist and revisionist interpretations of it.[50] Furthermore, these recollections demonstrate that the concerns of the people were with the immediate need for food, money or employment, rather than with the high politics of decision-making taking place in Dublin and London. The political and ideological framework of the Famine experience was provided by those who possessed a more overt political agenda.

The idea that the Famine was 'a visitation of God' – which emerges from both contemporary accounts and in the folk memory of the Famine – was refuted by nationalist writers. Throughout the Famine British politicians and paupers alike linked the food shortages with providentialism. The nationalist construct of the Famine challenged this viewpoint. O'Donovan Rossa believed that England had 'blasphemously charged God Almighty with the crime', which rightfully should have been laid at their door; Davitt echoed this view when he referred to this interpretation as a 'horrible creed of atheistic blasphemy'.[51] During the Famine years, a number of Evangelical Protestant groups used the excuse of providentialism to proselytise starving Catholics.[52] One journal, the *Achill Missionary Herald*, claimed that God was punishing the Irish for the 1845 Maynooth Act which provided a grant 'to endow a college for training [Catholic] priests to defend and practise and perpetuate this corrupt and damnable worship in this realm', whilst a religious tract written in 1847 claimed that 'in the heartrending scenes around us do we witness punishment for national idolatry'.[53] Although the success of the proselytisers was limited, the fact that it happened at all left a further legacy of bitterness and anger that God was invoked in such a cynical manner.

The recovery of the past, especially such a painful past, has been regarded by some as part of a 'healing' process in Ireland. This throws a great responsibility on historians and researchers, especially those who consciously allow current political concerns to constrain and shape their interpretation of the past. The recent revival of interest in the Famine period will undoubtedly throw up new challenges and insights regarding Ireland's greatest social catastrophe. The revisionist interpretation, which has so long dominated academic writing, is clearly being overtaken by interpretations which have more in common with the traditional nationalist perspective on the Famine. At the same time, some of the wilder claims of the nationalist writers have in turn been challenged. Whilst the old orthodoxies are being questioned or reworked, and fresh research, especially at the local level, is providing an ever more complex and subtle understanding of the events of the Famine years, fresh myths and orthodoxies are emerging. New methodologies, new orthodoxies and new interpretations, however, should not be allowed to disguise the fact that a truly terrible tragedy occurred at the heart of the richest and most powerful Empire in the world, and that much of this suffering resulted from ideological, political and commercial constraints, rather than the simple fact of a potato blight in Ireland.

CHAPTER 2

'A State of Degradation'.
Pre-Famine Ireland

Ireland's political involvement with England has its roots in the twelfth century, but expansion of English control in Ireland took place over several centuries. The process was sporadic and piecemeal, reflecting the personal interest of individual monarchs. The Protestant Reformation of the sixteenth century, however, was not embraced by the indigenous population of Ireland and resulted in a shift in the relationship between the two countries. Ireland was viewed no longer as a source of economic wealth and plentiful land, but was now seen as a highly dangerous security threat to the interests of her neighbour.

Initially, colonialism brought some benefits to Ireland, but increasingly it took place at the expense of the indigenous population, who became dispossessed or marginalised. This was frequently achieved through brutal methods, which left a bitter and enduring legacy. At the same time, various items of legislation, including the Penal Laws, codified the denial of the basic civil and religious rights of the majority of the Irish people. In 1800, the political relationship changed again when the Act of Union resulted in the absorption of the Irish parliament into the British parliament. The promise that Catholic Emancipation would follow was not kept. This contributed to the rise of a mass movement, led by Daniel O'Connell, initially to achieve Catholic Emancipation, but subsequently to repeal the Union. It also meant that the Union was created on a foundation of distrust.

By the 1840s Ireland was widely regarded as being poor, overpopulated and too dependent on a single crop, the potato. Yet the Irish economy was diverse and contained both a commercially successful linen industry and a substantial grain export trade. Also, whilst the Irish peasants were materially poor, their diet was highly nutritious and they had easy access to plentiful shelter and fuel. Culturally too, their lives were rich.

The Irish Famine was not inevitable. It was triggered by a potato blight which was unprecedented in its severity and duration. The blight occurred at a time when there was a widespread acceptance within the British government that Irish society needed to be restructured and her economy modernised. The Famine became an important tool in the regeneration of Ireland.

The Political Background: Dispossession and Disunity

Ireland's political association with England dates back to the twelfth century. Initially, it was prompted by a conflict between native Irish kings, which resulted in the overthrow and exile of Diarmaid MacMurrough, King of Leinster. Diarmaid sought support for his cause from the King of England. Henry II was reluctant, however, to become involved in a domestic Irish squabble. Yet Henry was not totally disinterested in Irish affairs; he had considered invading Ireland in 1155 and had gone so far as to seek the permission of the Pope for his action. In 1169, it was left to a Norman warrior, Richard de Clare, Strongbow, to lead an armed force to Ireland and restore Diarmaid to his throne. In return, Strongbow received Diarmaid's daughter, Aoife, in marriage and the promise of the kingdom of Leinster on Diarmaid's death. As a consequence of Strongbow's success, Henry II felt obliged to ensure that an independent Norman kingdom was not established on the border of his empire. Henry visited Ireland in 1171 and thus began the subjugation of Ireland by the English Crown. This brought Ireland into the Norman empire and helped to complete a programme of westward expansion by the Norman conquerors.[1] For the Irish, it marked the beginning of a new political relationship, which would prove to be both enduring and painful.

Although the Normans came to Ireland as conquerors, they were gradually absorbed into native Gaelic society and joined the Irish people in their struggles against subsequent English invaders. The descendants of the Normans who were involved in this process of 'gaelicisation' became known as the 'Old English'. A number of anti-Irish pieces of legislation were passed, including the notorious Statutes of Kilkenny (1366), which attempted to proscribe the use of the Irish language, customs and laws, but it was not until the reign of the Tudors (1485–1603) that a more concerted and systematic series of attempts was made to complete the colonisation of Ireland.

From a legal standpoint, the most significant stage came in 1541, when the Irish Parliament enacted that the English monarch Henry VIII should also be King of Ireland. Henry had felt this was necessary to tighten his grip on his Irish lands following his split with Rome, and to defend the Tudor state from any threat from Catholic Ireland. This continued to be a preoccupation throughout the sixteenth century, coupled with an effort to concentrate political power in the hands of a new English population 'planted' in Ireland.

The purpose of the 'Plantation' was to displace from the land disloyal Irish Catholics and replace them with loyal English men. This policy enjoyed little success until the beginning of the seventeenth century, when Elizabeth I finally brought Ireland under English subjugation through a series of vicious wars. The conquest was consolidated by the Plantations in Ulster.

The most extensive and successful plantation was carried out between 1608 and 1610 in six of the nine counties in Ulster – Armagh, Cavan, Coleraine (later renamed Londonderry after the city and merchants of London), Donegal, Fermanagh and Tyrone. Antrim and Down effectively became part of the Ulster Plantation, which thus covered most of the Province. The nature of that Plantation helped to ensure its permanence. New towns were built (including the city walls around Derry) and Scottish and English settlers were offered a pioneering opportunity, the consequences of which were long to outlive them.

The Ulster Plantation marked a significant development in bringing the whole of Ireland more completely under English control. Many of the new settlers brought in under the Plantation schemes were separated from the native Irish by their religion (they were usually Anglican or Presbyterian, whilst the native Irish and their so-called 'Old English' landlords were overwhelmingly Catholic) and by language, as Gaelic was still spoken by the natives. The settlers were forbidden to mix, marry or socialise with the native Irish, a policy that served to reinforce the cultural differences between the two communities. Although Gaelic culture did survive, for the most part it was forced to go underground and became the culture of the oppressed.

The period 1625–85 saw the gradual erosion of native Irish and 'Old English' power, which gave way to what was known as the 'New English'. This group were not just prominent in Ulster – other new landlords such as the Boyles and Jones (the earls of Cork and Ranelagh) staked claims in Ireland in the seventeenth century – but Ulster, and indeed Dublin, with its significant Protestant population, gave the Crown strategic and numerical support. It was possible for the Dublin administration no longer to have to rely on the Catholic population to provide its tax collectors, its JPs, its militia and its army officers: a new loyal Protestant group, who regarded themselves as English, were now available to fulfil those roles. The alienation of the Irish and Old English rulers led to rebellion; and defeat, in turn, led to further confiscation of land, and the transfer of these lands and of power to the hands of the New English.[2]

By 1685, the settlers controlled almost 80 per cent of the land. In the wake of the Jacobite wars between William III and James II, and particularly the battles of the Boyne and Aughrim in 1690–91, the area of land controlled by Catholics fell to 14 per cent.

These wars also provided the basis for an exclusively Protestant parliament to pass a series of 'Penal Laws' against the Catholics to prevent them from ever holding land or power again. The New English were determined that once their rivals who had claims on their lands were defeated, it would be virtually impossible for them to recover them. By 1775, only 5 per cent of land was in the hands of the native Irish.[3] Although some Catholic landowners retained their lands they were the exception; the majority of Catholics were reduced to the status of tenants or poor cottiers (labourers who rented small plots of land). A minority of Protestant landowners, known collectively as the 'Protestant Ascendancy', governed an overwhelmingly Catholic Ireland. However, despite Protestant triumphs on the battlefields in 1690–91 and legislative supremacy, their victory was tempered by a sense of chronic insecurity.

The ascendancy of the ruling elite was confirmed and extended by a complex body of anti-Catholic legislation known collectively as the Penal Laws, many of which emanated from the parliament in Westminster. To some extent, they were modelled on legislation already passed in Westminster against the small minority of English Catholics, but in Ireland the impact of the legislation was much more extensive. There, the laws were passed against the majority rather than the minority of the population. In 1691, for example, an Act was passed which effectively excluded Catholics from the Irish parliament and from holding public office. Between 1695 and 1729, a series of 'Penal' Laws was passed which included forbidding Catholics from owning a horse valued at over £5, acquiring an education either at home or abroad, or bearing arms. In 1697, an Act was passed to banish regular Catholic clergy and bishops, although this was never fully enforced. An Act of 1703 limited the rights of Catholics to inherit land or secure leases on it. A further Act of 1704 stipulated that parish clergy had to register, remain within their own county and enter into a bond promising to behave peaceably.[4] Although the Catholic Church survived, it represented alienation and disaffection to the ruling elite and Irish Catholics continued to be a potential source of insurrection. The justification for these extreme measures was compounded by the Jacobite rebellions of the eighteenth century, which served to underline the popular belief that Catholics could not be trusted to be loyal subjects of the Crown.

Although the Penal Laws were justified on the grounds of security, their impact was further to marginalise Catholics within Ireland. Ironically, however, sections of the penal legislation extended not only to Catholics, but also to other nonconformists, including Presbyterians, who were concentrated in the north-east of the country. The imposition of the tithe (tax) on all denominations for the maintenance of the Anglican Church in Ireland was widely

unpopular.[5] The establishment of a minority church in Ireland was
to be a running political sore until Gladstone achieved its dises-
tablishment in 1869.

In addition to the restrictive religious legislation, a number of
economic controls were also introduced – again at the instigation
of the Westminster parliament – which limited the ability of Ireland's
merchants to export their goods freely. This legislation was
symptomatic of a more ambivalent attitude towards Ireland by the
English Crown. On the one hand, Ireland retained a parliament
and was a 'separate kingdom', although its legislative programme
emanated from England: in this regard, the Crown did all it could
to support the New English and the Protestant Ascendancy. Yet,
on the other hand, in economic terms, the government treated
Ireland as a second division and separate province, whose well-being
could be subordinated to England's interests. This was clearly
evidenced by the Cattle Acts of 1666 which forbade the export of
Irish cattle (a key trade for Ireland) to England in order to protect
and nurture that industry in England. Even after the Protestant
Ascendancy had been installed, a more notorious Act was passed
in 1699 which controlled Irish woollen exports. More importantly,
the increasing dependence of Irish products on English markets
and the uneven industrial development of the two countries had a
detrimental impact on Ireland's economic development. This
restrictive legislation, combined with a rapid growth in population
and increasing competition for fertile land, contributed to a large-
scale exodus of Presbyterians from Ulster to colonial America in
the second half of the eighteenth century. Catholics also chose to
emigrate, but in smaller numbers.[6]

Throughout this period, Ireland continued to have her own
parliament in Dublin, although the Westminster parliament retained
the right to legislate for Ireland. The relationship between the
Dublin and the London parliaments was not clearly defined and
interference from the latter was generally motivated by self-interest.
This ambiguity was increasingly despised by Irish politicians and
resulted in the growth of a form of 'colonial nationalism' in the
seventeenth and early eighteenth centuries. Like the Dublin
parliament, colonial nationalism was the preserve of a small
Protestant and conservative elite. It desired economic self-sufficiency
and political autonomy for Ireland, but within the context of a
Protestant political nation. Colonial nationalism found an eloquent
and vituperative, but ultimately ineffectual, outlet in the writings
of Jonathan Swift and William Molyneux. The limitations of this
form of separatism could be seen in Swift's description of himself
as 'An Englishman born in Ireland' who, although a Protestant
clergyman, despised both Catholics *and* Presbyterians.[7]

The American Revolution in 1776 – in which many Ulster emigrants played a leading role – was a significant defeat for English colonial policy. The strong links between Ulster and America led to a new wave of Irish antipathy towards the British government.[8] The demand for autonomous government in Ireland coincided with a population boom, economic instability, increasing competition for land and a wave of popular democratic sentiment throughout Europe. Middle-class Presbyterians (especially the wealthy merchants of Belfast) and middle-class Catholics alike resented the political restrictions which had been placed on them. They also felt that their economic interests would be better served in an independent Ireland. As a result, anti-Ascendancy and anti-British sentiments fused into a demand for change.

In the 1770s, armed and uniformed 'Volunteer' forces were spontaneously raised throughout Ireland, ostensibly for the purpose of defending the country in the event of invasion. Increasingly, however, they were a vehicle for demanding political reform. Although predominantly Protestant, the Volunteers also supported the abolition of anti-Catholic legislation, arguing that being Irish should take precedence over religious affiliations. Essentially the Volunteers were middle-class moderates who ultimately were concerned with improving their economic position, but who wished also to maintain property rights and some form of Protestant Ascendancy (albeit a more liberal version) within Ireland.

The combination of war with America and the numerical strength of the Volunteer movement (within a few years its membership was in excess of 100,000) galvanised the government into lifting a number of petty restrictions on Catholics, both in Ireland and Britain. This resulted in the removal of commercial regulations, which had restricted the ability of Irish merchants to export their goods. In 1782, the constitutional standing of the Dublin parliament was revised when the law restricting its right to initiate change was revoked.[9] A more independent parliament was thus created under the leadership of Henry Grattan. This was followed by a Renunciation Act by the Westminster parliament, which acknowledged the exclusive right of the Dublin parliament to legislate for Ireland, and which recognised the jurisdiction of Irish courts. Although the Volunteers continued to demand more extensive parliamentary reform, this was rejected by the Dublin parliament. Ultimately, although armed and potentially a serious threat to both the Dublin and the Westminister parliaments, the Volunteers were not willing to use physical force to realise their aims. After 1784, when a number of constitutional reforms had been won, the Volunteer movement began to lose both its members and its focus.[10]

Impatience with the prevarication's of Grattan's parliament –
although it had achieved more independence it was still essentially
conservative – contributed to political agitation which supported
a new form of separatist ideology. In 1791, a number of Belfast
radicals formed the Society of United Irishmen, which like the
Volunteers, argued that Irishmen should forget their religious
differences and unite to win political concessions. One of the most
charismatic leaders of the movement was Theobald Wolfe Tone,
a middle-class Protestant from Dublin.[11] Tone believed that a
necessary precondition to Ireland's economic and political
development was separation from England and described the link
as 'the never-failing source of all our political evils'. He also
supported and campaigned vigorously for Catholic rights although
he disliked the 'priesthood and superstition' of some Catholics.[12]
Tone's ideas were particularly welcomed by Protestants in Belfast,
notably by Henry Joy McCracken and his sister, Mary Ann, Thomas
Russell, Samuel Neilson and William Orr. The threat posed by this
alliance was not lost on the British government, especially when a
number of influential Ulster Protestants began to call for a complete
end of British rule in Ireland. The significance of this ideological
transformation was such that 'for the first time an important group
of Protestants began to think of themselves as belonging to the
Irish nation'.[13]

The surge of popular egalitarian protest, especially the alliance
between traditional religious antagonists, worried the politicians
at Westminster. Their apprehension was further increased following
the storming of the Bastille in July 1789, an event which was
commemorated on the streets of Belfast. As the French Revolution
descended into its most 'revolutionary' period, signalled by the
execution of the monarch in 1793 and the coming to power of the
Jacobins, these fears intensified. The government in Westminster
responded to the challenge to traditional government by forcing
the Dublin parliament to pass a mixture of conciliatory and
repressive measures. Most of the former were directed towards
Catholics in the hope of undermining the alliance between the various
religious groupings. This resulted in the introduction of a number
of Catholic 'Relief' Acts, despite some Protestant opposition.
Overall, ideological and religious affinities were put to one side as
the British government chose a policy of appeasement with the
majority of the Irish population.

As a consequence of the relaxation of the Penal Laws, Catholic
40 shilling freeholders were given the right to vote, although they
still could not sit in parliament. Catholics were permitted to join
the army, which was desperately in need of additional manpower,
and a seminary for the training of Catholic priests was established
in Maynooth. In view of events taking place in France, a native

seminary that could be closely monitored by the state was a more attractive alternative to Irish priests going to Europe for their training where they would come into contact with revolutionary ideas. Furthermore, Catholics were permitted to act as solicitors and barristers and to bear arms. Concessions, none the less, were accompanied by a number of repressive measures, including the prohibition of large assemblies, which drove the United Irishmen and the remnants of the Volunteer movement underground.

The spread of popular egalitarian ideas throughout Ireland did not go unchallenged, as the 1790s also marked the emergence of another form of ideological politics. County Armagh, the centre of the linen industry, became a flashpoint for sectarian conflict. Armagh was then the most densely populated county in Ireland and contained almost equal numbers of Anglicans, Catholics and Presbyterians, unlike the neighbouring counties of Antrim and Down where Catholics were in a minority. The rapid growth in population after 1750 had increased competition for land. The land question became particularly sensitive following the repeal of the Penal Laws. In addition to local religious tensions, there were also economic pressures, with the result that 'an explosive religious geography reacted upon an unstable social structure and local economy'.[14] In 1795, a clash between armed Protestants and Catholic 'Defenders' (a generic name for secret societies) took place close to an area known as 'The Diamond', near Loughall. Twenty-one Catholics were killed in the conflict. In the wake of this skirmish, the Orange Order was founded, ostensibly as a means of defending Protestant interests.

Like the United Irishmen, the Orange Order was based on secrecy, oath-taking and active participation, features also associated with Freemasonry. However, the Orange Order differed in that membership of the United Irishmen tended to be middle-class, whilst that of the Orange Order was lower in the social order. From the outset, the authorities in Ireland recognised the potential of harnessing and controlling the more subversive dimensions of the Orange Order. This is evident from the following letter written by a local magistrate:

> As for the Orangemen, we have a rather difficult card to play; they must not be entirely discountenanced – on the contrary, we must in a certain degree uphold them, for with all their licentiousness, on them must we rely for the preservation of our lives and properties should critical times occur.[15]

The growth of the Orange Order was rapid; in 1796 over 2000 members attended a 12 July march to commemorate the Battle of the Boyne. Overall, the ideological rationale of the Order was provided by its professed attachment to king and country, but

more significantly, by its defence of the traditional order in a
society that was changing rapidly. In this regard, it had much in
common with other forces of 'counter-revolution' apparent in
popular politics throughout Europe. For the British government,
the re-emergence of a new form of sectarian conflict, together with
an increasingly confident Catholic middle class, and the spread of
a populist form of democratic and separatist ideology, presented
a real threat to their position in Ireland. The backdrop of war with
France and the persistent threat of invasion coupled with political
agitation and social discontent in England (notably during the
food shortages of 1795) increased these feelings of British insecurity.

Wolfe Tone and a number of other leading United Irishmen
resolved to take advantage of England's instability. This culminated
in an uprising in 1798, for which Tone had enlisted the help of
French troops (who arrived too late to be fully effective). Although
the United Irishmen and their supporters won a number of initial
victories, overall they lacked coherence and co-ordination. In parts
of the north, for example, the links with radical French ideas were
apparent and found an outlet in the singing of the 'Marseillaise'
by United Irishmen as they marched on Antrim. In other places -
especially where Protestants were in a minority and supported the
authorities – the uprising took on a sectarian dimension. The most
obvious instance occurred in Wexford, where a number of
Protestants (as many as 200) were shot or burned alive, thus
adding a new dimension to existing sectarian divisions. Eventually
the rebellion was crushed, with the loss of approximately 30,000
lives, including that of Wolfe Tone, who took his own life rather
than face the gallows and a public execution.[16]

Although the 1798 rebellion failed, it left a romantic legacy of
revolutionary struggle, rooted in a 'physical force' tradition. The
rebellion had a further and more immediate outcome: the abolition
of the parliament in Dublin and the creation of a new political entity
known as the United Kingdom. The British authorities' use of
bribery, threats, coercion and broken promises (all traditional and
recognised tools of parliamentary life) to bring the United Kingdom
into existence proved to be an inauspicious foundation for the
union between Great Britain and Ireland.

Union and Discord

On 1 January 1801, the Act of Union became law. Ireland lost her
own parliament and was formally integrated into the United
Kingdom. However, this union was not achieved as easily as the
British prime minister, William Pitt, had anticipated. The Dublin
parliament was reluctant to relinquish its recently achieved legislative

autonomy by voting itself out of existence. The first vote recorded a majority against the alliance. It was finally achieved through a concerted effort by leading English officials to convince the disparate elements within the Irish House of Commons that union would bring many individual and collective benefits. This optimism was short-lived as immediate disappointment followed in the wake of the legislation. Pitt had promised that Catholic Emancipation would follow union, but was unable to deliver this in the face of determined opposition by George III and British public opinion. Thus, there was no honeymoon period to usher in the alliance, and both partners were left feeling impotent and betrayed.

In return for agreeing to the Act of Union, Ireland received 100 parliamentary seats (out of a total of 658 seats) in the House of Commons at Westminster. In real terms, this effectively disenfranchised a number of Irish MPs. It also meant that the 'Irish interest' would always be a minority within the new parliamentary body, despite the fact that Ireland represented almost 40 per cent of the total population of the United Kingdom. Furthermore, the Irish electorate was smaller than that of other parts of Britain. Following the 1832 parliamentary reforms, when the number of Irish MPs was increased to 105, 1 person in 5 had the vote in England and Wales, compared to 1 person in 8 in Scotland, but only 1 in 20 in Ireland [17]

Following the Union, some political continuity was ensured through the resident Viceroy (also known as the Lord Lieutenant) in Dublin Castle. He was assisted by a Chief Secretary (who was an MP and thus provided a direct link to the House of Commons) and an Under-Secretary. These appointments were made in London, and the Lord Lieutenant and the Chief Secretary were usually English. Apart from the Viceroy and his entourage, further visible evidence of the British presence in Ireland became apparent with the establishment of a professional police force by Robert Peel in 1814 (which pre-dated the English Metropolitan police force by 15 years), and the erection of military barracks in most provincial towns throughout the country.

The economic impact of the Union was more complex, but again proved to be a general disappointment. As a consequence, Ireland became absorbed into a free trade zone in which, having a less well-developed economy, she was inevitably at a disadvantage. This was exacerbated by the rapid industrial growth of the British economy, allied with the general collapse of the agricultural sector after 1815. Also, as the economic institutions of the two economies were integrated in the decades following the Union, Ireland lost her remaining protective duties, leaving her vulnerable to British competition. The exception to this was Belfast, which made a successful transition to being part of a larger economic unit and which benefited from access to the new markets. However, Belfast's industrial development took place within an increasingly charged political climate in which the merchants and industrialists were predominantly Anglican and Presbyterian. Although the workforce was mixed, Protestants dominated the better paid craft industries, whilst Catholics were concentrated in lower paid casual employment. Consequently, the workforce became increasingly polarised not only economically, but also by religious and political ideologies.

The emergence of Dr Henry Cooke, a dogmatic Presbyterian, as leader of militant Ulster Protestants ensured that hard-line attitudes triumphed over more liberal ones in north-east Ireland.[18] At the same time, Irish politics were polarised as a number of leading Ulster Protestants viewed the Union as the reason for their increasing affluence. Politics, theology and economics became inextricably intertwined and the Union became the lynchpin of this ideological cocktail. This belief was articulated by Henry Cooke in 1841 when he stated:

> Look at the town of Belfast. When I was a youth it was almost a village, but what a glorious sight does it now present! The masted grove within our harbour – our mighty warehouses teeming with the wealth of every clime – our giant manufactures lifting themselves on every side – and all this we owe to the Union.[19]

From the outset, a minority questioned the legitimacy of the Union. An early reaction came in 1803, when Robert Emmet, a brother of one of the 1798 leaders, led an unsuccessful rising against the new regime. In many ways, Emmet's uprising had its roots in Tone's earlier rebellion. And, like the 1798 rebellion, Emmet's uprising made little impact at the time; in retrospect, though, it contributed much to the political rhetoric of the nineteenth century. The apparent decline of much of the Irish economy in the early nineteenth century was used by subsequent Irish nationalists as further proof of the failure of the Union. However, it is probable that even a native Irish government would have found difficulty in competing with the economic might of Britain, especially given the proximity of the two islands.

The disappointments of the Irish Catholics found an outlet in the person of Daniel O'Connell, a radical Catholic lawyer. In the 1820s, economic dissatisfaction combined with religious frustrations resulted in the revival of the demand for Catholic Emancipation. In 1823, O'Connell founded the Catholic Association, which swiftly became one of the most formidable mass movements in Europe. Its tactics included mass 'monster' meetings, the collection of a small subscription from each member and the organising of support for parliamentary candidates who endorsed Catholic

Emancipation. The challenge to the government of such a large and well-organised movement was considerable, although O'Connell always declared that he was opposed to physical force as a tactic and was loyal to the Crown.

The struggle for Catholic Emancipation came to a head in 1828 when O'Connell was elected MP for County Clare, a seat he was unable to take as Catholics were excluded from parliament. With their hand so completely and publicly forced, the British government (which included supporters of Emancipation) felt that it had no choice but to concede. It fell to the ministry of the Duke of Wellington and his Home Secretary, Sir Robert Peel, to introduce a Bill for Catholic Emancipation. They argued that Emancipation was necessary to safeguard the Act of Union. This action provoked a backlash from Protestant Tories, much of which was personally directed against Peel, whose staunch defence of Protestantism up to this point had earned him the sobriquet 'Orange Peel'.[20] Peel's apparent betrayal of his party was neither forgotten nor forgiven by a number of leading Tories. Following Emancipation, Catholics throughout the United Kingdom were allowed to hold most offices of state and to sit in parliament. At the same time, a number of poorer Catholics were disenfranchised as the vote was removed from 40 shilling (£2) freeholders and given to those with a £10 qualification. Overall, O'Connell's success in winning Catholic Emancipation raised his profile to cult status and won him many admirers throughout Europe.

The success of Catholic Emancipation meant that the need for mass politics disappeared as Irish Catholics were able to participate in constitutional politics. This also coincided with the ending of the long run in office of the Tory Party and their replacement by the Whig Party on a ticket of reform. During the 1830s, O'Connell's successful alliance with the ruling Whig Party resulted in various reforms within Ireland, including improvements in local government, education and health provision. An Ecclesiastical Commission was established which recommended Church reform and the hated tithe was abolished.[21]

The fall of the Whig government in 1841 and the return of the Tories under Peel ended the period of relative political calm, as the Tory Party was felt to be less sympathetic to Irish demands. In 1840, O'Connell, who was becoming increasingly disillusioned with the Whigs, had formed the National Association for Repeal of the Union. This movement gained more momentum during Peel's premiership. The reconstituted repeal movement adopted many of those tactics which had proved so successful in winning Catholic Emancipation. The close associations between the two organisations gave the new movement for national autonomy a more exclusively Catholic dimension than earlier separatist groups.

For Peel, the repeal agitation posed a threat not only to the existence of the United Kingdom, but also to the British empire as a whole. In a speech to parliament in May 1843, he stated unambiguously:

> There is no influence, no power, no authority which the prerogatives of the crown and the existing law given to the government, which shall not be exercised for the purpose of maintaining the union; the dissolution of which would involve not merely the repeal of an act of parliament, but the dismemberment of this great empire ... Deprecating as I do all war, but above all, civil war, yet there is no alternative which I do not think preferable to the dismemberment of this empire.[22]

Peel and O'Connell were old adversaries. In 1815, when the former was Chief Secretary for Ireland, he and O'Connell had come close to fighting a duel over a political difference. Peel's tactics in the face of the repeal crisis were a mixture of conciliation and coercion. In 1844, O'Connell was imprisoned for a year, charged with conspiracy. Later, the sentence was overturned by the House of Lords. At the same time, Peel increased the grant to Maynooth College and provided funding for the establishment of three university colleges. As part of his long-term plan for modernising and regenerating the Irish economy, a Commission was appointed in 1843 to enquire into the occupation of land in Ireland, with a view to recommending improvements and reforms. The findings of the Commission were published in 1845, but were overshadowed by the arrival of potato blight in Ireland.[23]

The repeal agitation came to a head in 1843, when the government banned a monster meeting due to be held in Clontarf, chosen for its symbolic significance as the scene of Brian Boru's defeat of Viking intruders in 1014. O'Connell complied with this order and cancelled the meeting. This disappointed not only many of his followers, but also a radical grouping within the repeal movement, known as the 'Young Irelanders'. The Young Irelanders tried to win support by using their newspaper, *The Nation*, as a medium for combining tales of Irish oppression and heroic struggle to become an independent nation with their own brand of nationalist ideology. After the humiliation in Clontarf, O'Connell lost much of his support, and the political initiative (although not the mass support) passed to the Young Ireland movement. In 1848, the movement attempted an armed uprising, led by William Smith O'Brien. This was the year of revolutions throughout Europe and thus the Irish uprising can be seen as part of a revolutionary continuum which was sweeping the Continent. The British government dealt with the uprising swiftly and decisively. The leaders were arrested and transported – sent into exile at a time when thousands of Famine victims were also leaving Ireland. In the wake of this insurrection, the repeal movement collapsed and many of its supporters were reabsorbed into constitutional politics.[24] In the long term, the 1848 uprising and the writings of its leaders, notably John Mitchel, shaped the subsequent development of Irish nationalism. Moreover, the transportation of its founders, together with the mass exodus of people from Ireland, ensured that Irish politics in future would be played out on an international stage.

The Pre-Famine Economy

Whilst the pre-Famine economy was predominantly agricultural, it was far from monolithic. In the early nineteenth century, Ireland not only fed her own population, but was a net exporter of food. It was also the world market leader in linen production. Despite this economic strength, in the century prior to the Famine the Irish economy, and in particular Irish agriculture, was generally regarded as backward and underdeveloped by contemporaries, especially those from outside Ireland. For example, Arthur Young, the celebrated agricultural improver, published accounts of his three extensive tours of England, and by English standards, he judged Irish agriculture to be backward. Like many subsequent travellers, he failed to take sufficient account of the different cultural and social mores of the two countries. Young gave the impression of a society dominated by small tenant farmers, underpinned by a massive subsistence population, who lacked both the resources and the vision to modernise. By using England as a benchmark, however, he was effectively measuring Irish agricultural performance against that of a country which had recently undergone a rapid agricultural transformation which was unique, even by European standards. Although Young was not impressed with Ireland's agricultural sector, he did note that Irish grain yields were impressively high.[25]

Young's gloomy diagnosis of Ireland's agriculture was frequently echoed in the decades preceding the Famine. This concern was given a sharper focus in the years following the Act of Union. The paradox of the Union was that, after 1800, Ireland continued to be both part of the empire and an integral part of the United Kingdom, and in her latter role, she contributed MPs, soldiers, emigrants and administrators who helped to rule the wider empire.[26] The economic implications of the Union were also complex. An integrated Ireland simultaneously presented economic opportunities and an economic threat to the prosperity of the United Kingdom. This potential threat was articulated by the influential economist and demographer Thomas Malthus, who informed a Parliamentary Committee in 1826 that if Ireland continued to remain economically backward, an increasing number of Irish would migrate to England to take advantage of her more developed opportunities. Ultimately, the impact of this would be to demoralise the English poor rather than improve the lot of the Irish poor. Malthus suggested that emigration needed to be regulated and he warned:

> It is vain to hope for any permanent and extensive advantage from any system of emigration which does not primarily apply to Ireland, whose population, unless some other outlet be opened to them, must shortly fill up every vacuum created in England or Scotland, and to reduce the labouring classes to a uniform state of degradation.[27]

As a consequence of the Union, Ireland lost not only her political and legislative autonomy, but also her economic independence. A number of radical measures were passed which included the abolition of trade barriers within the United Kingdom, the introduction of a common tariff, the unification of the two exchequers (in 1817) and the establishment of a common currency (in 1826). The integration of these key economic institutions and the opening of Ireland to international markets appeared to be disadvantageous to Ireland. However, the Union coincided with a period of economic dislocation and structural readjustment, which became particularly acute following the conclusion of the Napoleonic Wars in 1815. This downswing was exacerbated by a series of poor harvests throughout Europe, including Ireland, in 1816–17, 1821–22 and 1830. After 1830 prices did begin to recover and the Irish economy appeared to have adjusted to the consequences of the Union.

The decades after 1800 were marked by rapid and sustained industrialisation in much of Britain, which was due in part to the transition from domestic to factory production. At the same time a process of deindustrialisation was taking place in many parts of Ireland as factory production became concentrated in the Belfast region. For Belfast, improvements in internal transportation and shipping gave access to international markets and proved to be a positive outcome of the Union.

The decline in industrial occupations in Ireland intensified after 1815. The abolition of protective duties on Irish goods in the mid-1820s meant that Ireland effectively entered a free trade zone which left her open to competition from the most industrially advanced economy in the world. The Union and the subsequent removal of remaining protective measures brought together two economies which differed in size and industrial capacity. However, in view of the proximity and historical connections between the islands, it is probable that much of this trade would have taken place anyway, even if an Irish parliament had been in place. Furthermore, the Union coincided with major developments in transport, banking and labour-saving technology, all of which facilitated intercourse between different economies. The change to factory production and the consequent need for capital accumulation necessitated the need for large-scale rather than domestic production. All these changes made rationalisation and specialisation inevitable. By 1841, approximately 17 per cent of the male labour force of Ireland was employed in the industrial sector. This was a much lower proportion than in Britain, where 70 per cent of the male labour force was so employed (although, it was far higher than in mainland Europe). Within Ireland, only Belfast and its hinterland was able to make a successful transition to factory production and take advantage of new techniques, especially in textiles and engineering.

Much of Belfast's emergence as a major industrial city was due to the achievements of the local linen industry. Linen, like wool, had been a staple industry in Ireland since the sixteenth century. The early stages of linen production could be carried out in the home and so were ideally suited to family production. Weaving and spinning, for example, were done by outworkers who sold the finished goods to large merchants. This process created a system of proto-industrialisation within Ireland. Employment in linen production could be carried out in conjunction with subsistence cultivation, thus maximising output from a small plot of land. In this way, linen production and potato cultivation were complementary. By the end of the eighteenth century, linen was Ireland's most important export commodity. The linen exported was of the highest quality, whilst that kept for home consumption was of a coarser variety.

Most of the domestic linen industry was concentrated in the north of Ireland, notably in Counties Antrim, Armagh, Cavan, Derry, Down, Louth, Monaghan and Tyrone, and parts of Leitrim, Longford, Mayo, Meath, Sligo, Roscommon and Westmeath. The opening of the White Linen Hall in Belfast in 1785 was indicative of the ambitions of the rich merchants in the city who were determined to control the linen trade within Ireland. By 1821, Antrim (which included part of Belfast) Armagh and Tyrone dominated the Irish linen industry and accounted for over half of Irish linen sales. However, the success of these counties was achieved at the expense of the outlying districts. This geographic domination increased as new technical processes such as wet-spinning and the replacement of water by steam power, all facilitated a change from domestic to large-scale mill production.[28] As a consequence of the rationalisation of the linen industry, much of the proto-industry collapsed. Many small domestic weavers and spinners lost an important source of income. This forced them to depend even more on their small plots of land and, significantly, on potatoes.

Whilst linen production was one of the great successes of the Irish economy in the nineteenth century, Ireland's industry, like her agriculture, was diverse and regionally dispersed. At the beginning of the nineteenth century, cotton was successfully produced in Cork, Dublin, Belfast and, latterly, Waterford. In spite of restrictive legislation introduced in the 1690s, a small but flourishing wool industry had survived in Carrick, Cork and Kilkenny. The textile industry, however, became increasingly dominated by linen, which had benefited from changes in technology and from being part of a larger free trade zone. The ending of protective measures in the 1820s further undermined the cotton industry and it collapsed in many areas thereafter. Shipbuilding was another successful industry. Initially it had been centred in Cork, but by the late nineteenth century had made a rapid and successful transition to Belfast, facilitated by the export requirements of the local linen industry.

Other examples of industrial success were the distilling industry which survived the challenge of the Temperance Movement in the 1840s, the population decline after the Famine and the increase in duties. Brewing also flourished and, despite tough opposition from Cork, was increasingly dominated by the firm of Arthur Guinness, based in Dublin. Nevertheless, despite some initial regional diversity, in the decades preceding the Famine there was increasing regional specialisation within the industrial sector. Whilst there was some de-industrialisation, it appears to have been due to the development of labour-saving technology, the need for capital investment and the move to large-scale production, rather than simply the consequence of the Act of Union.[29] The opening of Irish markets to international competition did undermine a number of industries within Ireland which were no longer able to compete with opposition from Britain.

By the end of the eighteenth century, Irish agriculture was dominated by corn (a generic term for all types of grain) and potatoes. Potatoes were not indigenous to Ireland, but had been brought to the country, according to popular legend, by Sir Walter Raleigh during the reign of Elizabeth I. The potato thrived in the damp and temperate climate of Ireland and demonstrated an unusual adaptability in its ability to grow even in poor quality and rocky soil. Whilst there were some poor harvests, potatoes generally were as reliable as corn harvests, and it was extremely rare for them to fail in two consecutive years. Gradually, therefore, potatoes came to replace the traditional diet of grain (mostly oatmeal) and dairy products. By the beginning of the eighteenth century, they were the staple, subsistence food of many of the poorest cottiers and labourers, especially during the winter months. Also, as the Irish population increased in the latter part of the century, the cultivation of potatoes was able to keep pace with Ireland's rapid growth.

Initially, dependence on potatoes had been concentrated in the Province of Munster; however, it rapidly spread eastwards to Leinster and westwards to Connaught. Consequently, the section of the population dependent upon oatmeal retreated into the north of the country. The existence of a large 'potato economy' simultaneously allowed the expansion of tillage within Ireland. Paradoxically, the reliance both of potato production and tillage on low subsistence wages (literally a potato wage) and labour-intensive methods, also proved to be a barrier to technological and agricultural innovation within Ireland. Nevertheless, in the decades after the Union, high quality corn was grown extensively in Ireland (predominantly in the south-east). Like linen, it was grown primarily for sale and export, mostly to the bread-hungry towns of industrial England. By 1841, oats was the largest single item exported from Ireland and, in total, Ireland was exporting sufficient corn to England to feed 2 million people. This high level of dependence on Irish agriculture led to the description of Ireland as the 'bread basket' of the United Kingdom.[30] Ironically, it was the existence of the much despised potato economy which allowed English workers to enjoy cheap bread, probably ignorant of its origins. Ultimately, this combination of a highly commercialised export sector side-by-side with an under-resourced subsistence economy made it difficult for Irish agriculture to adjust to changing economic circumstances in the first half of the nineteenth century.

The expansion of the Irish corn trade had been rapid and remarkable, especially given the damp climate of Ireland. In the 1790s, Ireland had supplied Britain with only 16.5 per cent of its corn imports; this had risen to 57 per cent in 1810; and by 1830, Irish corn accounted for 80 per cent of British imports.[31] The reasons for this growth were many – the Corn Law of 1815 provided protection against cheap foreign grain; developments in transport, especially shipping and railways, facilitated cheaper and swifter carriage; and the availability of a cheap supply of labour who, instead of demanding higher wages, demanded more from the ubiquitous potato. Overall, this meant that an expanding and highly successful corn sector shared a symbiotic relationship with an overworked and under-resourced subsistence potato economy.

By the 1840s, the desire to modernise and restructure Irish agriculture had gathered pace within Britain.[32] In the 1830s, the Whig government had pursued a highly interventionist policy within Ireland which resulted in the introduction of elementary (primary) education, the establishment of a board of public works, the reform of the Anglican Church and the introduction of a Poor Law to Ireland. Nevertheless, poverty and discontent appeared endemic in Ireland. This impression was reinforced by a number of foreign travellers who followed in Young's footsteps and echoed

Young's analysis from half a century earlier. For example, the French social commentator, Gustave de Beaumont, observed that Irish people were more wretched than 'the Indian in his forests, and the negro in his chains'. The writer William Thackeray, who visited Ireland in 1842, made a distinction between different regions of Ireland, but was highly critical of the 'potato people', whom he observed 'sitting by the way-side here; one never sees this general repose in England – a sort of ragged lazy contentment'.[33]

A more sympathetic interpretation of Ireland's condition was provided by Mr and Mrs Hall who, like Thackeray, toured Ireland on the eve of the Famine. Although they could not ignore the widespread poverty within the country, they also noted that:

> A material change for the better has therefore taken place throughout Ireland, which is perceptible even in the remotest districts, but very apparent in the seaport towns. The peasantry are better clad than they formerly were, their cottages much more decent and their habits far less uncivilised.[34]

Even the Halls, however, like other visitors, were judging Ireland by an alien benchmark, which failed to take into account the social and cultural mores of Irish society. The so-called 'lazy-beds', in which potatoes were grown, allowed an efficient utilisation of available resources (Irish potato yields were amongst the highest in Europe), whilst the dung-heap outside many of the poorer cottages (which was highly offensive to many visitors) was in fact a visible reminder of a society that had access to and knew the benefits of manure.

The system of agricultural production more and more became of concern to successive British governments in the wake of the Union. Increasingly, members of both the Tory and the Whig Parties and Irish Nationalists came to believe that the system of landholding in Ireland, and in particular the relationships between landlord and tenants, had to be reformed as a precondition to modernisation. The large number of smallholdings, especially in the west of Ireland, was seen as an obstacle to this reform. During the eighteenth century, as English agricultural land was being consolidated under the Enclosure Acts, many estates in Ireland were being subdivided. This was because landlords, especially absentee ones, were letting their estates on very long leases to 'middlemen'. These middlemen in turn sub-let their holdings to small tenants, who were able to obtain relatively long leases. The system of subdivision was initially viewed as a way of maximising rental from an estate, although when prices fell, as they did after 1815, so did rentals.

The middlemen provided a link between peasants and small farmers and absentee landlords. After 1815, with the collapse in agricultural prices and the beginnings of de-industrialisation, a number of landlords dismissed the middlemen in an effort to boost their falling profits. As a consequence, shorter leases became more common, on the basis that they increased profit margins and made the process of eviction easier. A few Irish landlords, influenced by the changes in English agriculture, became filled with the desire to 'improve' their properties and thus take advantage of new technologies and processes. However, this also required the consolidation of property which, in the context of Ireland, meant the ending of subdivision.[35] This transition to a more capitalised system of agriculture represented a threat not only to the livelihood of the small tenants and cottiers, but also to the society and culture that was an integral part of it. In an effort to preserve this way of life and what they saw as their traditional or 'moral' rights, the smallholders and labourers responded to the threat of change by organising secret societies.

These secret societies adopted generic names, such as Whiteboys (who were most prevalent in Munster) or the Hearts of Oak and the Hearts of Steel in Ulster. They resorted to agrarian violence, which the authorities countered by arresting the ringleaders and introducing a series of repressive measures. These measures forced the secret societies to go underground but violent activities and a policy of non-cooperation continued, especially during periods of distress. The policy of coercion adopted by the government, however, was 'an admission that Ireland was in a state of smothered war'.[36] Overall, though, the objectives of the societies were to prevent change or redress a perceived grievance, and their activities were mostly sporadic and localised. Their main targets were landlords, middlemen or large farmers, but rarely the central government. In a number of counties, notably Tipperary and Armagh, the societies were particularly active, as it was in these areas where traditional roles were being eroded. The activities of these societies did appear to have a restraining influence on some Irish landlords.

The societies were a continual source of anxiety to the Irish propertied classes and a constant concern to the British authorities. The Irish poor acquired a reputation for lawlessness and, to some, this appeared to provide further evidence of their cultural inferiority. In a powerful speech to parliament at the beginning of 1846, Lord Grey, a Whig MP, drew attention to the level of crimes or 'outrages' in Ireland:

> The state of Ireland is one which is notorious. We know the ordinary condition of the country. We know the ordinary condition of that country to be one both of lawlessness and wretchedness. It is so described by every competent authority

... Ireland is the one weak place in the solid fabric of British power; Ireland is the one deep (I had almost said ineffaceable) blot on the brightness of British honour. Ireland is our disgrace.[37]

Unusually, Grey attributed the crime rates to misgovernment of Ireland rather than to a fault of the Irish character. The ruling Tory Party, however, responded by introducing a tough Coercion Bill which attempted to control agrarian disorder by imposing a collective fine on disturbed districts and introducing a rigid curfew, with transportation the penalty for ignoring it. The passing of this Bill (in June 1846) was significant for a number of reasons: it provided an opportunity for the Tory Protectionists to punish Peel for the repeal of the Corn Laws, and it meant that, as Ireland entered a period of famine and social chaos, the traditional response of the people to unfair treatment or eviction was denied to them.

Repression was not the only response of the British government. In November 1843, the Devon Commission was appointed to enquire into the state of law and the practice of landholding in Ireland. The Commission submitted its report in February 1845. Inevitably, they noted the extensive poverty and high level of dependence on potatoes but, unusually, they attributed the apparent apathy of Irish proprietors to insolvency. They believed that many landlords – even the well-intentioned – lacked the capital to finance their own improvements 'in some cases out of family charges, and resulting in others from improvidence or carelessness possibly of former proprietors'.[38] The Commissioners suggested that external finance and compensation were necessary to allow improvements and reforms to take place. Significantly, however, Irish landlords had been formally identified as a cause of Ireland's economic backwardness. The Report was not immediately acted upon and the first appearance of potato blight a few months later demonstrated with compelling clarity the underlying vulnerability of the Irish economy.

Poverty, Population and Poor Relief

In the years following the ending of the Napoleonic Wars, much of domestic political discourse at Westminster was concerned with poverty and how to alleviate it. The debate was both shaped and constrained by an eclectic mix of ideological concerns combined with the more pressing reality of post-war unemployment, a European-wide crop failure and political unrest which was challenging the political status quo. Although poverty and poor relief remained high on the political agenda, a solution that did not involve political suicide for the governing Tory Party appeared to be more elusive.

The problem of poverty was linked by many commentators with the issue of population control. To a large extent this association was due to the success of the theories of Thomas Malthus. At the end of the eighteenth century, Malthus, an Anglican vicar, had demonstrated a link between food production and population growth, predicting – with increasing confidence as various editions of his book sold out – that population increases would outstrip food production, with fatal consequences. Malthus's main concern was with the reproductive habits of the poorest classes. His solution was appealingly simple – stop giving poor relief to the lower classes and they would stop producing children.[39]

Notwithstanding Malthus's casual disregard of advances in agricultural production, his publication elevated him to the status of a demographic oracle. Although subsequent economists questioned or refined Malthus's findings, his ideas continued to influence political ideology in Britain, long after his death in 1834. In this regard, Malthus's timing had been perfect as, in 1801, the first census was undertaken in Britain and it demonstrated that the population had grown to almost 11 million – double its estimated level in 1700 – and showed no signs of slowing. This alarmed politicians who no longer regarded a large population as a valuable resource, but increasingly viewed it as a source of potential conflict and expense. In the immediate aftermath of the Napoleonic Wars, population growth had reached an unprecedented 11 per cent per annum and poor relief expenditure had risen to almost £7½ million per annum, compared with annual expenditure of just over £1 million in 1776.[40] Malthus's message thus fell on very receptive ears.

Despite Malthus's twinning of overpopulation with poverty, he showed little interest in Ireland as providing an example of his prognosis, preferring instead to use Holland and Sweden to provide case studies. Throughout his life, in fact, Malthus demonstrated little interest in Irish demography.[41] Yet, even by British standards, Irish population growth was remarkable. In 1800, the population of Ireland had been approximately 5.5 million, rising to 7 million in 1821 (the year of the first national census in Ireland) and to 8.5 million in 1841. Although the growth was rapid, after 1821 the rate of growth was showing signs of slowing down, partly as a consequence of high emigration, but also in response to the economic uncertainties of the post-war years. The distribution of this reduction, however, was uneven, and the highest growth rates remained concentrated in the poorest and most potato-dependent regions. The availability of potatoes had also contributed to a geographic redistribution of population as, in the space of two centuries, the population had shifted significantly from the east to the west of the country. Potatoes had contributed to a spatial and social polarisation within the country, and had ensured that the material expectations of the people who ate them remained low. At the same time, for landlords who wanted high financial returns for low investment, the potato communities or villages ('clachans') provided a ready source of income. For both groups, however, there was little opportunity to break out of this system of production, which was both underpinned by and constrained by the potato. The system was also relatively inelastic in times of crisis.

Malthus was superseded by a new generation of economists who argued that Ireland's poverty was not simply a result of her large population, but was primarily caused by a lack of investment and the absence of a spirit of enterprise within the country, especially amongst the landlord class. Consequently, both peasant and proprietor were viewed as impediments to Ireland's economic development.

Despite the high level of visible poverty within Ireland, the condition of the Irish poor was not unmitigated. For much of the year, they had a plentiful supply of food (potatoes) which was also highly nutritious. In fact, when combined with buttermilk, this diet provided all the nutrients and vitamins necessary for a healthy adult.[42] In fact, Irish peasants were amongst the tallest and healthiest in Europe.[43] Irish peasants also had ready access to fuel (turf) and rich fertilisers (manure or seaweed). Similarly, accommodation, although basic, could be quickly and easily constructed by using materials which were locally available, such as stones, clay and thatch. The combination of readily available food, fuel and shelter made possible earlier marriages. Whilst potato growing did involve hard labour, it also left plenty of time for leisure activities and this helped to keep alive a rich culture of music and story-telling. The weakness of this system was that this lifestyle depended on a system of monoculture, which periodically failed.

In England and Wales, the problem of poverty appeared to be resolved with the passing of the Poor Law Amendment Act in 1834 – the so-called 'new' Poor Law. This Act revised legislation which, with modifications, had been in place since the end of the sixteenth century. The new Poor Law, however, was shaped by the influential ideologies of utilitarianism and political economy, which sought to ensure that relief would be administered in an efficient and cost-effective way. To achieve this, the principle of 'less eligibility' was implemented to ensure that dependency on poor relief was less attractive and materially less comfortable than the life of even the poorest independent labourer. A key tool in achieving this aim was the workhouse. Workhouses were grim and austere institutions which had been used even before 1834, but following the passage of the Act it was hoped that all relief would be provided within them, thus making 'outdoor relief' no longer necessary. This aim was never achieved as a combination of active opposition and apathy by the local Boards of Guardians who disliked the inflexibility of the new system meant that outdoor relief was never fully abandoned. Despite this, in financial terms the new Poor Law was a success as poor relief fell from an average annual expenditure of £6–7 million, to £4 million.

The passage of the English Poor Law provided an impetus to tackle the question of poor relief in Ireland. Unlike England, Ireland had never possessed a national system of poor relief and the government was working with a clean slate. In 1833, a Royal Commission was appointed, chaired by the Archbishop of Dublin and the eminent political economist, Richard Whately.[44] The Commission sat for three years, during which time it collected a mass of detailed information, based on painstaking and thorough interviews. At the end of its investigation, it concluded that almost 2.5 million people in Ireland lived in poverty, many of whom had insufficient food during the summer or 'hungry' months, and would therefore require external assistance. In view of the magnitude of the problem, the Commissioners did not recommend an extension of the English Poor Law to Ireland, but proposed that the problem be tackled at its roots with an innovative programme based on public works and assisted emigration.[45]

The Commissioners' findings fell on deaf ears at Westminster for a combination of ideological and financial reasons. Instead, the Whig government sent an English Poor Law Commissioner, George Nicholls, to Ireland in an attempt to supersede the recommendations of the Commissioners. Nicholls had risen to prominence due to his ability to provide cheap poor relief in his local parish. His remit in Ireland was to investigate 'destitution' rather than 'poverty', as the Commissioners had attempted to do. Nicholls was also told that he was to concern himself with the suitability of the English workhouse system for Ireland. Following two short visits to Ireland, Nicholls reported that the number of destitute people in Ireland was in the region of 100,000, or approximately 1 per cent of the population, and that, not surprisingly, the new English Poor Law could be extended to Ireland. Nicholls' report was welcomed in England and provided an excuse to bypass the report of Whately and his Commissioners. As a consequence, in 1838 a Poor Law was introduced into Ireland, based on legislation which had been framed for a different country and which showed little sensitivity to circumstances which were unique to Ireland.[46]

Although the Irish Poor Law was modelled on the 1834 English Poor Law, it differed in three key respects: first, outdoor relief was expressly forbidden, which meant that in Ireland all relief was provided through the medium of the workhouse; secondly, no right to relief existed, which meant that if a workhouse became full, it was no longer the responsibility of the Guardians to provide relief; and thirdly, no law of settlement (which had been an integral part of the English Poor Law since the seventeenth century) was introduced, which meant that paupers did not have to have lived in an area in order to be eligible for relief. These differences indicated that from the outset, relief in Ireland was to be more stringently administered that in England. However, in all parts of the United Kingdom, poverty was regarded as the fault of the individual and the experience of receiving poor relief was made as unpleasant as possible.

The Irish Poor Law was implemented quickly in order to avoid many of the teething problems and opposition that it had encountered in England. The country was divided into 130 new administrative units known as unions, each of which was to have its own workhouse. Boards of Guardians were elected to administer the new institutions. In total, the workhouses could accommodate over 100,000 paupers, according to George Nicholls' estimate. In addition, a framework was established for the collection of taxes – poor rates – to finance the new system. An important component of the system of poor relief in both England and Ireland was that it was to be funded locally from taxes levied within a union, thus giving each area a vested interest in the level of poor relief expenditure.

Almost immediately after the 1838 Act was passed there were crop failures in all parts of Ireland but predominantly in the west. These shortages were most severe in 1838 and 1842 and coincided with economic slumps in Britain generally. On both these occasions, the government decided that it was beyond the remit of the new Poor Law to deal with a period of extraordinary distress. Instead, temporary relief measures were introduced to deal with the situation. This policy of distinguishing between permanent and temporary distress established a precedent which was adopted in 1845. On all of these occasions, the government recognised the limitations of the Poor Law in providing emergency or widespread relief. In 1847, the government departed from this policy and decided that both ordinary and extraordinary relief were the responsibility of the Poor Law. The outcome of this change of policy was disastrous as a Poor Law which had been designed to relieve approximately 100,000 paupers was forced to provide relief to almost $1\frac{1}{2}$ million people.

By 1845, 118 workhouses in Ireland were providing relief, but they were far from full and some Guardians were complaining that such large institutions were unnecessary. Within a space of a few months, however, the failure of the potato crop initiated a famine of unprecedented longevity and impact within Ireland. Although the Irish Poor Law had to be radically revised to cope with this crisis, the ideological premises on which this system was founded remained unchanged, even in the face of famine.

CHAPTER 3

Rotten Potatoes and the Politics of Relief

The appearance in 1845 of a mysterious disease which destroyed almost half the Irish potato crop heralded a prolonged crop failure the human consequences of which were without parallel in modern Europe. The extent of the potato blight was difficult to gauge initially. By the end of 1845, it appeared to have peaked. Furthermore, its greatest impact had been in the eastern counties of Ireland, away from the west, where a high level of dependence on the potato by a densely settled rural community represented a highly vulnerable situation.

Crop failures had long been part of the Irish condition but (with the exception of 1740–41) had usually been localised or confined to one year of shortages. Such failures had been countered through various measures, which normally involved a combination of restricting food exports and encouraging additional imports of food. Under the Act of Union of 1800, Ireland lost its own parliament. All legislative and executive power was therefore centralised at Westminster, which thus became directly responsible for relief measures in times of crop failure. An important effect of this constitutional change was to create a distancing of the responsibility for action from the source of the problem. Concurrently with these legislative changes, the ideological climate also changed. Poverty was seen increasingly as a result of the moral failings of the individual, whilst the autonomy of the marketplace became sacrosanct. These beliefs were incompatible with prolonged government intervention during a period of food shortages.

The response of the Peel administration to the 1845 crisis, although effective in alleviating the food shortages, was also an early demonstration that the design and management of relief policies in London would proceed on the basis of criteria very different from those of a localised parliament. Geographic distances were underpinned by cultural, social, economic and political separateness. Relief measures were influenced by a range of perceptions and prejudices regarding Ireland, which both justified and shaped the policy formulations of a ruling elite in London. As the blight reappeared over a further six seasons, the simple link between food shortages and the provision of relief was broken. A more complex web of considerations helped to determine the response of the government to the unfolding of a humanitarian disaster. Increasingly, the potato blight provided an opportunity to introduce radical legislation to restructure and regenerate Ireland. The early politicisation of the relief policies blunted their effectiveness as a response to food shortage. An ecological disaster was thus transformed into a famine.

Pre-Famine Famines

The scale and tragedy of the Great Famine of 1845–52 have tended to overshadow earlier famines and subsistence crises in Ireland. Although the circumstances and context of each of these famines were different, they help to illustrate the way in which the response of the local authorities and the government changed over time. An early tabulation of famines was created by Sir William Wilde, as part of the 1851 Census. Wilde claimed that Ireland's recent experience of 'plague, pestilence and famine, with which it had pleased Providence to afflict this country' led him to investigate earlier periods of suffering.[1] He identified over 500 years of Irish famines. For example, in 964, there was 'A great miserable dearth in Ireland that the father sould [sold] his sonn and daughter for meat'.[2] Subsistence crises, however, were clustered in the fourteenth, the seventeenth, the eighteenth and the nineteenth centuries, culminating in the extraordinary crisis of the 1840s.[3] Relatively little is known about early famines in Ireland. In general, they were caused by crop failure (often due to climatic conditions) or war, or a combination of both (as in 1640–41) and they were followed by a period of plague, pestilence and epidemics, which often took more lives than simple starvation.[4] Less frequently, as was the case in 1845, crop failure was due to an ecological aberration.

The numerous subsistence crises which occurred in the eighteenth century have been obscured by the devastating famine of 1740–42. Yet, throughout that century, there were a large number of crop failures and food shortages in the country. Until 1838, Ireland had no statutory system of poor relief, and the services which existed were under-resourced and inadequate. Consequently, each of the crises put considerable pressure on the relief services. To avoid high levels of mortality, a variety of *ad hoc* relief measures were introduced. The early part of the century was marked by a series of subsistence crises, caused mostly by unseasonable weather. In 1708–9, for example, bad weather caused crop failures throughout Europe and a corresponding rise in excess mortality. Ireland escaped from this situation relatively unscathed. This was due mainly to the action of the Irish Privy Council, which responded by placing an embargo on the exportation of grain from the country. Bad weather was also the cause of a series of poor grain harvests of 1725–29.[5] The government in Dublin, where the impact was particularly severe, responded by imposing price controls and authorising imports of grain from abroad. This appears to be the first instance of the authorities importing foodstuffs into the country to help alleviate distress. Despite these measures, there was a certain amount of excess mortality (that is, deaths additional to those which could have been expected in a normal season), particularly in Dublin and rural Ulster. A further consequence was that the poor began to replace their traditional oat diet with potatoes, which had been viewed previously as a winter food only.[6]

The famine of 1740–41, which was also known as *Blaidhain an air* (the year of the slaughter) was precipitated by an unusually long spell of extremely cold weather throughout Europe. This destroyed both the potato and the grain crops, although the impact was more severe on the former. The extreme temperatures also killed large numbers of livestock and even birds. By this time, many of the population, especially in the south and west, were dependent on potatoes as their main foodstuff. Hence this period of scarcity can be viewed as the first real potato famine. The geographical impact of the suffering – unlike in earlier famines – was felt to a greater extent on the west coast, thus reflecting Ireland's changing pattern of economic development. The food shortages throughout Europe were exacerbated by war. As a consequence, less surplus food was available to be imported, although, in June 1741, there were reports that 'large supplies of provisions arrived from America'.[7]

The government responded to the famine by prohibiting exports and by deploying the army commissariat to distribute relief. Large-scale private charity was organised by local landlords and gentry and by members of the Anglican Church (the Catholic Church in Ireland lacked the organisational structures to offer much assistance). The bulk of this private relief was provided free or as subsided grain or free meals. To some extent, such apparent generosity was motivated by fear of public disorder and food rioting.[8] Public activity may also have been inspired by a fear of the spread of epidemic diseases. This became more likely when large numbers of people took to the roads, either to beg or to move to the towns where they sought relief, employment or escape on an emigrant ship. By 1741, fever, typhus and dysentery were widespread and contributed to a sharp rise in deaths. Excess mortality during this famine was high, probably between 300,000 and 400,000 people, making the losses comparable, if not proportionately higher, than those suffered during the Great Famine.[9]

Although the decades after 1741 have sometimes been regarded as representing 'a gap in famines' the term is misleading. In fact, the late eighteenth century was marked by a large number of poor harvests and subsistence crises.[10] There were harvest failures, for example, in 1745–46, 1753, 1756, 1766, 1769–70, 1772–73, 1782–84, 1795–96 and 1800–1. They were all, however, local or regional, and excess mortality tended to be slight. To some extent, this highlights the importance of external factors in transforming a poor harvest into a famine. For example, the absence of war and a good harvest elsewhere could allow food to be imported. Crop failure was not inevitably followed by famine in a situation where trade (both internal and international) was an established part of economic relations. The role of local elites in responding to the scarcities was also important and suggests the rudiments of a system of 'moral economy' within Ireland.[11]

The food shortages of the eighteenth century highlighted the changing role of the state in welfare provision. Despite there being no Poor Law in Ireland until 1838, in the latter part of the eighteenth century, more than twenty county infirmaries and eight Houses of Industry had been established, giving the country the rudiments of a welfare system. Moreover, relatively low rates of mortality, even in these periods of distress, demonstrated that the state was becoming increasingly interventionist and sophisticated in responding to food shortages.

One of the most serious instances of food scarcity in the late eighteenth century occurred in 1782–84. It was prompted by cold, wet weather which resulted in a poor grain harvest, but was intensified by an international economic slump which contributed to high unemployment and inflated food prices. The impact of these shortages was felt mostly in grain-eating and industrialised Dublin and east Ulster and thus bore a resemblance to a similar situation in 1847. In Dublin, the House of Industry increased its capacity and public subscriptions were made, including a door-to-door collection by the Catholic Church.[12] However, the extent of the distress was beyond the resources of the fledgling system of poor relief and private charity, thus the greater portion of the burden fell on the government. The Lord Lieutenant responded promptly by placing an embargo on the export of corn, potatoes, flour and associated products, despite lobbying from the mercantile interest.[13] The 1782 Corn Law was also temporarily suspended and the Lord Lieutenant made available £100,000 as bounty payments on imports of oats and wheat. The impact of these measures was immediate and food prices started to fall. A contemporary newspaper observed that if the embargo had not been introduced, 'there would not be more than five pounds of bread for a shilling, by Christmas Day. A famine must have been the consequence.'[14]

Further bad weather in the winter of 1783–84 prolonged the subsistence crisis. Again, the authorities in Dublin demonstrated flexibility and imagination in alleviating the distress. More public and private funds were provided and the Dublin House of Industry, no longer able to admit the poor, gave outdoor relief for the first time in January 1784. This meant that in addition to the 1300 inmates, 5000 people were being fed daily on outdoor relief. The Dublin authorities were subsidising local parish committees, who were feeding a further 9000 people daily. They took only ten days to establish and implement this scheme.[15] Not only was the scale of relief considerable, the quantity provided to individuals was generous, especially when measured against the standards of the 1840s. The poor were fed a pound of bread, a herring and a pint of beer daily. On a wider level, the Lord Lieutenant was given increased control over the corn trade and used these powers again to control the export of corn. Although there was a certain amount of excess mortality, it was much lower than in other periods of scarcity. The response of the authorities in 1782–84 also suggests a qualitatively different response to the poor, when compared with the measures taken at the time of the Great Famine. In each subsistence crisis, policy formulations were shaped by a combination of practical, ideological and political considerations. The difference in the speed, scale and effectiveness of the response to food shortages in the two periods indicates that a different set of priorities, motivations and perspectives determined relief policies in times of shortage and high prices. Overall, this suggested 'that the abolition of the Irish parliament [in 1800] resulted in a disimprovement in the political response to such cases'.[16]

The distress of 1800 was again precipitated by unusually severe weather, which resulted in localised failures of the potato crop. Again, the local gentry were active in providing relief and the government responded by importing large quantities of rye flour and Indian corn (probably for the first time).[17] The years following the Napoleonic Wars were marked by an economic downswing throughout Europe. Unseasonable weather in 1816 resulted in poor harvests and food shortages in all parts of the Continent, resulting in the (inaccurate) epithet 'the last great subsistence crisis of the western world'.[18] In the United Kingdom, there was a high level of government intervention, partly motivated by fear of social unrest. In England, public works were introduced, but in Ireland, where the shortages were more severe, a more extensive package of relief measures was implemented, including the importation of corn into the west, which was then sold at subsidised prices. However, significant quantities of this corn were found to be of poor quality and some instances of fraud were reported. This led to the establishment of a Relief Commission in the following year of shortages, which decided upon public works schemes as the main mechanism for alleviating distress.[19]

Mortality during the 1817–18 subsistence crisis was in excess of 65,000 which, although lower than in a number of other European countries (notably Switzerland and Austria), was much higher than the example of the previous 50 years in Ireland. Expenditure by the central government was high (in the region of £500,000), but a shift in attitude by the central authorities was evident. The Chief Secretary, Robert Peel, deliberately chose not to impose embargoes on grain exports – a device which had been used to good effect in earlier decades. Peel justified this on the grounds that it would prove 'prejudicial to the cause of humanity, as it would induce individuals to relax their benevolent exertions if they found the state willing to become the dispenser of charity'. Instead, a proclamation in June 1817 suggested that 'persons in the higher spheres of life should discontinue the use of potatoes in their families and reduce the allowance of oats to their horses'.[20]

The subsistence crisis of 1821–22 was also caused by bad weather, which damaged the potato but not the grain crop. The resultant shortages were local and mostly confined to the south and west of the country. The government brought corn into the west and extended its programme of public works, placing them on a more permanent footing. As a consequence of this policy, many roads, piers and hospitals were constructed in the west in the decades prior to 1840. In 1821–22, a central Relief Commission was established to support and monitor the work of local relief committees. Following the precedent established in 1817, financial assistance to the committees was made dependent on local contributions. Again, the government spent approximately £500,000 on the relief of distress and, as had been the case in 1817, there was considerable generosity shown by the local landlords and gentry.[21] Substantial sums were also raised in England, Scotland and a number of British colonies.[22] Despite this high financial outlay, by the summer of 1822, there were reports of people in the west subsisting on seaweed and being too weak to bury their dead.[23]

In 1831, there were further food shortages in Ireland, although these were confined mainly to Counties Galway and Mayo. Again, private donations were significant. Subscriptions were raised throughout Britain and Ireland, which included donations from the House Committee in Dublin and the London Tavern Committee, both of which had been involved in raising money in 1821–22.[24] Yet attitudes within Britain – both public and private – appeared to be hardening. To some extent, this was evident in the contemporaneous debate on the issue of poverty which resulted in the draconian English Poor Law of 1834 and its Irish counterpart in 1838. As a consequence of this ideological shift, poverty came to be viewed as the fault of the individual and therefore should not be treated too sympathetically. At the same time, Irish landlords began to be blamed for the economic backwardness of the country; it was felt that they should take more responsibility for the consequences of Ireland's underdevelopment.[25]

There were partial failures of the potato crop in 1835, 1839 and 1842, mostly confined to the west of Ireland. In 1838, a permanent system of poor relief had been established in Ireland. None the less, the government refused to allow its relief administration or the workhouses to be used to provide extraordinary relief, on the grounds that they wished to keep the permanent (and limited) system of poor relief separate from any measures needed to help short-term distress. However, the establishment of a Poor Law in Ireland and the introduction of a system of local taxation to finance it, appeared to make local landlords less willing to contribute privately to relief. The precedent of keeping the Poor Law separate from temporary relief measures was again followed in 1845–46. Significantly, the government believed that it was not possible to expect local taxpayers to bear the burden of financing relief during a period of shortages.[26] This policy was reversed in 1847, when local ratepayers were expected to bear the burden of all famine relief.

Overall, the period of scarcities before the Great Famine demonstrated a long history of state involvement in famine relief. This intervention took a variety of forms which were frequently innovative and effective. The periods of scarcity also demonstrated a shift in the pattern of distress from the east to the west of the country, as an increasing percentage of the population became dependent on the potato. Although the famine of 1741–42 was in some ways comparable with the Great Famine a century later, there were differences that make simple comparisons invalid. First, the Great Famine was distinguished by its persistence, there being seven successive years of blight. Second, there were changes in the wider political and economic environment over the intervening 100 years. The infrastructure of Ireland had improved greatly, partly as a result of the facilities provided through the public works. As a consequence of developments in transport, especially shipping, Ireland was extensively linked to an international marketplace. Food surpluses could quickly be shifted from one part of the world to another in this situation. The scale and pace of change had been even more extensive in Britain, which had become established as the leading industrial nation in the world. These developments sharpened the contrast between the two countries and Ireland's allegedly poor economic performance was increasingly compared unfavourably with that of Britain. Economic regeneration, especially on the English model, became a concern and objective of successive governments, culminating with Peel's administration after 1841.

The nature of government involvement in social welfare had also changed. After 1838, 130 workhouses were built throughout the

country, providing Ireland with a national administrative machinery
for the relief of poverty. The new Poor Law, however, was the
legislative embodiment of an ideological hardening of attitudes
towards poverty. The intellectual context had also changed as the
ideas of Adam Smith, Thomas Malthus and their various devotees
helped to shape the philosophy of political economy, with its
preference for little and cheap government. Moreover, the spread
of evangelicalism had imbued a number of influential figures in
government with a view of a wrathful, vengeful God increasingly
demanding atonement from those who had committed the sin of
being poor. Perhaps of most importance in determining the response
to famines in the mid-nineteenth century was the fact that the political
context had changed. Overall, the impact of the Act of Union
appears to have

> increased the distance between the Irish people and the legislature
> responsible for their government, and resulted, in the main, in
> the transfer of responsibility for key decisions to a small nexus
> of Englishmen who were less sympathetic to Irish poverty and
> more disinclined to countenance interference with normal
> commercial activity than the more empathetic Irish-manned
> executive in the late eighteenth century.[27]

Potatoes and the Coming of Blight

Potatoes originated in the Andes region of South America and were
believed to have been brought to England in the middle of the
sixteenth century by Sir Walter Raleigh, who planted them on his
properties in Ireland in the 1580s. Initially, they were used as a
vegetable for the gentry. In the seventeenth century, however, they
became a field vegetable, especially in the province of Munster. At
this stage, potatoes were primarily a supplement to a diet of oats,
grain and dairy foods.[28] By the beginning of the eighteenth century,
potatoes had become the staple winter food of the poor, especially
in the provinces of Leinster and Connaught. As a consequence,
there was a decrease in the oat-growing zone which had previously
surrounded the potato districts. Increasingly, oats became centred
in the north of the country. Although these continued to be grown
alongside potatoes, they were no longer part of the diet, but were
grown as a cash crop. By the beginning of the nineteenth century,
the potato was the staple food for cottiers and small farmers
throughout the west of the country, but also in parts of Leinster
and eastern Ulster. This was due partly to the rapid and sustained
growth in the Irish population after 1750. The Napoleonic Wars
became an additional factor by increasing the demand for Irish corn
by the bread-hungry population of Britain. This meant that profits

from tillage farming were high. The resulting expansion and commercialisation of the Irish corn sector – and, by implication, Britain's industrial advance – were underpinned by the potato economy.

The cultivation of the potato throughout Ireland was helped by the country's temperate climate, as the vegetable's main enemy was frost rather than rain. Potatoes were easy to grow even in poor quality, boggy or rocky soil and in hilly areas. As the population expanded, this became of particular importance because increasing numbers of people were forced onto ever more marginal and higher land. Potato growing was well suited to a people who possessed no capital and who lived on small plots of land which were rented rather than owned.

Potatoes are a prolific plant – approximately 1 acre of poor ground can yield up to 6 tons. This level of output was necessary in nineteenth-century Ireland as consumption was high. The average daily intake of an adult male was 14 pounds (approximately 6 kilos). Potatoes were consumed not only by Irish labourers, but by other social groups. Even more importantly, they were eaten by pigs and other farm animals – as much as 30 per cent of the annual crop was consumed in this way. As a consequence, in years when the crop was poor, animals rather than humans bore the main brunt of the shortages. Potato growing, when combined with access to mountains for grazing, bogs for turf, the coast for seaweed and fishing, and pigs for producing manure and paying the rent, provided an integrated and effective system of production.

Until the disastrous 1840s, Irish potatoes were relatively disease-free, making them more reliable than grain. Potatoes required little effort to cook, unlike grain, which had to be processed before being consumed. The former provided a highly nutritious, high energy and low fat diet. They were also palatable and, whilst a potato diet may have been monotonous, the consumers appeared to enjoy it. After 1845, when potatoes were in short supply, they were missed as a basic food. Elizabeth Smith, a farmer's wife in County Wicklow, recounted the reaction of her labourers to this change in their diet: 'good bread, greens, milk, bacon, pork etc. yet no one is satisfied – all miss the potatoes. Even old Peggy is all lamentation, no other food is so strengthening.'[29] Potatoes were also highly nutritious – much more so than the grain-based diet of the poor in Britain. Many contemporary observers, whilst noting the poverty of Irish people, also commented on their health and good looks. The eighteenth-century economist, Adam Smith, commenting on the Irish in London, was unequivocal in attributing their health and handsome looks to the potato:

> The chairmen, porters, coalheavers in London, and those unfortunate women who live by prostitution, the strongest

men and the most beautiful women perhaps in the British
dominions, are said to be, the greater part of them, from the
lowest rank of people in Ireland, who are generally fed from
this root. No food can afford a more decisive proof of its
nourishing quality, or its being particularly suitable to the
health of the human constitution.[30]

Over generations, the system of growing potatoes had been
tailored to meet Irish soil, climate and landscape conditions. They
were usually grown in ridges or rows which were described
pejoratively as 'lazy beds'. This system, however, was an efficient
way of utilising land, maximising drainage and providing shelter
from inclement weather. Because growing potatoes was labour-
intensive, it absorbed the surplus agricultural population and
enabled further demographic growth. This was particularly necessary
following the ending of the Napoleonic Wars in 1815, when a
general agricultural depression combined with a series of bad
harvests, notably between 1817 and 1822. This slump also coincided
with a decline in Ireland's cottage industries, notably textiles. As
farm wages became depressed, potato cultivation provided an
alternative means of survival. The intensive use of the spade and
manure ensured good crop yields from the potato ridges. Crop yields
in Ireland were amongst the highest in Europe – all the more
surprising in a country frequently described as agriculturally
backward and inefficient.[31]

The probity and productiveness of the potato were not
unmitigated. Potatoes were difficult to transport and had little
commercial value (although there was a small export trade).[32] The
poorer varieties in particular did not store well. The crop lasted
9–10 months, which meant that the so-called 'meal months' of July
and August had to be supported by other means. Also, there were
periodic failures of the crop, usually due to bad weather or disease.
Paradoxically, a consequence of the potato economy was that
where population growth was most intense, the land was of the
poorest quality. This meant that west of a line from Sligo to
Waterford, the vast majority of the population depended on a
single crop for subsistence. This narrow economic base of production
supplied the food needs of 60 per cent of the population.

The potato economy also acted as a lynchpin within the wider
agricultural sector. As tillage expanded, it was underpinned by the
rundale and clachan system (community-based production), which
allowed massive exports of corn whilst the majority of the population
survived on potatoes. The potato economy provided farmers with
a cheap, well-fed workforce with few material expectations. Rent
was paid either in casual labour which could be supplemented
through seasonal migration, or through the sale of a pig (the

spailpin system). Surplus potatoes were used to feed pigs. Before being sold for rent, pigs produced good quality manure which, in turn, ensured a high potato yield. Potato growing, however, was increasingly associated with cultural backwardness. When linked with 'Papism', this proved to be a fatal combination. It also tied the peasants to the land and allowed them to continue to survive on land that was highly subdivided. However, the 'clachans' or communities in which the potato growers lived enjoyed relatively little interference from external bodies such as landlords, the Church or even the state (all of whom were becoming increasingly interventionist) and possessed their own economic, cultural and social cohesion.[33]

To outsiders, however, separated by either social class or nationality, the potato was the root of many social evils and its passing was to be welcomed rather than mourned. Thus Elizabeth Smith noted in 1846, 'The potatoe [sic] crop gone, here and everywhere the root I suppose extinct, and were we once this first year may be 'tis best, for the cheapness of this low description of food encouraged idleness, pauper marriages and dirty habits, and neither mind nor body could be fully developed upon such nourishment.'[34] This sentiment was given official endorsement by Sir Randolph Routh, the Chief Commissioner in charge of relief operations during 1845–46. In his opinion:

> The little industry called for to rear the potato, and its prolific growth, leave the people to indolence and all kinds of vice, which habitual labour and a higher order of food would prevent. I think it very probable that we may derive much advantage from this present calamity.[35]

This perception of the potato, and the social system that depended on it, shaped Britain's response to successive years of failure of the potato crop. Viewed from such a perspective, the blight could be seen not only as positive and providential, but as a fast track to economic regeneration.

One of the consequences of the post-1815 agricultural depression was an increasing dependence on the potato crop. However, not only were people increasingly relying on one crop, they were also mainly relying on one variety – the ubiquitous lumper or 'horse potato'. This was particularly true in Munster and Connaught. The provinces of Leinster and Ulster possessed more diverse economies and a greater range of potato varieties.[36] The lumper had gained popularity in the early part of the nineteenth century as it was easy to grow, even in very poor quality soils, and required relatively little manure or spade work. However, it was generally believed to be less nutritious and flavoursome than other more traditional potato varieties, such as the 'cup', 'black' or 'apple'.[37] In England, it was regarded primarily as an animal food. Overall, this meant that by the 1840s, a large portion of the Irish population had moved towards a system of virtual monoculture, in which the lumper potato was pre-eminent.

The Famine was triggered by *phytophthora infestans* or 'late blight'. This disease was caused by a fungus, which had probably originated in Mexico.[38] Extremely fast-spreading, being carried by wind or water, the fungus had the ability to recreate 'countless, asexually produced zoospores'.[39] Its spores germinated on the leaves and stems of the potato plant, or on the surrounding soil. The disease showed itself as dark spots on the leaves, followed by a furry growth. Thereafter, the stems and leaves decayed and the plant died. At the same time, the potato tubers became discoloured and turned into a dark pulpy mess. This was accompanied by an unpleasant odour, which for many potato growers was the first indication that their crops had blight.[40]

Blight had been observed on the potato crop in the United States in 1843, and from there was transmitted to mainland Europe, possibly by ships carrying manure. In 1845, blight was noted on a number of potato crops in Belgium, France, Germany and Switzerland. It then appeared in the Channel Islands, the south of England, the south of Scotland and the east coast of Ireland. The disease thrived in damp, humid conditions. The summer of 1845, being generally thundery, windy and with little sunshine, created ideal conditions for the spread of spores. The potato blight was first noticed in Ireland, in the Botanic Gardens in Dublin, at the end of August 1845.[41] By September, it had started to appear in the commercial sector. In that month, Dr Lindley, the editor of the prestigious *Gardener's Chronicle*, used a special issue of the journal to announce that 'the potato murrain has unequivocally declared itself in Ireland' and asked rhetorically, 'Where will Ireland be in the event of a universal potato rot?', thus giving an early indication of the impending disaster.[42] By the end of 1845, one-third of the crop had been lost to blight, although most of the losses occurred in the more prosperous east of the country. In 1846, almost 80 per cent of the crop was destroyed. In 1847, losses were again high, as much as one-third was destroyed of only a small crop. In 1848, approximately half was lost, although losses were primarily in the west. Between 1849 and 1852, blight reappeared, but was localised and centred mostly in the counties of the south-west of the country. Overall, the blight was unprecedented in its duration, geographic scope and tragic impact.

Diseases of the potato crop were not new in Ireland. The 'curl' had been in evidence from the 1760s and 'taint' or 'dry rot' since the 1830s.[43] But *Phytophthora infestans* was a new disease with no known cause or antidote. A number of observers believed that the disease was due to over-dependence on one potato variety, whilst the intensive use of land led others to believe that the disease was due to a degeneration in the potato. An influential interpretation, held by peasants, priests and politicians, was that the Famine was God's judgment, although their reasons for this judgment varied widely.[44] The British government, led by Sir Robert Peel, approached the appearance of disease calmly and clinically. In October 1845, a Scientific Commission was established with the dual purpose of assessing the true extent of crop losses and finding a palliative for it. Peel believed the first duty to be of particular importance within Ireland, on the grounds that 'there is such a tendency to exaggeration and inaccuracy in Irish reports that delay in acting upon them is always desirable'.[45] The Scientific Commissioners, however, were unsuccessful in both their missions. First, they overestimated the extent of potato crop lost, and second, although they devised various elaborate schemes for saving, storing or salvaging the diseased crop, none of these plans was successful. More importantly, they failed to find an antidote to the new disease.[46] The Commissioners initially misdiagnosed the blight, believing it to be a form of 'wet rot', whilst ignoring the claims of a number of botanists that it was caused by a fungus. More significantly, however, by overestimating the extent of the losses, they may have inadvertently caused Peel's government to give more relief than it would otherwise have done. As a consequence, the relief provided in the first year of distress was more extensive than Peel had intended it should be and, retrospectively, the assistance provided in 1845–46 appeared uniquely generous and effective.

Peel and the Politics of Repeal

When blight first appeared in 1845, Sir Robert Peel was prime minister of the United Kingdom. Peel was a skilled politician with over 35 years' parliamentary experience. During his long career he had angered and alienated many members of his own party, notably on issues concerned with Ireland, most particularly over his unexpected support for Catholic Emancipation in 1829 and, as part of his longer-term plan to change Irish society from above, by increasing the grant to Maynooth College at the beginning of 1845. Both of these actions were regarded as a betrayal of a cornerstone of the Tory commitment to the Anglican Church and a dangerous concession to Papism. Viewed in this way, it was convenient for some politicians, especially those imbued with evangelical spleen, to view the Famine as a judgment of God on Irish Catholics.[47]

Peel's involvement with Irish affairs was long-standing. His first parliamentary seat, won when he was aged only 21, had been Cashel in County Tipperary in 1809. In 1812, he was appointed Chief Secretary for Ireland in Lord Liverpool's new government. During his six years in this position, Peel acquired a reputation for dealing firmly with insurrection and outrages. An important part of his response was the founding of a permanent police force in Ireland in 1814. Peel's approach was underpinned by his belief that 'The Irish needed firm lessons because they could not understand oblique ones'.[48] He also acquired a reputation for opposing Catholic Emancipation, although he disliked the extremism of the Orange Order. In 1818, Peel resigned as Chief Secretary on the grounds of exhaustion; nevertheless, he was to be the longest serving Chief Secretary in the nineteenth century. After he left office, Peel never set foot in Ireland again.[49]

Before he left Ireland, Peel had gained direct experience of food shortages as a result of the localised potato failures of 1816 and 1817. Almost £40,000 was raised for famine relief through a combination of public works and additional foodstuffs (mainly oats and biscuits) being brought into the country by the government. In the second year of shortages, and to help to eliminate the abuses of the previous year, a Commission was set up to oversee the work of the local relief committees. Peel's response at this time was motivated as much by a fear of widespread violence as by his concern for the Irish peasants. He also viewed the public works as a means of contributing to the long-term improvement of Ireland, which was to become one of the cornerstones of his later Irish policies. As he was to do in 1845, he insisted on accurate information before he acted. He had reason to believe that this was judicious. At the beginning of 1817, the Lord Lieutenant had asked Peel to request that the government close the ports to potato exports from Ireland as a means of alleviating distress. Peel, following a characteristically thorough investigation, found that potato imports far exceeded exports. He wrote an exasperated note to the Lord Lieutenant stating:

> I cannot tell you how embarrassed I am ... After having had a meeting of the Government ... and seriously discussed the policy of immediately prohibiting the export of potatoes from Ireland, I must now inform those that attended that meeting that the imports into Ireland exceeded the exports from it in the last two months in the proportion of three to one.[50]

Peel's direct involvement in the alleviation of food shortages in 1816–18 was reinforced by his more indirect involvement in the distress of 1822 when as Home Secretary he also had overall responsibility for the relief measures. In 1845, these experiences combined with his ambitions for regenerating Ireland and his moves towards economic liberalism to shape a response to the potato failure.

The Tory Party had come to power in 1841 with a commanding majority of 76 seats. In Ireland, however, the Whigs had won a majority with only 41 per cent of seats there won by the Tories. The 1841 general election was a victory for Protectionist Toryism, that is, those who did not want to lose the protection of the Corn Laws. Yet at this stage, Peel was a proponent of economic liberalism, believing that agricultural and industrial capitalists had to be free from restrictions to exploit markets and thereby increase their profits. This inevitably meant the repeal of the Corn Laws. Peel also believed that social harmony would be a natural consequence of economic progress.[51] In Ireland, the Maynooth grant and the establishment of the Devon Commission to investigate the system of landholding in Ireland were the first steps in bringing about the economic and social reconstruction of Ireland. The Maynooth grant, however, was achieved at a cost to Tory Party unity as it was passed only with the support of the Whig opposition. The appearance of potato blight in 1845, therefore, has to be viewed within the context of the intellectual and ideological struggles which were taking place, not only between the Whig and Tory Parties, but also within the parties themselves.

The potato blight in Ireland exposed Peel's ideological differences with many members of his party, particularly the backbenchers. The 1815 Corn Law – the buttress of protectionism – had been modified and liberalised in 1828 and 1842. These relaxations provided clear indicators of Peel's commitment to free trade. For Peel in the mid-1840s, the challenge was to bring about repeal without losing the support of the majority of his party and also without appearing to concede victory to the Anti-Corn Law League. From the outset, the potato failure in Ireland became inextricably linked with the issue of the repeal of the Corn Laws. This concern not only helped shape policy formulations in the following nine months, but at times meant that Ireland's immediate needs were subordinated to Britain's long-term interests. By early October 1845, Peel was linking the potato failure with the need for repeal. Despite receiving alarming reports from Ireland, including a number from the Lord Lieutenant, Peel's past experience led him to believe that these were likely to be based on 'exaggeration and inaccuracy'. More importantly, he knew that the impact of food shortages would not be felt until the following spring and summer, which gave him an opportunity to plan a programme of relief measures. Even at this stage, Peel was clear as to what these measures should and should not include. Writing to Sir James Graham, his Home Secretary and loyal supporter, he commented, 'I have no confidence in such remedies as the prohibition of exports, or the stoppage of the distilleries. The removal of impediments to import is the only effectual remedy.'[52]

In the wake of the initial reports on the potato blight in Ireland, suggestions were made on how best to deal with the shortages. Few of these proposals linked relief measures with the need for repeal. Lord Heytesbury, the Lord Lieutenant of Ireland, suggested that the ports in Ireland should be opened to facilitate the importation of corn. Graham and Peel rejected this on the grounds that it would be unfair to give Ireland preferential treatment.[53] By the end of October, as the situation deteriorated, Heytesbury again wrote to Peel, asking if he could issue a proclamation prohibiting distillation from grain, adding 'this is demanded on all sides'.[54] Again, his advice was ignored. This suggests that Peel was placing more faith in his scientific advisers than in his official representative in Ireland, and that he already had a relief plan for Ireland which would entail more permanent changes. In Dublin, the Mansion House Committee, which had been formed in 1821 to raise subscriptions for distressed areas, was reconstituted at the end of October 1845. The Committee (whose members included the Duke of Leinster, Daniel O'Connell and Henry Grattan) organised a deputation to the Lord Lieutenant to present a programme of relief measures which included employing people in works of 'national utility', closing the ports against the export of corn, establishing public granaries and banning the use of grain in distilleries. The delegation, however, was treated curtly and their requests ignored, possibly for a mixture of political and partisan reasons.[55] Similar requests were made by influential organisations in Belfast, Cork and Derry, who suggested that the ports in Ireland be opened to facilitate the importation of food. Again, they were ignored.[56]

In late October, as part of Peel's determination to have full and accurate information from Ireland, he despatched 'two men of the highest eminence in the department of science to which they belonged, Professor Lindley and Dr Lyon Playfair' to Ireland.[57] Their preliminary findings appeared to confirm estimates already provided by the Lord Lieutenant, namely, that half the crop had been ruined and that as much as five-sixths could be lost in the season.[58] The news from Ireland coincided with reports of widespread potato failure in England (especially the south) and in Scotland, which gave credibility to the reports from Ireland. By contrast, in the harvest of 1846, the blight had almost totally disappeared from England, which made reports of a second catastrophic failure in Ireland less believable.

The gloomy prognosis from Ireland suggested that the food shortages were quantitatively different from earlier crop failures and that the crisis was national rather than local or regional. Peel responded promptly by putting in place a package of measures which would be available by the following spring. Once agreed, Peel gave the measures relatively little attention, leaving their implementation in Ireland to the Lord Lieutenant and Sir Randolph Routh, a Commissary General in the Army who had been brought out of semi-retirement to chair the Relief Commission,[59] as successor to Sir Edward Lucas. In London Charles Trevelyan was to oversee the financial aspect of the undertaking. The key aspect of the measures was the secret purchase of £100,000 of Indian corn (a form of maize) from North America and the financing of a programme of public works. The Indian corn was estimated by a government official to be sufficient to feed one million people for 40 days. In view of the losses estimated by the Scientific Commissioners this was insufficient to meet the food deficit.[60] Peel hoped that the government imports, however, would help regulate the market price of corn. By the end of January, the government's food purchases were beginning to arrive in Cork. By this stage, it was becoming clear that the Scientific Commission had overestimated the extent of the losses as, by the end of 1845, the blight appeared to have run its course. This meant that the ensuing shortages would not be as extensive as the Commissioners had anticipated. Consequently, Peel's relief measures appeared to be more generous than had been intended. The resultant efficacy of his response was, ironically, based on a miscalculation by his 'men of science'.

The repeal of the Corn Laws dominated political discourse and public discussion from October 1845 until June 1846 and this, rather than Irish relief, was Peel's major concern during this period. In October and November 1845, he held a series of meeting with his Cabinet in which he prepared the ground for the repeal of the Corn Laws. By way of persuasion, Peel referred to the crop failures in Russia, Belgium and Holland, where the governments had responded to the expected food scarcities by suspending their protective legislation.[61] Many members of his Cabinet remained ideologically opposed to the measure and two members resigned. A further crisis was precipitated, moreover, at the end of November by the publication in a number of London newspapers, of the so-called 'Edinburgh Letter' by the leader of the Whig Party, Lord John Russell, in which he declared his personal support for total repeal. In the wake of these two events, Peel resigned on 6 December, possibly as a tactical means of holding his fragmented party together. Russell, however, largely due to internal party divisions, was unable to form a government and so handed, in his own words, 'the poisoned chalice' back to Peel.[62] Following an absence of two weeks, Peel was again in power, his own position strengthened by the disarray of the Whig opposition.

At the beginning of 1846, when the news from Ireland suggested that the distress would not be as severe as had been feared, Peel continued to press for a repeal of the Corn Laws. A shift in emphasis was now becoming apparent as he increasingly used the 'Condition of England' question as much as the Irish potato blight as the imperative for repeal. Again, for Peel the timing was significant as the post-Napoleonic Wars surplus of European corn had long disappeared as a result of bad harvests, making repeal not only ideologically desirable but a safe option. The price of corn had fallen in Britain and profit margins had also declined. Perhaps even more pertinent, in the context of Ireland's recent experiences 'A situation in which the Corn laws protected the British farmer against continental post-war glut was giving way to one in which their retention threatened Britain with Famine.'[63] For Peel's colleagues, however, the Irish situation had been the instigator of the repeal crisis. The Duke of Wellington, for example, with characteristic bluffness, announced 'Rotten potatoes have done it all. They put Peel in his damned fright.'[64] Lord George Bentinck, who was emerging as the leader of the Tory Protectionist opposition, claimed that the fear of an Irish famine had been used as a pretext or 'mere pretence', which Peel had engineered by despatching a Scientific Commission to Ireland.[65]

By the spring of 1846, it was becoming increasingly evident in Peel's speeches that the repeal of the Corn Laws was unlikely to benefit the economy of Ireland either in the short or long term. The paradox of the 1815 Corn Laws had been that they had simultaneously contributed to and softened the blow of Ireland's post-war de-industrialisation. Their repeal would leave Ireland's agricultural sector vulnerable, especially to competition from pasture farming, which proved to be the case. Peel was aware of these outcomes, admitting that 'if there be a part of the United Kingdom which is to suffer by the withdrawal of protection ... it was Ireland'.[66] Instead, he made the 'Condition of England' question the imperative for repeal, arguing that, 'I do not rest my support of this bill upon the temporary ground of scarcity in Ireland ... the real question at issue is the improvement of the social and moral condition of the masses of the population.'[67]

The Corn Laws were repealed in June 1846 with a comfortable majority, but only because of the full support of the Whig Party. Peel's government fell shortly afterwards following the defeat of an Irish Coercion Bill, introduced to control 'outrages' in Ireland. Both directly and indirectly, therefore, an Irish question had again lost Peel the support of many within his own party. Following this débâcle, the Tory Party split into two groupings, the Peelites led by Peel and the Protectionists, led by Bentinck. Although Peel appeared to have been consigned to the political wilderness, he was frequently consulted in private by members of the Whig Party on issues of policy during the next three years. Overall, he disliked many of the relief policies of the Whig administration, believing that their famine measures were not bold enough to help regenerate Ireland.[68]

Although repeal was achieved in the summer of 1846, it was too little and too late to have any impact on food shortages in Ireland. Furthermore, the Corn Laws were dismantled in stages over a period of three years. As the Famine bit even harder in the winter of 1846–47, corn still continued to carry a duty of 4 shillings per quarter, although duty on Indian corn was only 1 shilling a quarter. If Peel's primary purpose had been to allow cheap food into Ireland in the wake of the potato blight, he could have used the precedent of issuing a temporary Proclamation, as had been suggested by the Lord Lieutenant. Peel chose not to do this, but to use instead the crisis created by the potato blight – especially in October and November 1845, when potato losses appeared to be considerable – to initiate the removal of remaining obstacles to free trade. His ideological conversion to free trade took precedence over the needs of one part of the United Kingdom. At this stage, nobody foresaw that the blight would return for seven consecutive years – for the potato crop to fail for two consecutive years was very unusual. Yet Peel used a temporary crisis to bring about permanent changes in the economies of Britain and Ireland. The fact that no one died during the first year of shortages – for which Peel has frequently been praised – was due more to the quirks of the potato blight than to Peel's commitment to the potato growers of Ireland.

The Provision of Relief

The potato blight was first identified in Ireland at the end of August 1845. Although scattered outbreaks were apparent in September, initially there was little concern. On 16 September, the government asked the local constabulary to make confidential reports on the blight's progress. When the main digging commenced in October, some of the tubers proved to be rotten. Concern intensified as potatoes which had been stored in pits, apparently in a sound condition, were also found to be blighted. Reports from the local constabulary were contradictory, due to the patchy nature of the disease. But early indications suggested that Ireland was in the throes of the worst crop failure for over a century and the threat of an imminent famine was very real.

Peel had responded to the diverse reports from Ireland by seeking more precise information through the appointment of a Scientific Commission. Although the Scientific Commissioners misdiagnosed the disease and were unable to provide an antidote, their evidence corroborated the seriousness of the potato losses. Peel, who in November 1845 had put in place a programme of relief measures, stated that he found the reports of 'the men of science ... very alarming'.[69]

By the end of 1845, the blight appeared to have peaked. At this stage it was evident that the Commissioners had overestimated losses from the disease. A further survey of its progress was carried out by the Irish constabulary in March 1846. Whilst the mechanics of collating the data were not standardised and some areas were omitted from the collection, it gave an indication of the areas most affected. The blight had been most virulent in Counties Armagh, Clare, Kilkenny, Louth, Monaghan and Waterford, which had suffered over 40 per cent losses.[70] The fact that its impact had not been so severe in the potato counties in the west also helped mitigate the impact of the blight in the first year of shortages. This was further helped by an excellent oat harvest in 1845.

The response of the British government to the blight was not dictated solely by the needs of the people who had lost their subsistence crop. Instead, an interpretative framework was provided, which reflected the ideological preoccupations of government ministers and their advisers as much as the needs of the destitute Irish. From these at times conflicting ideologies and interpretations, a model of relief was constructed which transcended political differences. This framework was shaped by several strands of thinking. For example, the writings of the political economists, particularly of Adam Smith, Thomas Malthus, Edmund Burke, Robert Torrens and David Ricardo, found favour amongst both policy-makers and the influential middle classes. A providential-ist interpretation of the blight cut across social barriers and found resonance with pauper and politician alike.[71] In the former, it contributed to a fatalist and quiescent approach to the disaster, which observers sometimes mistook for apathy. For politicians, especially those with ultra-evangelical or anti-Catholic views, a providentialist interpretation meant that the blight could be viewed as a warning and judgment on the Irish people (and, to a lesser degree, on the English for tolerating such travesties).[72]

Within both the Peel and Russell administrations, a number of key figures favoured a moralistic or providentialist approach to the catastrophe, which went beyond mere rhetoric. These included Sir James Graham (Home Secretary under Peel), Charles Wood (Chancellor of the Exchequer under Russell), Earl Grey (Russell's Minister for the Colonies) and Charles Trevelyan (Permanent Secretary of the Treasury under both Peel and Russell). Thus Graham, in a letter to Peel in October 1846, confided, 'I am greatly troubled by this Irish calamity ... It is awful to observe how the Almighty humbles the pride of nations.'[73] Furthermore, unlike the blight itself, the providentialist interpretation offered an antidote to this impiety: namely, atonement and repentance. However, even for those who did not apply a providentialist framework to the blight but preferred a more rationalist interpretation, the underpinning argument was the same – the potato failure was not only teaching the Irish people a lesson, but simultaneously providing an opportunity for change.

When choosing his package of relief measures, Peel had rejected demands from Ireland for an embargo to be placed on exports, ports to be closed and distillation to be stopped – all measures which had achieved a high level of success on previous occasions. He had also rejected a proposal from the Mansion House Committee that a tax be levied on absentee landlords.[74] Instead, Peel chose a combination of actions which blended short-term, temporary relief with the longer-term goal of repealing the Corn Laws. An unusual feature of the policy was the fact that the Treasury was given a key role in overseeing the distribution and expenditure of relief funds in order to ensure strict budgeting. As a consequence, Charles Trevelyan, Permanent Secretary at the Treasury, acquired an important role in the relief operations.

The short-term relief measures were to a large extent procedures which Peel had used successfully on previous occasions. In November 1845, he arranged for the secret purchase of £100,000 of Indian corn (maize) through the London merchant firm of Barings Brothers. Secrecy was employed in order not to deter other merchants from importing foodstuffs into Ireland. The bulk of privately imported corn did not arrive until the summer of 1846, and came mostly from the United States. On arrival in Ireland, the corn was stored in special depots from where it was to be released slowly onto the market. Local relief committees could purchase this corn and thereafter sell it at *cost* price, a feature which changed after 1846, when the Treasury insisted that government food had to be sold at *market* price. The main government corn depot was established in Cork and a number of smaller depots were established in other parts of the country. None was established in Ulster, where government intervention was considered to be unnecessary. Although the date for the opening of the depots was fixed at 15 May, the impact of the food shortages was felt as early as March. This resulted in a number of food riots taking place, notably in Carrick-on-Suir, Clonmel and Tipperary, most of the anger being directed against forestallers (speculators) and merchants who were charging 'famine' prices for their corn. The local authorities responded by asking for more military to be sent to these areas and for relief to be made available as soon as possible.[75] The extreme distress in a number of localities resulted in the depots being opened at the end of March.[76]

The Indian corn was not intended to meet the deficit caused by the potato shortages. Instead, it was intended to help to regulate food prices and to deter people from hoarding or speculating. A further purpose was the fact that corn was regarded as an ideal substitute for potatoes – it would allow the Irish to move up a cultural ladder, potatoes having tied the peasantry to the bottom rung for many decades. This substitution was viewed as an important step in Ireland's economic and social regeneration. Thus, the idea of using shortages as a mechanism for change was an important aspect of relief policy from the first appearance of blight.

A further strand of the relief policy was the establishment of a central Relief Commission in Dublin, initially chaired by Edward Lucas, the Under-Secretary at Dublin Castle. Following reorganisation in January 1846, Sir Randolph Routh was appointed Chairman. The duties of the Commission were to advise the government of the situation in the localities and to work closely with local relief committees. The latter were comprised of local landlords, large farmers and clergymen of all denominations. There were three main functions: to purchase and resell corn from government depots; to oversee employment on the relief works; and to raise voluntary subscriptions for the provision of relief. Funds raised were to be matched by money provided by the government of up to 100 per cent value, channelled through the office of the Lord Lieutenant.

During the spring and summer of 1846, almost 100 committees were formed throughout the country, the majority being in the south and west, with only a handful in Ulster. These raised almost £100,000 in donations, the largest sum ever raised by voluntary subscriptions. To this amount, the Lord Lieutenant added a further £65,914.[77] Despite this success in raising money, there were signs of tension between the local relief committees and central Relief Commission and between the central Commission and the Treasury. For example, the central authorities delayed allowing the local relief committees to provide relief. This was a deliberate tactic to limit demands on their resources.[78] More seriously, the high level of interference by Trevelyan in the day-to-day administration of the Commission annoyed the Relief Commissioners in Dublin, who complained of his actions. The outcome was the removal of Edward Lucas from the position of chairman whilst Trevelyan remained even more firmly in place.[79] From the outset, Trevelyan was stamping his own authority on relief proceedings in Ireland and was removing those people who opposed him.

The final plank of the government's relief measures was the public works. Public works had been used since 1817 to provide employment during periods of scarcities. In 1831, a Board of Works had been established in Dublin which was responsible for permanent improvements in roads, bridges, piers, harbours and the like. Following the appearance of blight in 1845, the Board of Works was also responsible for the provision of relief works. Instead of providing works of public utility, however, the work's main purpose was to provide employment and wages. The works were also regarded as a good way of encouraging Irish landlords to make improvements to their estates. This was encouraged by the government through a system of 'half-grants' and loans. Again, Trevelyan attempted to impose his authority on the scheme by insisting that the grant system be made less accessible to landlords, on the grounds that they were using 'the pretext of scarcity' for their own benefit.[80]

In order to cope with the extra demands being made on the Board of Public Works, a special relief department was established, complete with its own inspectors, engineers, surveyors, overseers and pay clerks. This bureaucracy, and the various checks demanded by the Treasury before a work could commence, delayed the effectiveness of the Board of Works in responding to requests for relief employment. This cumbersome machinery resulted in several complaints regarding the ineffectiveness of the scheme. At the same time, a number of abuses on the public works were reported in the British press, which served to reinforce cultural stereotypes regarding Irish indolence, and the greed and indifference of Irish landlords.[81]

The relief measures introduced by Peel's government in the first year of shortages were deliberately intended to be kept separate from the permanent system of relief based on the Irish Poor Law. The 1838 Poor Law, which permitted only indoor relief, was viewed as playing a subsidiary role to other relief. By 1845, 118 of the 130 workhouses planned for Ireland had been opened and were providing relief. The government did not want to permit outdoor relief – even on a temporary basis – on the grounds that it would become permanently embedded in the system. Whilst the number of paupers seeking relief in the workhouses did increase slightly, the main impact of the blight on the Irish Poor Law was the replacement in many workhouses of potatoes with Indian corn or, occasionally, rice.[82]

The relief measures introduced in the first year of shortages were largely successful. No excess mortality was recorded during this time. General satisfaction was expressed with the actions of the British government, and even the *Freeman's Journal*, generally critical of Peel, congratulated him on his handling of the crisis. Despite the widespread loss of the potato crop, Ireland did not experience famine in 1845–46. However, a number of aspects of relief proved to be less than satisfactory, especially in their implications for future relief policies. For example, the high degree of success in combating the results of the blight was regarded as an indication that relief provided by the government had been too generous. It was felt that this had depressed the need for local efforts. Consequently, despite the money raised and the effective input of many local relief committees, there was a growing belief in the press and political circles that Irish landlords were shirking their duty.[83] Public opinion was beginning to target the Irish landlords as a scapegoat for many of Ireland's ills, juxtaposing their alleged lack of involvement in famine relief with the extensive efforts made by British taxpayers. A general consensus emerged that the blight was an opportunity to bring about the long-desired regeneration of Irish society.

Whilst the importation of Indian corn had generally been successful, it had not displaced the potato as the staple Irish diet. Unlike potatoes, maize required considerable preparation before it could be eaten and the method of grinding and cooking was alien to the Irish. Sir Randolph Routh, who regarded himself as an expert on Indian corn, produced a pamphlet which served only to reinforce the complexity and slowness of this process. The corn, which became known popularly as 'Peel's Brimstone' or 'Yellow Male', had to be kept in kilns for 8 hours, dried for 48 hours, ground, allowed to stand for 70 hours, and then left to cool for at least a day before it was placed in sacks.[84] Many people fell ill from incorrectly preparing it. More importantly though, 1 pound of Indian corn did not satisfy the large appetites of a people used to a potato diet, either in terms of bulk, taste or nutrition. Despite the shortages of the previous season, most of the seed potatoes had been kept intact and in the spring of 1846, approximately 80 per cent of the usual acreage was planted. For the poor of Ireland, Indian corn was not a long-term alternative to the potato. The return to potatoes had not been achieved without some sacrifices. This often included the early selling of the pig, the main capital asset for paying the rent, or the pawning of other items of value, including winter clothes or fishing tackle. Consequently, the number of items pawned increased substantially in 1845 and 1846.[85] This high-risk strategy proved to be injudicious for, as early as July 1846, there were isolated reports of sightings of potato blight throughout the country, which suggested the ominous possibility of a second year of blight.

A further dimension of the relief policies introduced in 1845–46 was that, from the outset, they were highly politicised and debated in the public arena to an unprecedented extent. Despite the widespread praise for Peel's policies, his government fell in the summer of 1846, although his long-term ambition to repeal the Corn Laws had been achieved. Within Parliament, the Tory Party split into Protectionists and Peelites, the division hampering any effective or united opposition during the remaining Famine years. The fall of the Tories resulted in the coming to power of the Whig Party under Lord John Russell. They were to remain in office until 1852. Russell had come to power in 1846 as head of a minority government and his inability to form a government in December 1845 had demonstrated that the divisions within the Whig Party were as sharp as those within the Tory Party. This meant that from the outset Russell's position as prime minister was precarious. Following the general election in 1847, the Whigs gained more seats in parliament but they were mostly won by opponents of Russell which meant that he was increasingly isolated within his own party. Furthermore, many of the new seats were won by radical free traders who supported little and cheap government and demanded financial retrenchment, especially in the provision of relief to Ireland. This meant that within Westminster there were four main blocs. Irish MPs tended to identify themselves with the main political groupings, with the exception of the Repeal Party, which was also torn by internal divisions. In 1847, Irish MPs did unite in an attempt to influence the relief programme, but the coalition was short-lived and had no impact on policy.[86] Consequently, throughout the years of the Famine, relief policies were in the hands of a ruling elite whose political and ideological motivations were shaped by concerns which at times had little basis in the needs of the destitute Irish, but had more to do with preconceived notions of Ireland and perceptions of how the country should be restructured to suit the needs of its political partner.

CHAPTER 4

Putrefying Vegetation and 'Queen's Pay'

In 1846, the potato crop failed for the second successive year. The destruction of the crop was rapid and comprehensive, with a 90 per cent failure. The food shortage could no longer be viewed as a temporary or localised calamity. A national crisis had arrived.

The success of Peel's government in dealing with the scarcities in the previous year had unwittingly raised false expectations about the extent to which the government was prepared to intervene to combat food scarcities. After 1846, there was a sharp increase in the scale of food losses within Ireland and there were food shortages throughout Europe. At the same time, the Tory government had been replaced by a Whig administration dominated by political economists and free traders. A Whig government was initially welcomed by the majority of Irish MPs. But this welcome proved to be short-lived.

Despite the shortfall in food supplies after the 1846 harvest, the government decided not to intervene in the import or export of food from Ireland. The commitment to free trade was one of the few policies on which the members of the new Whig government could agree. As a consequence, massive amounts of food were exported from Ireland to feed the population of Britain. In the winter of 1846–47, food exports exceeded food imports to Ireland, resulting in a 'starvation gap' in supplies.

After 1846, the government chose public works as a means of alleviating distress. This policy was disastrous. The works were frequently of little benefit to the community, and as a mechanism for saving lives they failed. In the winter months, hundreds of thousands of destitute Irish died from disease, starvation, exposure or exhaustion. Simultaneously, social displacement caused by evictions and emigration soared. By the beginning of 1847, the name Skibbereen had become associated with suffering and human tragedy, not just in Ireland, but throughout the world.

The Whig government, like its predecessor, was committed to a policy of local responsibility and accountability. This policy was reflected to an increasing extent in various relief policies. Although they achieved little, the public works were expensive, costing over £5 million. Most of this money was provided as a loan which was to be repaid by Irish taxpayers. Following the failure of the public works, there were increasing calls within the British government for financial retrenchment and for landlords to support their own poor. These demands were welcomed in Britain, which was itself in the throes of an economic depression. Yet Ireland was not unique in undergoing crop failure and food shortages. Throughout Europe, both the corn and potato crops were poor. As in Ireland, the poorest groups in society were forced to depend on external sources for a livelihood. It was only in Ireland that the shortages were accompanied by such high levels of suffering, mortality and long-term political resentment.

Party Politics and the Triumph of Ideology

The return of blight in the summer of 1846 meant that the potato disease could no longer be viewed as a temporary calamity. Moreover, the blight was more extensive than it had been in the previous year and the final potato yield represented only one month's supply of sound potatoes.[1] For the potato crop to fail in two consecutive years was very unusual. Yet a number of factors ensured that the blight was far more devastating in 1846 than it had been in the previous year. Despite the appearance of blight in 1845, Irish labourers had remained loyal to this food source and 80 per cent of the crop had been sown in the spring of 1846. Throwing the diseased potatoes on the same land where the new crop was sown had served to reinfect the crop. Climatic conditions also played a part. The mild winter of 1845–46 had helped the disease to survive and the spores to propagate. Throughout Europe the summer of 1846 was hot, but in Ireland and Scotland the heatwave was followed by heavy rain and thunderstorms, which helped the blight to spread. In Ireland also, the winds that summer helped to carry the disease from the east to the west of the country.[2]

In 1846, the disease appeared early (there were numerous sightings throughout July) and it spread rapidly, travelling at an estimated 50 miles a week.[3] The rapid spread of the blight and its destructive impact were noted by many people, including the Irish Temperance leader, Father Mathew. On a journey from Cork to Dublin in July, he observed 'this doomed plant in all the luxuriance of an abundant harvest. Returning on 3rd. inst. [August] I beheld with sorrow one wide waste of putrefying vegetation.'[4] By mid-September, blight had affected the potato crop throughout the country, including the north and west, with only isolated areas escaping.[5] A month later, newspapers started to carry reports of deaths from starvation.[6]

Apart from the reappearance of blight, the summer of 1846 had been marked by a political crisis which resulted in the fall of Peel's government. The Whig Party, led by Lord John Russell, lacked a clear majority in parliament and was also divided by both ideological differences and personality clashes. In the wake of the 1847 General Election, the divisions between the traditional, aristocratic, landowning Whigs (of whom Russell was one) and the liberal free trade radicals became more marked, the latter group gaining an increased number of parliamentary seats.[7] If Russell had been a strong leader, he might have overcome these divisions; instead he was increasingly isolated and marginalised not only within his party, but also within his Cabinet.

The Cabinet's internal conflicts were brought into sharp focus by the crisis in Ireland. Lord Bessborough (Lord Lieutenant in Ireland until his death in 1847) was sympathetic to the victims of the potato blight; Lord Clarendon, his successor, was initially unsympathetic to the Irish destitute, but increasingly became alienated from his colleagues in London and their parsimonious policies. Lords Lansdowne, Clanricarde and Palmerston (all Irish landlords) were followers of the ideology of political economy and favoured minimal government intervention. Lord Grey, the Colonial Secretary, and George Grey, the Home Secretary, held a providentialist interpretation of the blight and viewed the food shortages as providing an opportunity for moral improvement; Charles Wood, the Chancellor of the Exchequer, combined a moralistic interpretation with a strategy of economic non-intervention, a viewpoint enthusiastically endorsed by his Permanent Secretary at the Treasury, Charles Trevelyan.[8] As the Famine progressed, Wood and Trevelyan were allowed increasing autonomy in their interpretation and implementation of relief policies.

The power of Trevelyan in issues relating to the Famine had been recognised in the wake of the first potato crop failure. This increased in the second year of distress when Trevelyan and Wood forged a formidable partnership at the Treasury. All matters relating to the provision of relief had first to receive Treasury approval, which became a source of frustration and annoyance to the Central Relief Commissioners, the Board of Works and the Executive at Dublin Castle, especially as Trevelyan's interpretation of policy was far more parsimonious that they believed was practicable. At the beginning of 1847, relations between the Treasury and the various relief departments in Dublin had become strained. Henry Labouchere, a member of the Irish Executive, wrote from Dublin Castle to Russell asking if he would intervene to persuade Trevelyan to release more funds to Ireland. He warned that the response of the Whigs compared unfavourably with that of the Tory Party and pointed out that 'up to this day we have only given £12,000 to assist the extremity of destitution which exists where workhouses are full. The late government gave £75,000 in a state of things which, compared to the present, was one of comfort and abundance.'[9]

From the outset, members of the Whig government sought the advice of Peel regarding the handling of the crisis in Ireland. This was especially true of Charles Wood, the Chancellor of the Exchequer, who sought Peel's advice on a number of financial issues. Despite the difference in approach between the two governments, Peel was largely in agreement with the Whigs' early policies, especially their decision not to intervene in the marketplace. However, by 1849, Peel had become frustrated with Russell's failure to make sufficient progress in the regeneration of Ireland and began to criticise his policies publicly. The Whig Lord Lieutenant, Clarendon, nevertheless, remained in frequent communication with Peel and confided in him his own frustrations with what he had come to regard as the inadequate response of the government to the crisis in Ireland.[10]

Initially, the Whigs' return to power had the support of the majority of Irish MPs, including the enfeebled but still influential Daniel O'Connell. In the early 1840s, Russell had presented himself as a champion of Irish issues. He believed that the food shortages could be used to bring about beneficial changes within Ireland which would serve to strengthen the Act of Union. Following the first appearance of blight and whilst in opposition, he had argued:

> I consider that the Union was but a parchment and an insubstantial union, if Ireland is not to be treated, in the hour of difficulty and distress, as an integral part of the United Kingdom.[11]

Russell's aspirations for Ireland proved to be elusive.[12] In spite of his declared good intentions, his approach combined repression and pragmatism with a determination that Britain should not suffer financially at the expense of Ireland. This was evident as early as August 1846 when Daniel O'Connell pleaded with the government to give prompt assistance to what he believed was becoming 'a death-dealing famine'. He also warned 'there is the greatest danger of outbreaks in various parts of the county of Cork of the population driven to despair by want of food'.[13] Russell responded personally to this plea. He informed O'Connell that public works would be established, although they were to be financed by the local rates. At the same time, he rebuked O'Connell for the fact that there had been a shortage of Irish harvest labourers in Britain despite the fact that they could have earned 'high wages ... The inference has been that they have employment in their own country'.[14]

Despite the inadequacy of the relief measures and the ever-increasing financial burden placed on Irish landlords, the Irish elite did not put up a successful or coherent challenge to the Westminster government. Many Irish MPs (the vast majority of whom were landowners) were critical of the inadequate provision of relief and, at the end of 1846, numerous meetings were held throughout the country to challenge the government's policies. At a meeting in Cork, for example, the chairman, Horace Townsend, suggested that the verdict on every person who died of starvation should be 'died from an overdose of political economy administered by quacks'.[15] By the middle of 1847, the concerns of many landlords changed as they became victims of a policy of fiscal rectitude. Despite this, they remained loyal to the party political system in London. In the general election of 1847, following a year of mass mortality and suffering, only 38 Repealers were returned to parliament (compared with 42 Conservatives and 25 Whigs).[16] A number of repeal MPs did use the Famine as an opportunity to renew demands for a domestic legislature. However, at the end of 1846 the split between the constitutional and the radical members of the Repeal Party deepened and O'Connell publicly denounced the violent threats of the latter.[17] O'Connell's death in May 1847 further weakened those who wanted a repeal of the Union. The radical Young Ireland movement was not regarded as a threat to the government despite its call for an armed rebellion. Thus Clarendon was able to assure Russell two weeks before their uprising that 'Young Ireland has no money, some talent, very little influence, and is losing ground.'[18] The uprising in July 1848, led by William Smith O'Brien, served to alienate rather than win support for radical nationalism. Despite the Famine, therefore, and regardless of being made scapegoats for the country's social ills, Irish landlords for the most part chose to remain within mainstream British politics.

In 1847, the radical MP, George Poulett Scrope, asked Russell to provide additional relief rather than repressive policies in Ireland, on the grounds that:

> Coercive measures, whether extra constitutional law or increased military and police, can only make the people more desperate, encourage the landlord to exterminate them still faster, and aggravate the existing social evils.[19]

Ignoring his request, a few days later, in a confidential letter, Russell offered a further 2000 mounted police and armed forces to the Irish government.[20]

The choices made by the Whig government were shaped not only by political differences but also by a combination of ideological and intellectual factors. These, however, were not static, but changed as the Famine progressed. Policy formulation combined elements of political economy, classical economics, utilitarianism, philanthropism, racism, providentialism and the gloomy prognoses of Malthus. In the context of these abstract principles and the shifting adherences to them, the forceful and unified approach of Wood and Trevelyan was able to take precedence.

In addition to these theories, parliamentary response was shaped by public opinion, especially that of the influential and newly enfranchised middle class. The financial crisis in 1847 had alarmed this class, whilst the General Election in the same year had provided them with a powerful political tool. Russell was aware of the dilemma posed by any attempt to do justice to the people of Ireland, especially if it involved a financial outlay. In the wake of the election results which had been personally disappointing for him, he lamented, 'We have in the opinion of Great Britain done too much for Ireland and have lost elections for doing so. In Ireland, the opposite is true.'[21] Overall, the conflicting approaches meant that any policy choice would have offended another group. This was clearly stated by Clarendon in 1847. When discussing the condition of the Irish, he posed the rhetorical question, 'We shall be equally blamed for keeping them alive or letting them die and we have only to select between the censure of the Economists or the philanthropists. Which do you prefer?'[22] Two years later, Russell, lamenting that he was unable to do more for the starving Irish, stated:

> The great difficulty this year respecting Ireland is one which does not spring from Trevelyan or Charles Wood but lies deep in the breasts of the British people. It is this – we have granted, lent, subscribed, worked, visited, clothed the Irish; millions of pounds worth of money, years of debate etc. – the only return is calumny and rebellion – let us not grant, clothe etc. etc. any more and see what they will do.[23]

In the face of such large-scale food shortages, the options facing the Whig government were limited and would have involved conflict with one or more vested interests. The policy choices made by the government not only failed to save lives, but contributed to mass starvation.

The 'Male' Roads and 'Queen's Pay'

A distinguishing feature of the relief policies of the Whig government was its decision not to enter the market place and import food as Peel had done, but to leave this task to private enterprise. This decision had the approval of Peel who had only ever viewed his intervention as a short-term expedient. Instead, the cornerstone of the government's policy was a programme of public works. Relief works had been used on a number of occasions earlier in the century to alleviate distress and, in 1831, a Board of Works had been established to co-ordinate and extend these activities. In the localities, public works were monitored by Grand Juries, unelected bodies of landowners. During the Famine, the most efficient relief works tended to be located in areas with resident landlords who played an active role in the relief operations and who were financially sound. In areas where landlords were absent or bankrupt, public works were less effective. Ironically, it was the poorest areas where absenteeism was most extensive.

The relief policies which had been introduced by Peel's government were due to end on 15 August 1846, when it was anticipated that the new potato crop would become available. By this stage, blight had appeared in every county in Ireland. A new relief programme had to be put in place and, owing to the early devastation caused by the blight, it had to be implemented immediately. This was very different from the previous year when Peel had almost six months to organise for the food scarcities. To prepare for the approaching distress, the public works system was radically overhauled. Many of the changes initially had been recommended by Trevelyan. They were indicative that the Whig government was going to place more of the financial burden for relief on Irish taxpayers rather than the Treasury, and that they were determined to adopt a more stringent approach to the provision of relief. Both these actions were an attempt to force the Irish people to be more morally and financially responsible for the destitution. To ensure that this was the case, a number of changes were made in the relief works. A significant modification occurred in the funding methodology. In 1845, public works had been financed by Grand Jury 'cess', a tax levied on occupiers of land. After 1846, the public works were to be financed through Poor Law taxation, which placed more of the financial burden on landlords, especially those whose estates were highly subdivided.[24] Also, in the previous year, the Tory government had matched the funding raised in the localities. After 1846, the government's contributions could not exceed 50 per cent of local funds. The effect was to throw a greater financial burden on the localities. None the less, because the money was initially provided as a loan by the government, there was some recklessness in applying for these loans on behalf of the local authorities and attempts by landlords to get preferential treatment for their own tenants.

A further significant change was the fact that the level of wages paid to those on relief works had to be lower than the local market rate. Furthermore, instead of a daily rate being paid to workers, task work was to be introduced (that is, people were paid according to the amount of labour which they performed). At the same time, the local relief committees were no longer to have the authority to nominate people to work on the public works. Instead, they had to draw up lists of candidates, which were submitted to officers of the Board of Works for their approval. The lists were also sent to the Lord Lieutenant's office for scrutiny. More importantly, decisions regarding the workforce and other aspects of the relief works required the sanction of the Treasury.[25]

In an effort to eliminate the abuses of the previous year, a number of bureaucratic checks were also insisted upon. The rules governing the relief committees were revised and a new tier of inspecting officers was appointed. Two new members were appointed to the Central Board. Trevelyan, who was the architect of many of these changes, defined the role of the new Board as being 'to confine relief works to the destitute and to enforce a reasonable quantum of work'.[26] As a consequence of the changes, the various employers of the public works in each area were Gangsmen (who were paid out of the wages of the labourers), Stewards, Check-Clerk, Office-Clerk Storekeeper, Draughtsman, Surveyor, Head Steward or Overseer, Pay-Clerk, Baronial Check-Clerk, Valuator, Assistant Engineer, District or Conducting Engineer, Inspecting Ticket Officer and Inspector of Finance.[27] Apart from delays, the employment of such a large staff led to accusations of high overheads and incompetence. The Officers of Board of Public Works strenuously denied these accusations, pointing out that the cost of the staff had accounted for only 8 per cent of total expenditure, whilst the staff based in Dublin had been paid by the government. They also denied the accusations of the 'inutility' of the work carried out, but suggested that 'the numbers had become so great as to defy control'.[28]

The changes in the operation of the relief works were not popular with the workers themselves, especially as the various bureaucratic procedures resulted in long delays before work could begin. In some cases this meant that the labourers were weak even before they started work. An engineer employed on the works described this sort of scene thus:

> Often in passing from district to district have I seen the poor enfeebled labourer, young and old alike, laid down by the side of the bog or road, on which he was employed, too late for kindness to avail, nevertheless, giving his dying blessing to the bestowers of tardy relief.[29]

Payments for the works were also frequently delayed, owing to a shortage of pay-clerks and small coins and the complications of paying for task work. Payment was usually made on a Saturday evening, but the process was time-consuming and sometimes was not completed until midnight. In some cases, the local Boards of Works officials tried to make the payments from their own pockets.[30] The delay in payments led to a widespread adoption of the 'truck' system, whereby labourers would purchase goods on credit at highly inflated prices. This meant that they had often spent their wages before they received them.[31] One local priest reported that 2000 of his parishioners were without food and that 'they scarcely have a rag to cover them, having long since left in the huxter's shop every article of value in pledge for meal'.[32]

William E. Forster, a Quaker, who was working in Mayo and Galway in January 1847, came across one case of workers who had not been paid for three weeks owing to a mistake by the local officials. He was amazed by the docility of the people but this may have been due to exhaustion and malnutrition. In Bundorragha, for example, he noted, 'Out of a population of 240, I found 13 already dead from want. The survivors were like walking skeletons; the men stamped with the livid mark of hunger; the children crying with pain; the women in the same cabins too weak to stand.'[33]

The system of task work was particularly unpopular and some of the workers protested against it by refusing to work. In all such cases, the Treasury decreed that the public works were to be stopped and could only commence when such 'outrage' ceased.[34] Food riots were widespread although, as the people became weaker through lack of food, they became more infrequent. The crime rate also increased, although most of the crimes were against property rather than people. Many of them were an attempt to obtain food, and the plunder of mills, or even boats carrying grain, became common.[35] The people were harshly punished for their crimes (although jail or transportation no longer appeared to be a deterrent) and additional police and troops were deployed to the areas affected.

The work was physically demanding: each worker was expected to work a 12-hour day from 6 a.m., six days a week. And, as many of the labourers lived some distance from the works, their day began far earlier than this, as they had to walk to the site. The physical energy expended required a high calorific intake but, as the winter progressed, the hunger gap widened and the shortfall between wages and food prices increased. The average daily wage on the works fell to 8d a day, although on occasions, workers earned as little as 2d a day. At the same time, food prices were rising and the wages did not make any allowance for clothing, fuel or rent. The labour was hard and had to be done out of doors. Initially, to increase the need for labour, the Board of Works stipulated that pack animals should not be used. But when this proved to be impracticable owing to 'the weak emaciated state of the people', a limited use of animals and wheelbarrows was permitted. Despite this, one engineer reported that some labourers were 'scarcely able to lift the handful of material placed in the barrows for removal'.[36] There were a number of accusations that the workforce was lazy but this may have been the result of an inadequate and unnutritious diet. Without their usual potato diet, which was rich in vitamin C and protein, the workers developed a number of dietary-deficiency diseases including scurvy, marasmus (which made even children appear old and wizened and sometimes produced additional body hair), pellagra, characterised by burning or itching, diarrhoea and inflammation of the skin, and oedema (swelling of the body).

In an effort to boost family wages, at the end of 1846, women and children flocked into the relief works, although they were paid even lower rates than the men.[37] The winter of 1846–47 was particularly harsh, with snow falling as late as April 1847. The destitute were ill-prepared for this as they had not collected their usual supplies of turf and many of them had inadequate clothing which offered little protection when working outdoors. At the suggestion of the Board of Works, Trevelyan permitted a system of half-pay when conditions were too bad to work. Wages were so low already, however, that some labourers kept working even in snow and black ice.[38]

Despite the harsh conditions, the demand for employment always exceeded supply. The public works had been reopened officially at the beginning of September, but many were not operative until October. By the end of that month, 100,000 men were employed and by December, this had risen to 441,000. By January 1847, 570,000 people were employed, and by March, 734,000. Approximately one in every three adult males was employed by the public works, although there were wide regional variations in demand.[39] It also meant that in the region of 2 million people were dependent on this relief either directly or indirectly.

At the end of January 1847, the government decided to end the public works and to transfer the responsibility for all relief to the Poor Law. The new system was to become operative in the autumn and in the intervening months a network of soup kitchens was established to provide relief. Yet, despite the government's decision to close the public works, the numbers on them continued to increase. This resulted in the Treasury imposing a 20 per cent reduction on 20 March 1847 which was to be followed by further reductions, regardless of the fact that many soup kitchens had not yet opened. The arbitrariness of this decision was widely criticised, especially by relief officials who had been left without the means for providing relief. The radical Irish newspaper, *The Nation*, was highly critical of the action of the Treasury, which they described as a 'murderous absurdity' which would result in even more 'death by starvation'. However, they viewed this decision as indicative of the British government's 'utter apathy to the tremendous responsibility with which they are trifling'. They felt that its real purpose was ideologically motivated, and was to 'drive men into the market where there was no market'.[40]

The response in the press to the new public works was initially mixed, but by the end of the year, the general consensus was that they had failed.[41] Newspapers were carrying daily reports of death from starvation or famine-related diseases. This was variously attributed to the laziness of the Irish people, the selfishness of the landlords, the inefficiency of the Board of Works or the inappropriate policies of the government. The *Illustrated London News* suggested that as Ireland had already suffered from years of misgovernment, during the crisis the government should provide more rather than less intervention, on the grounds that 'neglect, carelessness and laissez-faire do not make a cheap system of government'.[42] However, apart from the cost in human lives, the works had disrupted agricultural production and this would have implications in the forthcoming harvest.

Overall, the public works were regarded as being inefficient, inadequate and ineffective. 'Famine roads' came to symbolise tracks that led to nowhere and performed no useful function. Yet, the public works did provide a vital life-line in the winter months of 1846–47, a fact that was reflected in the popular description of them as 'male' (meal) roads or 'stirabout drains'. The wages were known as 'Queen's pay', which may have reflected the belief that they were being paid for by England.[43] The Board of Works itself was aware of many of the problems with the relief works, but it argued that both the demands and the restrictions placed on it had limited the Board's effectiveness.[44]

Despite the numerous criticisms made about the high expenditure of the scheme, over 90 per cent of the Board of Works income was used to provide relief. Also, although the expenditure was compared unfavourably with the relative cheapness of the soup kitchen scheme (they cost under £2 million compared to the £5½ million expended by the public works) the relief works operated over a much longer period and had the more difficult task of providing employment and relief rather than assistance alone. Public works were also felt to be ideologically acceptable as they made the recipient perform a task of labour, which was regarded as a valuable 'test' of destitution, rather than providing gratuitous assistance. They also involved a high degree of local involvement, especially as they were ultimately to be financed from local taxation. However, despite the commitment of the Whig government to non-intervention, the relief works skewed the labour market by taking people away from their usual pursuits and by imposing a wage ceiling on wages but not on prices. As a mechanism for providing relief they were also slow and cumbersome, which was inappropriate for the immediate needs of the Irish destitute. Ultimately, the public works scheme provided a harsh test of destitution, which failed many of those people it was supposed to be saving.

Food Supplies and Food Exports

The most controversial aspect of Whig policy was its decision not to continue Peel's programme of importing Indian corn, but to leave food supply to market forces. The intervention of the Tory government in the market place in 1845 had angered many merchants and corn producers, who were traditional supporters of the Whig Party. Many Whig politicians were also ideologically committed to a policy of free trade and minimal state intervention. One of the first actions of the new administration, therefore, was to assure the merchants that the role of the government would be reduced in the second year of shortages, and that only a limited number of government food depots would operate in the west of Ireland. Moreover, despite being faced with the most extensive food shortfall for over a century, they decided not to close the ports to keep food within Ireland nor to forbid distillation of grain to take place. These measures were all traditional responses to food shortages and the refusal by the Whig government to implement them marked a radical departure of official policy from earlier subsistence crises.

Whilst the staple crop of the poor had failed massively in 1846, the potato represented only about 20 per cent of total agricultural production in Ireland. Throughout Ireland, grain production exceeded potato production. Often, both crops were grown side by side, but grain was grown as a cash crop. In 1847, even taking into account the fact that a smaller crop than usual was sown, grain cultivation far exceeded potato production – whilst 0.3 million acres were under potatoes, 3.3 million acres were under grain. In the same year, despite a widespread programme of slaughtering and an increase in cattle exports, there were an estimated 2.5 million cattle in Ireland, 2.2 million sheep and 600,000 pigs (the first animal to be sacrificed in times of scarcity).[45]

In 1846 the corn harvest was below average, not just in Ireland, but throughout Europe. This meant that there was less surplus available for sale. As a consequence, the demand for existing supplies was heavy. The removal of protective legislation allowed other European countries to purchase supplies within Britain and in 1846–49 grain exports from Britain to Europe *increased*. Some of this grain originated in Ireland.[46] Simultaneously, many European ports were closed to exports in an effort to protect their own supplies.[47]

The decision by the government not to import food into Ireland (except in a few isolated western areas) and not to interfere in the supply or distribution of food was partly motivated by an ideological commitment to free trade. Additionally, the policy was an attempt to appease Irish merchants, who felt their position had been undermined by government intervention. After 1846, therefore, food supply in Ireland was left to the workings of the market. None the less, in those parts of the country where distress was most severe, a market system did not operate. Whilst many of the ports in the west had participated in the export trade in the years prior to the Famine, they had no experience of imports and the necessary communication and distribution networks did not exist. Furthermore, the import trade was hampered by a cumbersome body of legislation known as the Navigation Acts, which allowed goods to be imported into the United Kingdom only if they were carried on a British ship. The effect of these Acts was to hamper the free movement of goods, and they acted as a ceiling on the amount of food that could be imported into Ireland at any one time. Furthermore, freight charges continued to be imposed on goods entering the United Kingdom. After the harvest of 1846, they rose to three times their usual rate. Despite claiming to leave food import to market forces, a number of restrictive regulations still existed which limited the ability of the market to respond adequately to the demand for food in Ireland, and which worked to the disadvantage of the Irish poor.

One of the most outspoken critics of the government's policies came, not from a nationalist, but from an Irishman who was also a unionist and a political economist. Isaac Butt, who had been Professor of Political Economy at Trinity College from 1836 to 1840, criticised the Whig government's relief policies and the paradox of their free trade programme. He described the Navigation Acts as 'the climax of infatuation', and he suggested that the freight charges could have been removed temporarily by an Order in Council. He believed that if the government had acted differently, far more cheap food could have been imported into Ireland in the crucial winter months of 1846. He also believed that such actions weakened the foundations of the Act of Union. Butt believed that it was wrong to treat Ireland in such a way during such a crisis. He posed the question:

> If ministers resolved to trust the lives of the Irish people to private enterprize, was it not common sense and common justice to them that private enterprize should be unencumbered by any restrictions in the execution of the task of supplying, at the notice of a few months, provisions to five millions people?[48]

The validity of Butt's criticisms became apparent in January 1847 when the prime minister introduced a Bill to suspend until 1 September all duties on foreign corn and to lift the restrictions imposed by the Navigation Acts. This legislation was subsequently extended until March 1848. This new policy did facilitate the import of more food to Ireland in the spring of 1847 and beyond, and food prices did begin to fall. It was too late for many people, however. The victims of the 'starvation gap' in food supplies and food prices in the preceding winter were the casualties of a system where the party of the 'free market' imposed restrictions on that same market. Restrictive legislation compounded the problem of food shortages to create famine conditions in Ireland.

In the winter of 1846–47, food prices within Ireland rose dramatically. They only started to fall in the spring of 1847, helped by good weather and the removal of restrictive legislation. By this stage, it was too late for many Irish people, whose only source of income had been the low-paid public works where wages were too low to sustain life. Although the government did not keep official records of mortality during the Famine, the local Irish constabulary estimated that in the winter months of 1846, 400,000 people died, either directly or indirectly, through want of food.[49]

Concurrently with people dying of famine or hunger-related diseases in Ireland, massive amounts of food were being exported from Ireland, not just from the east of the country, but also from ports in the west. The high level of exports demonstrated that food production was still high even as people starved in Ireland. A major area of debate within Famine historiography has been in regard to the export of grain from Ireland, especially in the crucial years 1846–47. The debate has tended to be polarised between John Mitchel's emotive assertion that exports vastly exceeded imports and the counter-claim that, by 1847, the opposite was true. The latter claim has tended to be based on Austin-Bourke's much quoted work on import and export data for 1847. Yet, as he admits, these figures are not based on accurate returns, but on imperfect statistics recorded by the government.[50] The government did not keep accurate aggregate figures of the trade between Ireland and Britain. Since the Act of Union, trade between Ireland and Britain had come to be regarded as inter-regional rather than international, and there was little need to keep precise records.[51]

Whilst most of the debate regarding the export of food from Ireland has centred on the export of grain, there were massive exports of other foodstuffs, the quantities of some of which increased after 1846. Furthermore, the exports of grain in other forms – converted into flour, farina, whiskey or porter, for example – also continued. Moreover, corn from Ireland was not only exported to Britain but also to other parts of the world. Ships arrived in the United States carrying Famine refugees alongside vessels laden with food, their arrival overshadowed by those carrying human cargo. A New York newspaper noted in the summer of 1847 that 'Arrivals of wheat from Ireland, either of home grown or foreign returns during the last fortnight have been very considerable.'[52]

Table 4.1 provides an example of goods arriving in Liverpool from Ireland on a single day in December 1846. The vessel, *Maiden*

City, was even carrying 47 bags of potatoes. *The Shamrock* came from the port of Sligo in the west of Ireland.

Table 4.1 Exports from Ireland to Liverpool, 20 December 1846

Name of Vessel	Cargo Composition		
Maiden City	209 pigs	24 bags oats	26 barrels of coarse meat
	5 calves	43 bags wheat	11 pounds bacon
	7 sheep	338 bags oatmeal	550 firkins butter
	28 pigs		56 kegs butter
			237 barrels butter
			47 bags potatoes
			3 tierces lard
			83 boxes of eggs and butter
			1 hogshead ale
Erin	13 cows		489 firkins butter
	137 pigs		
	106 sheep		
St. Patrick	124 cows	201 pounds oatmeal	8 barrels butter
	202 pigs		3 boxes eggs
	300 sheep		
Boiroimhe	153 cows	255 pounds oatmeal	4 hogsheads ale
	381 sheep		3 barrels ale
	40 pigs		
	1 horse		
Faugh-a-Ballagh	839 sheep	12 barrels oats	85 crates butter
	101 cows	100 pounds oatmeal	6 boxes eggs
Dundalk	10 boxes fowl		180 firkins butter
	23 pigs		58 crates butter
			24 puns whiskey
			2 hogsheads whiskey
Shamrock	62 cattle	60 bags oats	14 firkins tongues
	190 sheep		2 hogsheads hams
	40 pigs		2 barrels bacon
			80 kegs lard
			14 boxes eggs
			650 firkins butter[53]

Faced with a shortage of traditional supplies of food and an inadequate official response, many Irish people developed their own strategies for obtaining sustenance. Initially some attempts were made to convert the rotten potatoes into other food. In 1845, the government had suggested that the workhouses should purchase potato machines for this purpose.[54] However, the potatoes were so putrid that this proved to be impossible and gave stomach cramps to those who attempted to eat them. Without a supply of potatoes, animals, which were traditionally a source of income, became competition for food. The slaughter or sale of pigs was widespread. Once they had gone, however, other food supplies became more difficult to access. The bleeding of cattle was widely practised, blood being obtained by cutting a vein in the neck of the animal and extracting blood, then suturing the vein. The tails of bullocks were also stolen and then roasted.[55] The theft of ducks, geese, sheep and other livestock initially increased, but farmers who possessed anything of value employed men to guard their fields and the use of mantraps became common. Instead, the people searched their localities for alternative foods: birds, frogs, rats, dogs, cats, snails, nettles, weeds, seaweed and even ice and grass were eaten. The latter contributed to the folk memory of people dying with their mouths stained green.[56]

Stealing and crimes against property became widespread and the crime rate rose until 1849, roughly mirroring the years of shortages. Crimes against individuals, despite receiving much publicity when they did occur, remained constant with their pre-Famine levels. The assassination of the Roscommon landlord, Major Denis Mahon, at the end of 1847, for example, was widely publicised in Ireland and Britain and was even debated in the British House of Lords.[57] Most of the crime involved petty theft, often of food or livestock, and was generally non-violent. Food riots were widespread but tended to be focused on mills where corn was being stored, or the carts and canal boats which were taking grain to be exported. Increasingly, these vehicles were provided with armed escorts and the government placed patrol boats in the harbours and ports.[58]

For people living in the coastal regions fish and shellfish were only a limited food source. However, during the Famine people did comb the shores for shellfish or seaweed to eat. But neither of these items provided a substantial diet and some people became sick from eating shellfish which had not been properly treated or cooked. Also, despite Ireland's plentiful rivers and shorelines, many of these were owned privately and taking anything from them was regarded as theft and was therefore punishable. A number of landlords did turn a blind eye to a limited form of poaching, but this was not always the case. The landlord in Creeslough, County Donegal, for example, appointed a watchman to guard his stretch of shoreline.[59]

Before the Famine, many fishermen had grown potatoes for their main subsistence. The most profitable fishing was deep sea, but fishing tackle had been pawned to pay the rent in the previous year of shortages. The movement of herring, which had been plentiful earlier in the century, from the west of Ireland in the 1830s to other seas, also limited the catch available. A further reason was the primitive state of the equipment used by fishermen. The Quakers who visited the west of Ireland noted the paradox of people who lived on the coast starving, but they felt part of the explanation was that:

> So rude is their tackle and so fragile and liable to be upset are their primitive boats or coracles, made of wickerwork over which sail cloth is stretched, that they can only venture to sea in fine weather, and thus, with food almost in sight, the people starve.[60]

Whilst Butt had publicly expressed doubts about the wisdom of the government's food programme, a number of government ministers were privately concerned about the wisdom of such policies. At the end of 1846, as food prices rose in Ireland and mortality soared, Sir Randolph Routh, the Commissioner in charge of relief in Ireland, pleaded with Trevelyan to allow the supplies remaining in the few government food depots to be released onto the market. The Treasury refused until 28 December, and then insisted that the food be sold at the market price, which at that time was highly inflated. Routh believed this decision to be a mistake, but by this stage matters regarding relief policy had been left in the hands of Trevelyan who refused to allow any deviation. In a terse note to Routh, Trevelyan informed him that 'If we make prices lower, I repeat for the HUNDREDTH TIME, that the whole country will come upon us.'[61] Ireland was to be left to market forces. The Famine, however, had distorted the price of food, so that even that which came from government depots was inaccessible to those most in need.

By the beginning of 1847, the policies of the Whig government were being increasingly criticised, especially in Ireland. The Lord Lieutenant, Bessborough, warned Russell that there was a growing belief that the government should have done more to make food accessible to the destitute. Bessborough believed that the main fault lay with the Irish merchants and he reflected:

> I cannot make my mind up entirely about the merchants. I know all the difficulties that arise when you begin to interfere with trade, but it is difficult to persuade a starving population that one class should be permitted to make 50 per cent profit by the sale of provisions whilst they are dying in want of these.[62]

He went on to say that the merchants had broken their promises regarding the importation of food, 'and, as I am assured, have done as little as they could even if the government had entered on the trade'. At the same time, they had 'done their best to keep up prices'.[63]

Within Ireland, it was widely believed that the British government had let the people down and had failed to force the corn merchants to behave responsibly. Lord Clarendon, who succeeded Bessborough as Lord Lieutenant, warned Russell that public opinion in Ireland had turned against the Whigs and Russell personally. He informed him that 'no-one could now venture to dispute the fact that Ireland had been sacrificed to the London corn-dealers because you were a member for the City, and that no distress would have occurred if the exportation of Irish grain had been prohibited'.[64] The events of 1846–47 demonstrated the duality of the Irish economy; that food scarcities, deprivation and excess mortality existed side-by-side with a buoyant commercial sector.

Food Shortages and Famine Elsewhere

The appearance of the potato disease in 1845 and 1846 and consequent food shortages and social dislocation were not confined to Ireland. The potato blight had first been noticed in Belgium in June 1845. From there it spread to neighbouring districts in the Netherlands and northern France. By early September, the disease had appeared in parts of Germany, Russia, Scandinavia, England, Scotland and Ireland. The cause of the disease was unknown, but it was generally attributed to the dull, wet summer of 1845. There were a few proponents of the fungal theory of the disease, but they had little support.[65] In the areas where the blight appeared early, the resultant losses of the crop were high. Where the potato blight appeared late – as in Scotland and Ireland in 1845 – the impact tended to be more localised and hence limited. The fact that there was a good grain harvest throughout Europe in 1845 and that the winter of 1845–46 was relatively mild also helped to soften the impact of the first year of blight.

None the less, in Belgium, France, Holland and Ireland, the respective governments, alarmed by this new disease, appointed Special Commissions to investigate its cause and impact in more depth.[66] A number of European governments also implemented a series of practical measures to help combat the inevitable food shortages. In Belgium, Turkey, Alexandria, Russia and Sweden, the export of certain foods was restricted. Some governments responded by lifting restrictions on the importation of food. The governments in Belgium, Holland and Russia, for example, introduced a temporary suspension of duties on foreign grain. Their actions were cited by Sir Robert Peel when he was trying to win the support of his Cabinet for a repeal of the Corn Laws, and he quoted the fact that in Belgium the vote had been unanimous.[67] Peel, unlike some of his European counterparts, rejected the introduction of short-term – and immediate – solutions, preferring to use the blight as an opportunity for total and permanent repeal of the Corn Laws.

In addition to encouraging imports of food, a number of European governments and merchants sought actively to purchase potatoes in foreign markets, including in Ireland itself. This resulted in an increase in potato exports from Ireland to mainland Europe, especially to Belgium and Holland. In the first few weeks of September, potato exports to Holland were as high as 6000 tons.[68] The export of potatoes from the Irish market alarmed a number of people, including the Lord Lieutenant, and there were increased demands for the ports to be closed.[69] Peel, however, was determined not to interfere in the Irish export market.[70] There may have been some small consolation in the fact that some of the potatoes which had left Ireland in a sound condition arrived at their destination rotten from blight.[71] It was not only potatoes that were in demand. Agents of the Belgian government on a single day purchased all the rice in Liverpool market, resulting in a price rise of 75 per cent.[72] In contrast to the response of the British government, the governments of Bavaria and Prussia placed a temporary embargo on the export of potatoes to protect themselves from the increasing purchases of the merchants in Holland and Belgium.[73]

The losses of the potato crop in a number of European countries in 1845–46 were higher than in Ireland. An estimated 85 per cent of the crop was destroyed in Holland and 75 per cent in Belgium. The losses of the potato crop in 1846–47 were generally lower (with the exceptions of Scotland and Ireland) but the consequences were more serious owing to the conjunction of a poor grain harvest and the onset of a widespread depression in the industrial sector. In addition to the food shortages, the potential for social disorder concerned a number of European governments. This fear prompted them to provide more extensive relief than they believed was ideologically acceptable. In France and Holland this proved to be the case, despite both countries' governments being committed to orthodox liberal theories of non-intervention, as was the Whig Party in Britain.[74] In these two countries, the governments' relief policies were a balance between minimising the risk of social revolution and limiting government intervention as much as possible. The Dutch government, like the British government, also used the blight as an opportunity to repeal the Dutch Corn Laws and to move closer towards the policy of free trade.[75]

In Holland, potato consumption was second only to that in Ireland, which meant that the consequences of the blight were

potentially devastating. The role of the potato in the Dutch economy
had many parallels with the Irish situation. In both countries, by
the second half of the eighteenth century, the potato had become
the staple foodstuff of the poor – in Holland, it replaced rye as the
main foodstuff. This dietary change had been accompanied by rapid
population growth, especially in the potato growing districts. This
had increased the pressure for land, even of poor quality, and
consequently rents were high. As was the case in Ireland, most of
the potatoes were grown for home consumption and exports were
negligible. After 1815, economic dislocation and economic
restructuring in Holland further increased dependence on this
single crop.

As in Ireland, there were a number of advantages associated with
potato consumption. Unlike corn, the potato crop had rarely failed
in Holland and therefore was regarded as a safeguard against
famine. Also, potato prices were low and stable, unlike corn prices
which were far more volatile. Potatoes provided a cheap and
abundant animal food, thus allowing peasants to keep at least one
animal, usually a pig. They could also be used for the production
of farina and starch and were used extensively in gin and syrup
distilleries. As a consequence of their high nutritional content, the
health of the Dutch population had improved. Scurvy, for example,
had almost completely disappeared from the Dutch countryside.[76]
Regardless of the advantages of growing and eating this vegetable,
the high level of dependence on the potato was disliked by a
number of social and political commentators within Holland. Their
observations were redolent of those being made regarding the Irish
poor and their relationship with this vegetable. On a dietary and
social benchmark, potatoes were regarded as a 'low' type of food,
which had contributed, allegedly, to the 'laziness and indolence of
the working-classes'. This alleged fecklessness had been exacerbated
by a correspondingly high consumption of alcohol by the Dutch
poor – the alcohol itself being made from potatoes.[77]

Blight first appeared in Holland in July 1845. Its impact was most
severe in the wet clayland districts of the country, where dependence
on the potato was highest. Approximately 75 per cent of the crop
was lost in the first year. The disease reappeared in 1846 but was
not as destructive as it had been in the previous year. However,
owing to the shortages of 12 months earlier, a smaller crop had been
planted. In 1846 also the grain harvest was small, the result of a
combination of vermin and drought. Unlike the previous year, the
winter of 1846–47 was long and hard, snow falling extensively
throughout Europe, even in Ireland. The combination of a poor
potato and a small grain harvest meant that food shortages after
1846 were more serious than in the previous year.[78]

The second year of shortages was swiftly followed by a rise in pauperism, begging, plundering, petty thefts, rioting and social unrest.[79] Again, as was the case in the United Kingdom, potato blight was linked with providentialism and the need for restitution. It was claimed that in the years before the blight the Dutch people had forgotten their religion and had turned to pleasure, drink and 'sensual drives'. As the main alcohol consumed by the poor was potato-gin, the association of the potato with the ills of society was confirmed. This interpretation was reinforced by the announcement by Royal Decree of a Day of Prayer on 2 May 1847 to ask for forgiveness.[80] This mirrored a Day of Prayer called by Queen Victoria in England a few weeks earlier.

From 1845 to 1847, the Dutch government was dominated by ministers who were in favour of free trade economics and minimal government intervention in social welfare. They were admirers of the English classical economists and also opposed the idea of a state system of poor relief, preferring relief to be ad hoc or paid for by charity. When faced with a potential famine, the government believed that the only ideologically acceptable course was to encourage imports. In September, therefore, import duties on a number of foods, including grain, were reduced. Corn prices were so high that there was little impact. The increase in rioting in 1846 and early 1847 worried the government and the king, who were concerned that the unrest could take on a political dimension. One of the most serious riots occurred when the central government refused to close the ports, and a shipment of potatoes left for England in 1847. The government responded by drafting more militia into the affected areas and imposing a curfew. At the same time, the need for more relief was recognised. The central government was reluctant to provide direct relief itself. Instead, they encouraged municipal authorities to provide limited assistance. The government suggested that if extensive relief proved to be necessary, public works were the preferable option.[81] The inadequacy of the relief measures undertaken in Holland was apparent in a sharp rise in mortality in 1847, deaths exceeding births for the first time in decades. Many of the deaths were from the fever which characteristically accompanies food shortage and other famine-related diseases, and the loss of life was heaviest in the potato growing areas.[82] The social cost of government non-intervention was high. The revolutionary uprisings in 1848 in Holland may have been part of the political cost to the government.

The French government, like those in Holland and the United Kingdom, was opposed to direct intervention in the marketplace. In each of these countries, attitudes towards the poor and the relief of poverty were dominated by a doctrine of individualism, a dislike of government intervention and the belief that poverty was due to the moral failings of the pauper and therefore poor relief was not to be encouraged. These principles were tempered, however, by a fear of mob rule, which made them realise that charity and poor relief could also be a form of social security. The extensive food shortages after 1845, and more particularly after 1846, forced the French authorities to provide additional assistance to the poor. There were a number of requests for the reintroduction of a law, first introduced by Napoleon in 1812, which had set an upper limit on the price of grain. By the 1840s, the ideological climate had changed in France and the government was reluctant to intervene in the marketplace. It refused to regulate food prices, but introduced a number of measures to encourage the movement of foodstuffs, including the lowering of customs tariffs and reducing rail charges on the movements of grains.[83]

Whilst the central government did not want to intervene in the marketplace, it encouraged the local authorities to initiate relief measures. In November 1846, the Minister of the Interior impressed on the local prefects the desirability of establishing public works, both as a means of providing relief and as a way of keeping the lower classes occupied. The relief works were to be financed from local taxation and charitable donations, although, at the beginning of 1847, the French government allocated 8,000,000 francs for this purpose. The wages paid on the public works were low, but the families of the workers were also supplied with cheap bread.[84] This was different from the situation in Ireland where the low wages paid on the public works were the sole means of support for a family.

In addition to the public works, relief was also available from the *bureau de bienfaisance*. In 1847, over one million people received assistance from these boards. In addition to bread being provided, an allowance was made for soap, coal, wood, medicine and rent.[85] This was different from the situation in Ireland where outdoor relief was restricted to food. The role of the notables and Catholic clergy in providing relief was also important. For the most part, their involvement took the form of purchasing food and reselling it at cost price, an action they believed would simultaneously keep down prices and prevent speculation. Again, they were partly motivated by a fear of social unrest.[86] Within France, the provision of private charity was politicised, especially in Paris. A placard announcing a charitable ball was superimposed with a notice describing those who were to attend as 'the rich, the grain merchants and fat rentiers'.[87]

The impact of the blight in the Highlands of Scotland also had parallels with the Famine in Ireland. Although the period which followed is generally referred to as the Highlands 'famine', excess mortality was low compared with Ireland. It was also lower than

in a number of continental countries including Belgium and
Holland. Yet Scotland exhibited several indicators of social distress,
which paralleled the experience in Ireland, including widespread
malnutrition, disease, evictions, migration and emigration. Births
and marriages fell as mortality rose, creating a demographic crisis.
The population of the Highlands never recovered from the
demographic losses in the famine decade of 1846–55.[88]

In 1845 the blight appeared late in Scotland, and the Highlands
emerged relatively unscathed. As a consequence, there was an
increase in the demand for Scottish potatoes and seed potatoes and
exports to the rest of the United Kingdom and to the Continent
increased. In 1846, however, the blight was reported as early as
June, and the destruction was comprehensive. By September, the
entire crop had been destroyed. Like the Irish Famine, a providentialist interpretation of the blight was widespread, which regarded
it as 'The Hand of God' punishing the Scottish poor for their
moral failings.[89]

As in Ireland, the role of the central government, the landlords,
philanthropists and other local elites was a key factor in determining
the level of suffering. This was especially important given the
limitations of the 'new' Scottish Poor Law of 1845, which reflected
a national stringency in its attitude towards poverty and had
specified that the able-bodied had no legal right to relief.[90] Moreover,
neither the English, Irish nor Scottish Poor Laws were designed
to cope with periods of food shortages.

In Scotland, as in Ireland, the British government sought to play
a secondary role to landlords in the provision of relief. A mixture
of moral and financial pressure was applied to ensure that this was
the case. Two government depots were established – one in Skye
and one in Mull – from which grain could be sold at controlled
prices. In autumn 1846, the government imported a limited amount
of grain for distribution in Ireland and Scotland. Although the
shortages were more extensive in Ireland, it insisted that the
imported food should first be taken to Scotland. This caused alarm
amongst relief officials in Ireland. Sir Randolph Routh, who was
increasingly critical of the government's involvement in the Irish
Famine, commented, 'I shall be very glad to hear that Scotland is
supplied.'[91] The main form of government intervention in Scotland
was through the availability of grants for public works and the
improvement of estates. Approximately £500,000 was provided by
the government to the landlords for this purpose, but the take-up
of these grants alarmed the government.[92] It meant that the majority
of the money provided by the British government was directed to
the landlords rather than the destitute.

A common feature of the Scottish and Irish Famines was the use
of the same personnel by the government, including Sir Edward

Pine Coffin, Commissary-General Dobree and Captain Pole. More importantly, both famines were put under the control of Charles Trevelyan of the Treasury. Trevelyan made his mark on the provision of relief in Scotland early. In October 1846, he produced guidelines outlining what he expected the role of the landlords to be. His document stated:

> It is by no means intended to afford relief in such a way as would relieve the landowners and other persons of property from the obligations they are under to support the destitute poor ... any assistance contemplated would be in the form rather of giving a proper organisation and direction to the efforts of the proprietors.[93]

Whilst the role played by Scottish landlords varied, for the most part they responded generously to the food shortages, and were praised by the government for doing so. One landlord, James Matheson, was even knighted for his services to the Scottish poor. The Highland landlords were praised by Trevelyan in particular, who was dismissive of their counterparts in Ireland. In his private communications, he repeatedly drew comparisons between the two groups. In 1847, for example, he stated that 'the Treasury have been quite delighted with the whole conduct of the Highland proprietors in the present crisis ... it was a source of positive pleasure to them to turn from the Irish to the Scotch case – in the former every thing both with regard to the people and proprietors is sickening and disgusting'. In a subsequent communication, he reiterated this, noting:

> there is this important difference in the proprietors and larger classes of Farmers, that in Ireland the general disposition of these classes is to do nothing while in Scotland they are disposed to do what is in their power ... If Skye were in the west of Ireland, the people would be left to starve in helpless idleness.[94]

The economic situation of landlords in Ireland and Scotland was different, however. For the most part, Scottish landlords were financially more buoyant than those in Ireland. In the decades after 1815, many estates in the Highlands had changed hands and the new proprietors generally had alternative sources of incomes,[95] which meant that Highland landlords were able to survive a period of reduced rentals and diminished income. Many of these landlords also took advantage of the government grants made available for improvements and used the Famine as an opportunity to modernise their estates and implement clearances. This meant that it was 'possible to detect a hardening of attitudes among the other sections of the landed classes ... [as] ... the strategy on some estates moved decisively from the provision of relief to the promotion of the destitute population through a massive increase in clearance, removal and assisted emigration'.[96]

A further common feature between Ireland and Scotland was the duration of the crisis – the Famine did not end in 1847 in either country, and in both countries excess destitution continued to be high well into the 1850s. In Scotland, the worst year of suffering was 1849. Within the Highlands, there was a marked geographic diversity in the demand for relief. An average of 35 per cent of the Highland population was dependent on external relief, but on Barra, dependency was 89 per cent.[97] For the most part, there was a high correlation between dependency and areas of high dependence on a single crop, subdivision of land and pre-Famine poverty.

The failures of the potato crop in other parts of the United Kingdom and mainland Europe demonstrated that the impact of the blight was an international phenomenon. However, the variations in outcome reflected a combination of the severity of the loss of the potato crop, the relative importance of this food in each society, and the nature of the response by central and local authorities to the appearance of a shortfall in the supply of food within a part of their jurisdiction.

Within Europe, Ireland had the highest consumption of potatoes, although the poor in Holland and the Highlands of Scotland also had high levels of dependency. The blight did not affect all areas equally. For example, the west of Ireland and the Highlands of Scotland emerged relatively unscathed in 1845, but in 1846, the blight appeared in these areas with unparalleled severity. In other parts of Europe, the conjunction of a poor grain harvest and an industrial depression meant that levels of destitution and suffering remained high.

The impact of the potato failure did not necessarily result in social disaster but the blight took place in a wider economic and political context. In each area affected by the blight, the role of the central authorities was pivotal in determining the outcome in terms of the extent and persistence of famine and associated disease and mortality. A common feature that helped to determine the way in which governments responded to the onset of the crisis was the ideological climate. The popularity of political economy was characterised by a quasi-religious belief in the sanctity of the free market, minimum intervention by the state and in the particular case of the poor, an emphasis upon the idea that poverty was a self-imposed condition. The response to the food shortages by the central authorities was shaped also by such factors as fear of social unrest, and a concern not to offend the new politically powerful groupings in society, which had arisen from industrial and commercial expansion. The corn merchants were one such group.

In the United Kingdom and Holland, from the outset, the blight became linked with wider political issues and created an opportunity to repeal the Corn Laws. The governments of these two countries were those with the greatest dogmatic adherence to the philosophy of political economy. Coincidentally, it was in these two countries that providentialist interpretations of the blight were most often expressed. Additionally, in Holland, as in France, anxiety about social unrest, informed by the revolutionary experiences of 1789 and 1830, compelled more intervention than was ideologically acceptable. Most of the relief, however, was provided by the local authorities rather than by central government and, as far as possible, through the mechanism of the public works or private charity. In France especially the involvement of the Catholic clergy and the landed elite in the provision of charitable donations was motivated as much by fear as by compassion or moral obligation. In Scotland, the involvement of the landlords in the provision of relief was motivated by self-interest, which manifested itself through state-sponsored land improvements, to such an extent that the government became anxious about the high level of demands made on their grants by Scottish landlords. On the other hand, in Ireland, the landlords were criticised for not having sufficient capital or commitment to improve their estates and take advantage of similar grants. The government was thus able to use the Famine as an opportunity to facilitate a social revolution, both through the clearance of subdivided estates and the sale of estates which were in debt or 'encumbered'.

Throughout Europe, the potato blight and the simultaneous failure of the grain crop in 1846 resulted in widespread excess mortality, although it was particularly high in Holland and Ireland. The variations in impact reflected the different social, political and ideological climate of each country. A common feature, however, was that it was the poor – those most dependent on the potato – who suffered the greatest losses. In the Highlands of Scotland but more especially in Ireland, the potato blight changed the demographic profile of the local population. Even after the blight had disappeared, the population decline continued. The population of Ireland never recovered from this demographic shock. It is perhaps no wonder that in Ireland, more than in any other European country, the food shortages and Famine of the late 1840s have been regarded as such a tragedy.

CHAPTER 5

'Black '47'

In popular tradition 'Black '47' is remembered as the height of hunger and distress. It was in 1847 that the Famine was at its worst in Ireland. Apart from high levels of mortality and disease, other indicators of social distress were reflected in soaring crime rates, evictions and emigration. The small town of Skibbereen in west Cork came to epitomise the multiple evils of famine, and its name is indelibly associated with suffering, starvation and a society which no longer protected its poorest and most vulnerable members. Reports from there and elsewhere touched the hearts of the international community. 1847 was thus marked by fund-raising activities on behalf of Ireland throughout the world.

By the beginning of 1847, it was clear that the relief policies introduced by the government only a few months earlier had failed. The commencement of the parliamentary year was marked by new legislation for Ireland, some of which was temporary, such as the suspension of the Navigation Acts and the introduction of soup kitchens. A more permanent measure was the extension of the Poor Laws in August 1847, a move intended to provide a solution to the need for both ordinary and Famine relief in Ireland.

Yet 1847 was a year of paradox. A new policy twist resulted in the closure of the public works and the transfer of relief measures to soup kitchens. This change caused much initial hardship and resulted in mortality peaking in the spring of that year. Nevertheless, the opening of the soup kitchens in the spring and summer was generally successful as, for the first time, hungry people were offered food directly. At its peak over 3 million were being fed daily through this mechanism. More importantly, the soup kitchens demonstrated the ability of the government to feed the hungry people of Ireland.

The Crisis of Starvation

On 1 January 1847, the *Freeman's Journal* described the impact of the Famine in County Mayo and announced 'the long feared crisis of starvation has arrived'.[1] At this stage, it was apparent that the various relief measures introduced only a few months earlier had failed to save lives. At the beginning of the year, the government hastily introduced a series of measures to salvage its earlier policies, but they were too late. Many people were already irreversibly weakened by months of undernourishment. The hunger marches and food riots that had marked the winter of 1846 increasingly gave way to despair, exhaustion and flight. Whilst the soup kitchens introduced in the spring and summer of 1847 increased access to food, the relief provided by the government still made no provision for medicine, clothing, fuel, shelter or rent. Malnutrition and disease, rather than starvation, became the main enemy of the Irish poor after 1846.

The three main diseases were fever, dysentery and smallpox, each of which was highly contagious. Other less common but also deadly illnesses were bronchitis, diarrhoea, influenza, measles and tuberculosis. Furthermore, in 1848–49 there was a cholera epidemic, which was particularly virulent in towns and ports.[2] Although such diseases were most prevalent amongst the poorest classes, especially those who were weakened by hunger, they were also greatly feared by other social groups. Fever, in particular, claimed the lives of many relief workers both in Ireland and overseas. The fear of catching it probably restrained people from helping each other, as those who were suspected of succumbing to it became outcasts. As one person recalled:

> When a person in any house got fever the people of the house would hide it from the neighbours. If the neighbours suspected there was any fever in the house, they used to steal up to the house at night time and put an onion on the window sill. They would split the onion in two. If the onion turned green they would know that there was fever in that particular house and they would avoid it.[3]

The spread of disease was exacerbated by the type of relief provided and the methods of obtaining it. The substitutes offered in the place of the traditional potato diet (most often Indian corn or soup) were low in nutritional content. Malnutrition, food deprivation and unsuitable food, such as certain types of shellfish or undercooked corn, increased the vulnerability to infection. The dislocation caused by food shortages also helped spread disease. Large gatherings of people on the public works, the congregation of people in towns or on emigration ships, queues for food rations or soup and overcrowding in workhouses all proved ideal for the transmission of body lice and disease. Furthermore, a combination of exhaustion, apathy and lack of access to fuel or soap meant that the clothing and the homes of many poor people were increasingly unhygienic.

Death from starvation or disease became so common that a number of newspapers ceased to report on them.[4] The high mortality also impinged on other aspects of life, including traditions associated with death and burial procedures. Wakes and other rites of passage disappeared and many bodies were buried without coffins or in communal burial pits.[5] However, one of the chief horrors of the Famine was not simply the number of people who died, but the way in which they lost their lives. There were numerous reports of bodies being eaten by animals. In Skibbereen, a man who had buried his wife in the garden heard scratching throughout the night but was too weak to investigate. The next day, his neighbour brought back the head of the unfortunate woman, saying 'that his dog had brought it home'.[6] Occasionally, the victims attacked by animals were not even dead but were too weak to resist. One report from Sligo described the inquest of Thomas M'Manus of Kilmactranny thus:

> both the legs, as far as the buttocks, appeared to be eaten off by a pig; is of the opinion his death was caused by hunger and cold. There was not a particle of food found in deceased's stomach or intestines. Those who saw the body were of the opinion, from the agonised expression on M'Manus's countenance, that he was *alive* when the pig attacked him.[7]

In the midst of this suffering a reporter from the *Freeman's Journal*, based in Mayo, noticed a new development, that of landlords evicting tenants who had not paid their rents and turning over the land to grazing for sheep and cattle. Whilst the reporter acknowledged that many landlords had been placed in 'a situation of tremendous difficulty', he felt that some protection was necessary for those in this situation.[8] Evictions continued to increase and were a major source of suffering and discontent in 1847. A number of landlords, such as Lord Lucan in County Mayo, gained an unsavoury reputation for initiating a programme of ejectments on their estates.[9] In 1846, 3500 families had been evicted, but this number virtually doubled the following year, when it reached 6000.[10]

Many of the evicted, especially those who had neither the capital nor the strength to emigrate, sought shelter in the local workhouse. At this stage, the Poor Law, which had been intended only to supplement extraordinary relief measures, was in crisis.[11] By December 1846, over half the workhouses were full and, due to the strict provisions of the 1838 legislation, were having to refuse admittance to new applicants. For those who were admitted, conditions were generally cramped and insanitary. Few workhouses had been prepared to accommodate such a sharp increase in the intake of paupers, especially sick paupers, and there were widespread shortages of bedding, clothing and medicine. This led to the practice of giving the clothes of paupers who died of fever or any other disease to new paupers, without first washing them. There was also a shortage of coffins, and many burial sites were situated within the grounds of the workhouse, sometimes next to the water supply. As the Famine progressed, the Guardians frequently had to choose between using their limited financial resources to see to the dead, or to spend it on the living.

In a number of workhouses the situation was made more precarious by the fact that some of the workhouse officers were incompetent – even in the frequently praised northern unions – or, occasionally, dishonest. This was partly the result of their low wages and the increasingly dangerous nature of their work. Despite all these problems, in many unions the Guardians and the workhouse officers attempted to provide relief despite their lack of capital and the various regulations imposed on them. In the winter of 1846–47, over half of the Boards of Guardians were giving food to paupers who were not residents of the workhouse. This was illegal and was strongly condemned by the Poor Law Commissioners. The introduction of soup kitchens in 1847 took much of the pressure off the workhouses, although they continued to be refuges for those who were old, young, sick, infirm or had no other shelter. In the autumn of 1847, the Poor Law became responsible for providing both 'ordinary' and Famine relief. At the same time, the Commissioners were given new powers to dismiss Boards of Guardians who contravened regulations or did not collect sufficient poor rates.[12]

Whilst suffering was widespread in the winter of 1846–47, one area achieved a grim notoriety for its depth of suffering. Skibbereen came to represent the plight of the Irish destitute in the winter of 1846–47. The pressure for relief was felt early in the town and in November 1846, the local workhouse which had been built to accommodate 800 paupers contained 890 inmates. By January, this had reached 1169, of whom 332 had fever. The overcrowding was particularly evident in the fever wards, where 121 patients were sharing 40 beds.[13] Although the use of public works in the area was extensive, there were frequent delays before the works were given Treasury sanction and the payment of workers was often late.[14] This led one local jury to announce that a worker who had not been paid for two weeks had 'died of starvation owing to the gross negligence of the Board of Works'.[15] At the beginning of 1847, the local Church of Ireland minister estimated that mortality in the union had reached 10,000 out of a population of 100,000. Sir Randolph Routh believed that the apathy of the local proprietors was largely to blame for such a high level of suffering. He forwarded to Trevelyan a list of local landlords who he estimated had an annual income of £50,000 and posed the question: 'Ought such destitution prevail with such resources?'[16]

The suffering in Skibbereen was brought to the attention of an international audience through a series of articles and letters describing the conditions in the area, including an open letter to the Duke of Wellington, which was published in *The Times* on 24 December 1846.[17] In January 1847, a deputation from the union met the Home Secretary in London. They also distributed 1000 copies of an appeal to peers and members of the House of Commons.[18] This publicity encouraged other journalists and observers to visit the area and witness the suffering at first hand. The visitors included a reporter from the *Illustrated London News* and two Oxford students, all of whom wished to verify the accuracy of the reports. One of the students was Lord Dufferin, whose family came from County Down. He and his companion, the Honourable George Frederick Boyle, travelled to Skibbereen and were unequivocal about what they saw there:

> We have found every thing but too true; the accounts are not exaggerated – they cannot be exaggerated – nothing more frightful can be conceived. The scenes we have witnessed during our short stay at Skibbereen, equal anything that has been recorded by history, or could be conceived by the imagination.[19]

When Dufferin and Boyle returned to Oxford, they began to raise subscriptions for Ireland and published an account of their journey, the proceeds of which were sent to the stricken town.

The suffering in Skibbereen and other southern unions was also reported in the north of Ireland. One Ulster journal carried frequent reports from newspapers published in the south and west of the country. It summarised the descriptions contained in the papers thus: 'Death is found in every paragraph; desolation in every district; whole families lying down in fever; hovels turned into charnel houses; entire villages prostrate in sickness, or almost hushed in the last sleep.'[20]

Ulster, including its prosperous eastern counties, did not escape the impact of the blight. Many small tenants depended on potatoes for subsistence and the crop had been destroyed in 1846. The oat and flax harvests, which many small weavers relied on, were also poor in that year. The situation was made more serious by the fact that the second failure of the potato coincided with an economic depression in England. This had repercussions within Ireland, most notably Ulster, where many linen workers either lost their jobs or were put on short-pay. The impact of this recession was particularly serious in Belfast and in Counties Antrim, Armagh and Down. In February 1847, a local newspaper, describing the destitution, wrote: 'It would be impossible to find more distressing cases, short of the horrors of Skibbereen, in any part of Ireland than those narrated by our reporter from the eastern divisions of Down.'[21] A minister from Armagh reported that not only agricultural workers but weavers too were in great distress and added, 'starvation is pictured in their countenances'.[22]

As was the case in other parts of Ireland, in the winter of 1846 many Ulster workhouses were filled to capacity, disease and death rates increased, and emigration and evictions became more commonplace. A number of local landlords, such as the radical MP William Sharman Crawford of County Down and Lord George Hill in Donegal, attempted to alleviate the suffering of their tenants by lowering rents or providing cheap grain.[23] Others were absentee or appeared indifferent to the suffering of their tenants. This led the Reverend Clements of Tartaraghan, County Armagh to complain:

> There are only two resident proprietors within the parish ... The largest estate is under the administration of the Lord Chancellor for debt with no help whatsoever being obtained from it for its starving tenantry. A large portion of the parish is bog, the property of absent proprietors and upon it are located a large number of the most wretched tenants who are not assisted by the landlord.[24]

A number of landlords, such as Lord Londonderry, were criticised for doing too little to help their tenants. In a series of newspapers articles, Londonderry was attacked for his parsimony. An example was his contribution of £20 to relief and £10 from his wife, whilst in 1848 they spent £15,000 renovating their house in Mount Stewart. However, when criticised, Londonderry (supported by his agent) vigorously defended his actions: 'My conscience acquits me of ever having wrongly acted as a proprietor, a landlord or a Christian.'[25] His claim to have acted in a Christian manner was in turn scorned by the editor of the *Londonderry Standard*, who pointed out, 'His Lordship is then in a most enviable state of inward blessedness for we imagine that some of the Apostles themselves could scarcely have made such a declaration.'[26]

The impact of the Famine was also felt in other areas in the east of the country. Elizabeth Smith, of Baltiboys, County Wicklow, kept a diary of her life as the wife of a small landowner. Whilst tenants on her husband's estate appear to have been protected from the worst effects of the food shortages, by the beginning of 1847 she recorded, 'Alas! the famine progresses; here it is in frightful reality to be seen in every face ... here they are starving around us, cold, naked, hungry and well nigh houseless.'[27] Mrs Smith, a Scot, blamed the situation on the Irish peasants, whom she described as 'Idle, improvident, reckless, meanly, dependent on the upper classes who they so abuse' and on 'indolent landlords' who were content to throw the burden of providing relief on a few 'willing horses'.[28]

By the beginning of 1847 it was clear that the relief being provided was insufficient to meet the needs of a hungry people. The government, recognising the failure of its relief policies, wound down the public works and passed a series of temporary measures to increase supplies of cheap food within the country. By this stage, however, Skibbereen had become a symbol of the failure of the British government to protect the lives of its most vulnerable members.

Soup or Starvation?

The introduction of the Temporary Relief Act in February 1847 provided for the establishment of soup kitchens in the ensuing spring and summer. Because of this, the Act became popularly known as the Soup Kitchen Act or, less commonly, Burgoyne's Act, named after its chief administrator. The transfer to a new system of relief was an admission that the public works scheme, introduced only a few months earlier, had failed. The Act marked a radical departure from earlier, and even subsequent, legislation due to the high level of entitlement to relief by those in need. It was intended, however, as an interim measure to facilitate a transition from the unsuccessful public works to a new and permanent system of relief based on an extended Poor Law.

Regardless of the high level of expenditure by the central government on the public works they had failed to provide even a minimal level of subsistence for thousands of people during the winter of 1846–47. Consequently, the rate of mortality had risen dramatically and, by the beginning of 1847, the Whig government was admitting that 'instances of starvation occur daily'.[29] The Temporary Relief Act was rushed through parliament in February 1847. Simultaneously, the government announced that the Act would be used to extend the Poor Law to allow it to become the main channel for providing relief after the autumn. In order for this to be possible, outdoor relief – which had been expressly forbidden by the 1838 legislation – was to be permitted for the first time. The soup kitchens and the extended Poor Law were to be financed by the local poor rates, although government loans would initially be made available. This meant that, after the autumn of 1847, local taxation would be responsible for both ordinary and extraordinary relief.

The Temporary Relief Act denoted a significant change in the provision of relief in two main ways. First, it facilitated the unique but short-lived introduction of a direct attack on starvation by giving food to those in need without the imposition of burdensome bureaucratic hurdles, which had been a feature of the public works. Second, however, the Act increased the pressure on hard-pressed local resources by transferring the responsibility for the payment for relief from being a national (or imperial) responsibility to a situation where local needs had to be met from local resources. These new policies marked a major step towards the government's desire to enforce a high level of local accountability and financial liability.

The Act provided that free cooked food was to be provided in government soup kitchens. Thick soup or 'stirabout' was recommended.[30] The food was to be cooked and ready for immediate consumption as it was thought that it would thereby have little transfer or resale value. Although the quantities provided were not generous, the fact that the provision of the soup was free and not subject to a means test or dependent on employment on the public works marked a break with earlier precedents. By providing free food to the starving Irish, the Temporary Relief Act reversed the earlier policies of Peel and Russell, which had been opposed to the provision of gratuitous relief. However, from the outset, the Act was regarded as a short-term expedient which would mark the end of the government's financial involvement in the Famine.[31]

Whilst the government was opposed to the provision of free food, even in a period of crisis, free soup had traditionally been given by a number of charitable organisations as a cheap and effective means of feeding large numbers of destitute people. In Ireland, the early and total failure of the potato crop in 1846 placed an unprecedented pressure on the relief services, which they were unable to meet. In Kilcoe in west Cork, for example, a soup kitchen was opened as early as September 1846.[32] As the public works collapsed, privately run soup kitchens became the mainstay of a debilitated peasantry and were used extensively to fill the void in official relief. Many of these soup kitchens were financed by the Society of Friends who had become directly involved in Irish relief at the end of 1846. A number of landlords also were supplying soup as a way of providing cheap and immediate relief. At the beginning of 1847, in a complete reversal of previous policy, the government encouraged the distribution of soup by private charities and, even more radically, began to make plans for the next phase of relief to be based on the establishment of a national network of soup kitchens.[33] Following this decision, the government set about the task of reorganising the system of relief in Ireland and, at the same time, finding a way of making the provision of free food by the government both morally and ideologically acceptable.

In England, the provision of free soup during periods of food shortages and high prices was a traditional response by private charities and philanthropic individuals. In the wake of a poor potato harvest in England in 1845, a number of charitable soup kitchens had been set up. The most famous of these was established in London in Leicester Square by Alexis Soyer, a French society chef employed in the exclusive Reform Club, the haunt of the Whig Party and their supporters. Whilst creating gourmet dishes for dignitaries and politicians, he had become interested in the mechanisms of feeding large numbers of poor people economically and efficiently.[34] To this end, Soyer designed a new type of soup boiler and published a series of recipes for cheap soup, some of which were created specifically on behalf of the Irish poor.[35]

Soyer's soup recipes required little or no meat. For this reason, he claimed that a quart of nutritious soup could be made for $^3/_4$d. Largely as a result of Soyer's flamboyant personality, the provision of free soup became the subject of lively debate in the columns of the British and Irish press. In England, claims and counter-claims appeared regularly in *The Times* regarding the cost and quality of Soyer's soup, critics declaring that it was not so much 'soup for the poor' as 'poor soup'. One protagonist suggested that Soyer should feed his cheap soup to the members of the Reform Club for two weeks and see how they fared.[36]

This debate was followed by leading members of the Whig Party. At the beginning of 1847, the Whig government decided to provide free food in Ireland, despite its being contrary to prevailing doctrines on the relief of poverty. In what appears to have been a public relations exercise, Soyer was approached by a member of the government and asked to travel to Ireland for the purpose of establishing a 'model' soup kitchen in Dublin. Soyer agreed and quickly achieved the same high profile in Ireland as he had in England. Soyer's model soup kitchen was opened on 5 April 1847, just as the Temporary Relief Act was becoming operative. The kitchen, a large tent, was located just outside the Royal Barracks in Dublin. The opening ceremony was accompanied by the maximum publicity. This included a fanfare of music with the tent decorated with flags and banners. The Lord Lieutenant of Ireland, the Lord Mayor of Dublin and a hundred other dignitaries were invited to attend. More importantly, both the English and Irish press were invited to observe the proceedings. The guests were permitted to sit at the benches in the tent and sample the soup. They all declared it to be 'delicious'.[37] After they had finished and left the premises, a hundred paupers from the Mendacity Institute were then admitted to the tent and allowed to taste the soup. Again, they claimed that it was delicious. Overall, the day was a well-orchestrated publicity stunt, it even being recorded for posterity by an artist from the *Illustrated London News*. The destitute of Dublin, however, had to wait a further day before being allowed access to the soup kitchen.[38]

In addition to providing cheap soup, Soyer's aim was to distribute the rations quickly and efficiently. To make this possible, the process of receiving the soup was strictly regimented. Entry to the tent was through a narrow zigzag passage; a bell signalled that the paupers could enter the main tent; while they ate, the next group waited in the passage. Within the eating area, there were long tables which were set with bowls and spoons, attached to chains. A prayer was said before eating commenced. A quart of soup was provided per person, and a further quarter pound of bread was to be handed out to be consumed outside. The whole process was estimated to take no longer than 6 minutes.[39]

Apart from feeding the paupers in the main tent, Soyer's soup kitchen also made sufficient soup to supply other relief centres within Dublin. Soyer estimated that in this way, 5000 meals a day could be provided. This figure turned out to be an underestimation as, between 6 April and 11 August 1847, an average of 8750 persons were fed daily either directly or indirectly from Soyer's soup kitchen.[40]

The efficiency and economy of Soyer's model soup kitchen impressed the Whig government, who purchased it for the use of the South Dublin Poor Law Union. The Guardians estimated that as a consequence of Soyer's methods, the cost of providing outdoor relief was reduced by 50 per cent.[41] In the middle of April 1847, Soyer returned to London in a blaze of publicity, public dinners being held in his honour in both Dublin and London. Before leaving Dublin, Soyer was presented with a snuff box from the 'citizens of Dublin' as a token of their appreciation for making cheap soup 'palatable'.[42] Overall, largely as a result of Soyer's efforts, the provision of free soup as a form of relief had been made cheap, efficient and (in the short term, anyway) ideologically acceptable.

Whilst Soyer was convincing politician and pauper alike of the benefits of his soup kitchens, within Ireland preparations were underway for the implementation of the Temporary Relief Act. In view of the deficiencies of the public works, the Act was implemented instantly. In February 1847, a Board of Temporary Relief Commissioners was appointed, based in Dublin. Sir John Burgoyne, formerly of the Board of Works, was appointed Chairman. The Relief Commissioners were put under the control of the Treasury, which ensured the continuation of the Treasury's involvement in the provision of relief. In effect, this meant that the Relief Commissioners were answerable to Trevelyan on matters of policy and for the day-to-day administration of the scheme, including staff appointments. More importantly, loans to the local relief committees from the central Commissioners could not be made without the prior sanction of the Treasury.[43]

It was estimated that it would take approximately 4–6 weeks for the complex administrative machinery for the new Act to be operative. During this time, 10,000 account books, 80,000 pro-forma sheets, and 3 million card tickets were issued. Although the

issue of cooked food could commence as early as 15 March, the
bureaucracy was rarely in place this quickly. Despite this delay, at
the end of March, the Treasury announced that the public works
were to be wound down, beginning with an immediate reduction
of 20 per cent of the workforce. A dogmatic adherence to this policy
meant that in a number of districts the destitute were left without
access to any form of relief. In addition to the bureaucratic delays,
many of the poorest areas lacked either the infrastructure or the
apparatus to establish the soup kitchens. This was evident in regard
to the availability of large cauldrons for the cooking of the soup.
The central Relief Commissioners had arranged to import and
distribute them in the west and south of the country, but they did
not arrive in Ireland until early April.[44]

The period between the public works being closed and the soup
kitchens being opened was marked by widespread suffering and a
rise in mortality as the administrators in the localities were left without
the means to provide relief. The Grand Jury in Kerry, for example,
described this decision as being equivalent to signing a 'death
warrant' on the poor of Ireland.[45] An increase in riots and social
disorder in the spring of 1847 was met by the deployment of
additional troops to the disturbed areas.[46] Although there were many
accusations that the government was 'withholding food from the
starving population', the Treasury refused to deviate from this
policy on the grounds that it was preferable 'to incur partial present
inconvenience, than be the means of introducing measures
productive of eventual injury to the community'.[47] At the beginning
of June, the Guardians of the Galway Union attributed the high
level of mortality in the locality to the tardiness in opening the soup
kitchens.[48] In the Roscommon Union, when no soup kitchen had
opened by mid-June, the local Government Inspector provided
interim relief from his own pocket. The final soup kitchen was not
opened until 15 June in the Skibbereen Union, an area which had
achieved so much publicity in the previous year for the suffering
of the local population.[49] In the areas which were without access
to official relief in the spring of 1847, it was left to private
philanthropy, notably the Society of Friends, local clergy and other
charitable individuals, to meet the nutritional deficit.

In the local areas, the distribution of soup was under the control
of newly constituted relief committees, working alongside a separate
finance committee. To ensure a high level of local involvement and
to avoid any possibility of proselytising, a representative from each
of the main religious denominations was asked to sit on the relief
committees. The finance committees were appointed by, and
answerable to, the Lord Lieutenant. To facilitate the government's
longer-term aim of transferring all Famine relief to the Poor Law,

the new relief committees were superimposed on the existing administrative and fiscal structure of the Poor Law.[50]

Many local relief committees were unsure as to what was meant by the term 'soup' – did it imply the inclusion of meat? The Relief Commissioners reassured them that this was not the case; soup meant 'any food cooked in a boiler, and distributed in a liquid state, thick or thin and whether composed of meat, fish, vegetables, grain or meal'.[51] The Relief Commissioners recommended that the amount of food to be provided was to be 'miserable and scanty', the typical daily ration to be one bowl of soup and one pound of biscuit, flour, grain or meal. If the soup had already been thickened, only one quarter of these rations had to be provided.[52] Whilst the quantities suggested had received the prior approval of the Board of Health, the latter were apprehensive that the local committees would mistake 'bulk for nutrient' and they repeatedly recommended that the soup should be 'solid' rather than 'fluid'. They also advised that the ingredients of the soup should be varied as much as possible.[53] However, these recommendations were not fully adopted and a number of local relief committees reduced both the quantity and quality of their rations in an attempt to keep down costs. By the summer, the Board of Health was worried by the appearance of disease resembling 'sea scurvy' and it recommended that more fresh vegetables should be added to the soup.[54]

The transfer from relief in wages to relief in cooked food was not universally popular, especially as the soup varied so much in quality. In Clonmel, a Juror described the local soup as being 'totally unfit for human food'.[55] In a number of areas, the soup kitchens were attacked and a few were destroyed. In Kells in County Meath, a crowd gathered around the local soup kitchen in an effort to stop people from taking the soup – an event which the local newspaper described as a 'Stirabout Rebellion'.[56] One newspaper undertook its own experiment based on tastings of rations from a variety of soup kitchens. It judged most of the soup to be of poor quality with the notable exception of that provided by the Mullingar relief committee, which it described as 'three pounds of well cooked and wholesome stirabout'.[57]

On the model of Soyer's soup kitchen, each government soup kitchen was expected to have two doors – one for entrance and one for exit. To minimise the congregation of crowds and the possibility of any disturbances at the soup kitchens, each person was allocated a number on a relief list and a time to attend. Any persons who caused disturbance whilst in the queue were required to wait until the end of the day for their rations.[58] Rations left over at the end of the day could be sold, although this was rare as the demand for relief was so great.[59]

The government had initially attempted to impose a ceiling of 75 per cent of a local population being entitled to receive rations of soup. This proved to be impossible, especially in some western unions where the take up of relief was registered as 100 per cent. The number of rations provided peaked on 3 July 1847 when over 3 million people (that is, at least 37 per cent of the population) were in receipt of free rations of soup. On the same day, a further 80,000 rations were sold by the relief committees.[60] There were, however, considerable regional variations in the demand for relief. The highest demand for relief occurred in unions in the west of Ireland, notably in Ballinrobe, Clifden, Gort, Swinford, Tuam and Westport. In contrast, in the unions of Antrim, Belfast and Newtownards (all in the north-east) no government soup kitchens were opened, although rations of food were provided privately.[61] In Belfast, it became a matter of civic pride *not* to have to depend on financial assistance from the government.[62] The sharp contrast between the areas of high and low demand for official relief provides an insight into the geographic diversity of the food shortages and the localised impact of the Famine.

Parliament voted £2,250,000 for the support of the Temporary Relief Act. This meant that after the public works, the soup kitchens were the most generously supported of the government's relief schemes. A feature of the provision of this money, which had been evident in earlier relief schemes, was that government funds could not be released without the prior approval of the Treasury which, in effect, meant Trevelyan. The majority of this money was provided as a loan to the local relief committees, to be repaid out of the local poor rates. The poorest unions did receive a combination of grants and loans. Despite the large numbers of people who were supported by the soup kitchens in the summer of 1847, not all the money voted by the government was spent.[63] The Irish Executive asked if the residue of this money (approximately £500,000) could be reallocated to medical relief, which they considered to be underfunded. The Treasury refused on the grounds that to do so would only further the 'unhealthy dependence' of the Irish people on central government.[64]

The relative cheapness of financing the soup kitchens demonstrated that direct relief could be provided efficiently and economically. This was helped by an increase in food imports to Ireland after the spring of 1847 and a temporary relaxation of import duties, both of which helped to bring down the price of grain.[65] As a consequence, the cost of a full ration fell to approximately $1\frac{1}{2}$d a day. In contrast, the wages paid to the government officials who administered this system were high – Government Inspecting Officers being paid 21 shillings a day. The Officers also received 10 shillings for each night spent away from home, plus 3 shillings lodging money, in addition to their travelling expenses.[66]

Although the Temporary Relief Act had stipulated that the soup kitchens could remain open until 30 September 1847, the government decided to begin closing them in August. On 15 August, the Treasury ordered that relief was to end in 55 unions, most of which were situated in the east or midlands of the country. On 29 August, relief was stopped in the remaining unions, with the exception of the 26 poorest unions where relief was allowed to continue until 30 September. To expedite this process, in July the government decreed that all able-bodied men in receipt of poor relief were to be made to work on the roads as a test of destitution.[67] Following the closure of the soup kitchens, all relief became the responsibility of the amended Poor Law, including repayments of loans for the soup kitchens. This meant that in addition to financing relief, after the autumn of 1847, the poor rates also had to pay the outstanding debts of the Temporary Relief Act.

Despite the delay in opening a number of soup kitchens, when they were operative they were successful as a means of providing large-scale relief. Moreover, uniquely of all Famine relief, they provided a liberal and demand-determined response to the food shortages. Whilst the relief provided was cheap and kept to a minimum, by the summer of 1847, the general health of the population had improved and mortality appeared to have fallen, even in the poorest unions of Skibbereen and in Kerry.[68] In the long term it is doubtful if a soup diet could have sustained the population, especially one used to the high-bulk content of a potato diet. In the short term, the soup kitchens were successful in that they tackled the problem of food shortages and hunger directly.

The soup kitchens were not universally popular, however. At a public meeting convened by the landowners in Roscommon, they criticised the Temporary Relief Act for demoralising the poor and leaving them 'free to idleness and acts of crime'.[69] A Dublin newspaper, which had advocated that government intervention should be kept to a minimum, stated that the introduction of this Act had 'submerged the last vestiges of self-confidence that the useless works suffered to remain among the people'.[70] One of the harshest critics was Archbishop MacHale of Tuam, a vociferous critic of the Whig governments earlier policies who prophesised that:

> Future historians will have to record that, with a joint stock firm of the professors of French cookery and the itinerant followers of Tubalcain, a Prime Minister of the richest empire in the world, succeeded in snatching from the jaws of famine a remnant of the Irish people.[71]

Despite the criticisms of the Temporary Relief Act, at its peak over 3 million people were receiving food rations daily, making it individually the most availed of relief measure. The administrative machinery which supported this system had been, for the most part, established in under two months. This relief scheme demonstrated that the British government and its agents possessed the administrative and logistical ability to provide relief on a massive scale – and to do it at relatively little cost. By doing so, the Whig administration contravened a number of their own key ideologies. After the autumn of 1847, however, relief was again provided in such a way as not to undermine these doctrines.

Private Philanthropy

An important although sometimes overlooked aspect of relief provision was the amount of money, food and other items provided by private charity for Ireland. The practice of raising private subscriptions during a period of food shortages was traditional. However, the scale and geographical scope of contributions provided during the Irish Famine was unprecedented. Donations were raised in each of the five continents and cut across national, religious, cultural, sexual, political and social divisions. As a consequence, for a brief period during the Famine, an international community, with little in common except the desire to help Ireland, responded with speed and unparalleled generosity.[72] The role of private charity became particularly urgent after December 1846, when the Home Secretary announced that it was 'the conviction of the government that they cannot by any means within their power meet all the cases of severe privation and distress'.[73]

The first international donation came from Calcutta at the end of 1845, as a result of a fund-raising initiative by members of the British army, many of whom were Irish-born. The success of their activities resulted in the formation of the Indian Relief Fund, which raised almost £14,000 for Famine relief within a few weeks. This fund attracted donations from Madras, Bombay and Ceylon. The money raised was channelled through a committee in Dublin, which included both the Protestant and Catholic archbishops of the city.[74] Concurrently with subscriptions raised in India, thousands of miles away in Boston a fund-raising committee was organised. News of the potato blight had reached Boston in November 1845. At the instigation of the Boston Repeal Association, a charitable fund was established, making it the first formal fund-raising structure in the United States.[75] Within a few weeks the Committee had raised several thousand dollars, mainly due to the exertions of local parish priests and political activists. At the beginning of 1846 donations fell off sharply as there was a growing suspicion that reports from Ireland had been exaggerated. Also, there was a fear amongst some that the fund-raising activities were diverting funds from the repeal agitation.[76] The first of these fears appeared to be confirmed by newspapers received from Ireland and Britain during the spring and summer of 1846, which were dominated by the Corn Law debate and (in Ireland) the struggle between Daniel O'Connell and the Young Irelanders. To an outsider, it appeared that the Famine was over.

The reappearance of blight in the late summer and autumn of 1846 again placed Irish distress on the political agenda. In the wake of the second crop failure, newspapers throughout the world carried stories of the suffering in Ireland, although there was often a time lag of 3–6 weeks before the papers reached overseas readers. By the end of 1846, there was a sense of urgency that had not been apparent 12 months earlier. As a result, many of the philanthropic activities on behalf of Ireland were concentrated in the year after the second and more devastating failure of the potato crop. In the wake of this second appearance of potato blight, a number of charitable organisations were specially constituted to encourage and co-ordinate relief activities. The most successful of these were the General Central Relief Committee for All Ireland, the British Relief Association for the Relief of Distress in Ireland and Scotland and the Central Relief Committee of the Society of Friends. The Irish Relief Association, which had been formed to assist with the food shortages in 1831, was also reconstituted, but the membership of the Duke of Manchester (who owned 12,000 acres in County Armagh) led O'Connell to accuse it of ultra- Protestantism.[77] These fears were not without foundation: in January 1847, the Duke of Manchester and a number of leading Ulster Protestants published a letter in the Belfast newspaper, *The Northern Whig*, in which they said that 'the present favourable crisis' was providing an opportunity 'for conveying the light of the Gospels to the darkened mind of the Roman Catholic peasantry'.[78]

The General Central Relief Committee was formed in Dublin in December 1846. Its Chairman was the Marquis of Kildare and its membership comprised a number of prominent Irish men including Daniel O'Connell, his son John O'Connell and the radical nationalist, William Smith O'Brien. The Committee was closely supported by the Bank of Ireland, which acted as Treasurer. Donations came from all over the world, from Toronto (£3472) to Buenos Aires (£441 1s 10d), Grahamstown (South Africa) (£470) and Delhi' (£296 9s 1d). Within a period of 12 months, the Committee disbursed 1871 grants, ranging from £10 to £400.[79] Most of this money was given to Connaught (£20,835), although a considerable amount was provided for the poor in Ulster

(£11,300), especially in Counties Cavan and Donegal.[80] The Committee began to wind down its activities at the end of 1847, following a harvest that was small but relatively free from blight. They were apprehensive, however, that the ending of public works and the transfer to Poor Law would have tragic consequences and warned prophetically that 'in some respects the condition of the peasantry is this year more lamentable than it was during the past season'.[81]

The British Relief Association was constituted at the beginning of 1847 in London by a well-respected Jewish banker and philanthropist, Lionel de Rothschild. Its members included a number of bankers and businessmen, who set an example by each providing a donation of £1000. The Association decided that a sixth of all money raised should be used for the famine in the Highlands of Scotland, unless the donor specifically named the destination.[82] From the outset, their approach to famine relief was organised and professional. They appointed a Polish nobleman, Count Paul Edmund de Strzelecki, to act as their agent in Ireland. It was believed that Strzelecki, who had been educated in Edinburgh and had undertaken a scientific exploration of the interior of Australia in 1839, would be an impartial distributor of relief.[83] However, by deciding to work closely with the government – in effect, with Charles Trevelyan of the Treasury – the British Relief Association was seen by many as an arm of government relief. As the Famine progressed, a number of ideological conflicts emerged between Strzelecki and Trevelyan, especially over the issue of providing relief to children in the west – a scheme which the British Relief Association had successfully pioneered but which Trevelyan regarded as too generous. The British Relief Association closed its operations in the summer of 1848 as its funds were exhausted. In September, Strzelecki left Ireland, refusing to accept payment for the work he had done. When the Association ceased its operations they were still providing a vital life-line to many people, including a scheme that was feeding 200,000 children daily in the west of Ireland.[84] In 1848, blight reappeared on the potato crop, making a fourth year of food shortages inevitable. Nevertheless, with the exception of private remittances and small donations channelled through the Catholic Church, local taxation in Ireland was expected to bear the burden of the forthcoming distress.

The Quakers became involved in providing famine relief in November 1846. A relief committee was established in Dublin at the suggestion of Joseph Bewley, followed a few weeks later by the formation of a similar committee in London. In England also a 'Ladies Irish Clothing Society' was formed, which worked closely with its sister organisation in Dublin, the 'Ladies Relief Association',

with the purpose of collecting clothing and money for Irelar
May 1847, the Committees had received £4800 from Irish Qu
£35,500 from English Quakers and £4000 from non-Quakers in
both countries. The donations which were received from the United
States, however, far exceeded these amounts.[85] At the end of 1846,
the Irish Relief Committee had made contact with Quakers in
America, sending a circular asking for support. This was to prove
to be one of the most successful mechanisms for raising funds for
relief. In New York, Jacob Harvey, a wealthy merchant and
philanthropist, helped mastermind a massive relief operation which
extended throughout the United States.[86]

The approach of the Society of Friends differed from that of other
relief agencies in that they became personally involved in running
the day-to-day provision of relief. A number of Quakers from
England and Ireland travelled to the west of Ireland in order to assess
the true extent of food shortages and to oversee the distribution of
relief. They were appalled by what they saw and sent full and frank
reports to their co-religionists and to the national newspapers.[87]
The Quakers were equally critical of the response of absentee
landlords and of the British government, which they considered
to be inadequate.[88] Their reports helped counter-balance the
negative accounts of Irish distress which appeared regularly in *The
Times* and *Punch*. The private correspondence of the Quakers,
however, provided an even more pessimistic view of events in
Ireland. William Forster the Elder, who had considerable experience
of both Ireland and working with the English poor, wrote to his
wife from Galway:

> I have not the nerve – there is no need to tell my weakness – to
> look upon the suffering of the afflicted; it takes too much
> possession of me, and almost disqualifies me for exertion ... It
> was enough to have broken the stoutest heart to have seen the
> poor little children in the union workhouse yesterday – their flesh
> hanging so loose from their little bones, that the physician took
> it in his hand and wrapped it round their legs.[89]

The Quakers used their international network of Friends to
increase awareness and raise funds for Ireland. Because they were
held in such high regard, their appeal for donations cut across
religious and national divides. The role of fund-raiser occasionally
presented them with a moral dilemma. For example, the Quakers
were active campaigners against slavery. When the slave cities of
Baltimore and Charleston raised money for famine relief, they
were undecided as to whether or not to accept it. After much
discussion, they decided to take these donations.[90] They were
emphatic, however, in refusing a donation from a theatre company

in London, on the grounds that such venues were 'inconsistent with the gravity and sobriety required of professors of Christianity'.[91]

At the end of 1847, the Quakers decided to withdraw from providing direct relief in Ireland, although they continued to give indirect relief in the form of seeds and capital equipment, such as spades and fishing tackle. They did so on the grounds of exhaustion, preferring thereafter to channel their resources into providing long-term benefits to the country. During the previous year, the relief provided by the Quakers had been vital in saving lives, especially in the spring of 1847, when the government ordered the closure of public works schemes despite the fact that alternative relief was not available. They had also pioneered the use of soup kitchens, a scheme which the government had briefly used with great success in the summer of 1847.[92] In 1848, as famine raged, the British Treasury secretly offered the Quakers £100 if they would resume their relief operations. They refused to accept on the grounds that more radical measures were necessary.[93] Overall, the involvement of the Quakers was brief but successful. The personal cost of their efforts, however, was high: Jonathan Pim collapsed from exhaustion, and Joseph Bewley, Jacob Harvey and William Todhunter all died from the same cause, whilst Abraham Beale of Cork, Matthew Jenkinson of Carlow, J.C.Harvey of Leitrim, and about a dozen other Quaker workers died from famine epidemics.[94]

Although it possessed no formal committee or fund-raising structure at all, the role of the Catholic Church was extremely important in raising money in Ireland. Pope Pius IX, a great admirer of Daniel O'Connell, became involved in Irish relief on an unprecedented scale.[95] In January 1847, Pius sent 1000 Roman dollars to the country and organised three days of prayer on behalf of the starving Irish. The prayers, preached in Italian, English and French, reinforced the idea of the Famine as requiring international assistance. In March of the same year, the Pope took the unusual step of issuing an encyclical to the Catholic community world-wide, requesting them to set aside three days of prayer for Ireland and to make further charitable donations.[96] The early involvement of the Pope helped give prominence to the need for international help in Ireland, although some of the fund-raising activities preceded any involvement by Rome. Throughout the international Catholic community, collections were made for Ireland from churches in Venezuela, to those in Canada, South Africa and Australia. A remarkable feature of the Catholic donations was the fact that they continued to be sent even as late as 1850, when other donations had already ceased or were showing evidence of 'donor fatigue'.[97] In England, The Tablet, a Catholic newspaper, repeatedly urged its readers to send more funds to Ireland, offering to act as a channel for 'a few pounds from this country to the starving poor of Ireland'.[98] A number of English Catholics used the paper's columns to attack the policies of the British government and to counter the editorials in *The Times*.

Although donations from the Society of Friends were the best known, fund-raising for Ireland was truly an ecumenical affair. The Wesleyan Methodists in England collected £500 for Irish relief and the Anglican Church in Amsterdam raised £561.[99] Members of the Franklin Street and Crosby Street Synagogues, both in New York, contributed $80 and $175 respectively. In New York also donations were received from a Baptist Church in Amity Street, a Protestant Dutch Church in Franklin Street and a German Lutheran Church in Walker Street.[100]

The desire to assist the suffering in Ireland became a *cause célèbre* which attracted the interest of a number of powerful and influential people. Queen Victoria, the Pope, the Sultan of Turkey and the Tsar of Russia, for example, made strange bedfellows, but each gave a personal donation to Ireland. In doing so, they encouraged others to follow their example. As a consequence, donations came from a variety of disparate – and unlikely – sources, ranging from heads of state and British ambassadors to London policemen, English convicts and former black slaves in the Caribbean. Society ladies throughout the world (including Belfast and Dublin) organised charitable events, such as theatre outings, fashionable balls and lavish dinners, to raise money for the starving Irish.[101]

One of the most remarkable international donations to Ireland was made by the Choctaw Nation of America. The Choctaw Indians were familiar with suffering and marginalisation, having been compelled to move from their land in 1831 and forced to resettle in Oklahoma. During this journey, so many of their people died that the journey became known as 'The Trail of Tears'. The Choctaws had been told of the suffering in Ireland by their government agent, Colonel William Armstrong. A collection was made 'by Red men and white' and $170 dollars raised which was forwarded to the Society of Friends. The local Relief Committee in their acknowledgement of this contribution described it as 'the voice of benevolence from the western wilderness of the western hemisphere'.[102] This act of generosity did not go unnoticed in the local press. The *Arkansas Intelligencer* stated:

> What an agreeable reflection it must give to the Christian and the philanthropist, to witness this evidence of civilisation and Christian spirit existing among our red neighbours. They are repaying the Christian world a consideration for bringing them out from benighted ignorance and heathen barbarism. Not only by contributing a few dollars but by affording evidence that the labours of the Christian missionary have not been in vain.[103]

In England, fund-raising was also extensive. Private subscriptions had been sent from England in earlier periods of food shortages but in 1845, Sir Robert Peel had predicted that:

> There will be no hope of contributions from England for the mitigation of this calamity. Monster meetings, the ungrateful return for past kindness, the subscriptions in Ireland to Repeal rent and O'Connell tribute, will have disinclined the charitable here to make any great exertions for Irish relief.[104]

Peel was wrong, however, and contributions cut across political and religious divides. The involvement of the Church of England was formalised when Queen Victoria issued a Queen's Letter in January 1847, calling for collections to be made in each parish church on behalf of Ireland and Scotland. On 24 March of that year, a day of Fast and Humiliation was proclaimed for a similar purpose. These collections were widely supported and raised almost £172,000. At the same time, however, they helped link the Famine with the need for atonement and thus reinforced providentialist interpretations of the potato blight. In October 1847, a second Queen's Letter was issued. By this time, however, the tide of public opinion had turned against giving assistance to Ireland and only £30,000 was donated.[105]

Individual cities and towns in Britain established relief committees in the early months of 1847. One of the most successful was in Manchester and Salford where almost £8000 was raised. Other large donations were received from Newcastle and Gateshead (£3902), Hull (£3800), Birmingham (£800), Leeds (£2500), Huddersfield (£2103), Wolverhampton (£1838) and York (£1700). Smaller amounts were raised in a number of other towns, including Birkenhead, Bristol, Cardiff, Chester, Glasgow, Liverpool, Neath and Rugby.[106] Donations made by the British press included £50 from the *Observer*, £100 from the *Morning Herald* and £37 from the *Daily News*. The most surprising contribution of all, in view of its vitriolic attacks on Irish distress, was £50 donated by journalists of *Punch*.[107]

In Ireland itself a number of fund-raising committees were established, mostly centred in Belfast and Dublin. Again, imaginative ways were devised for raising funds. An art exhibition of Old Masters was organised by the Royal Irish Art-Union on behalf of the distressed Irish, whilst officers stationed in a garrison in Dublin donated £15, the proceeds of an amateur dramatic production.[108] In Belfast, an area traditionally not believed to have suffered much during the Famine, a Ladies' Relief Association was formed, which provided food and clothing, mostly in the distressed Ballymacarrett area of the town, although the committee also sent relief to parts of the west of the country. A Ladies' Committee was established in Dublin, which received a donation of £3000 from soldiers in the Regent's Park barracks in London.[109]

The largest and most successful fund-raising activities took place in the United States, where at least one million dollars was sent through established channels. The tradition of giving assistance to Europe had been established in the 1820s when America had sent donations to Greece, although the scale of relief to Ireland (and to a lesser degree Scotland) was far larger than previously known, helped by the close personal links between Ireland and the United States.[110] Information about the blight in Ireland had first reached America in early October 1845. News of bad harvests throughout Europe generally followed swiftly. Farmers and merchants within the United States viewed these problems as an opportunity to increase their exports, especially of Indian corn. Reports of the second and more extensive failure in 1846 initially was overshadowed by national concerns, notably the war between the United States and Mexico. Also, the extensive public works scheme which the British government had decided to implement was regarded as being sufficient to cope with the distress. Faith in the public works scheme was short-lived and by November 1846 tragic stories of starvation were appearing in the American press and were being reinforced by private letters sent from friends and family in Ireland. The circular sent by the Society of Friends in Dublin at the end of 1846 was widely publicised and used as a basis for fund-raising activities by non-Quakers throughout North America. The respect for the Quakers and their first-hand accounts from the west of Ireland led to a new wave of sympathy. In New York, a meeting in Tammany Hall raised 800 dollars and acted as a spur to other organisations to contribute the proceeds of social events. The seriousness of the Irish situation overcame much traditional native hostility to Ireland and to Catholics, which had been evident in 1846 when the president of an Irish Protestant organisation was jeered by his members for having given money to a Catholic fund.[111] Instead, the main division emerged between those who believed that the Famine arose from British mismanagement and those who supported the response of the government.[112]

The *Tribune* newspaper actively sought to encourage the inhabitants of New York to do more for Ireland, optimistically suggesting that 'the more unfeeling portion of the aristocracy of Ireland and Britain would feel rebuked and humbled by this exhibition of trans-Atlantic benevolence; they would be impelled to take effectual measures to prevent a recurrence of the occasion for it'.[113] This did not prove to be the case. The Prime Minister, Lord John Russell, personally thanked the inhabitants of the United States for their generosity and allowed the removal of freight charges on charitable goods imported from the United States, but his administration did not feel impelled to do more themselves. In fact, the government frequently relied on private benevolence to provide relief where it was unable or unwilling to do so itself. This was most evident in the case of the Society of Friends who, as early as October 1846, were providing free soup – an action to which the government was ideologically opposed, despite it being both cheap and effective in saving lives. Ironically, as its own system of public works relief failed, the government was forced to resort to opening soup kitchens itself for a few months in 1847.[114]

By the beginning of that year, there was extensive coverage of events in Ireland in the American press and also reports of suffering from individual localities. Meetings were held and appeals made to give generously or, as one speaker in New Orleans described it, 'The Old World stretches out her arm to the New'.[115] By February 1847, the cities of New York, Philadelphia and Baltimore had raised over one million dollars and collections were continuing.[116] Again, as in the previous year, the trade of the United States was benefiting from the food shortages throughout Europe. Their generosity was also helped by the fact that America had enjoyed a bumper food harvest in 1846 and therefore had a considerable agricultural surplus. It was suggested that the country should use this opportunity to increase its exports of Indian corn, which was now in demand not only in Ireland, but in Holland, England, Germany, Belgium and Hungary, all of which had suffered from poor corn harvests.[117] A Charleston newspaper, for example, when urging its readers to donate money, reminded them: 'We must not forget that the increase to our national wealth in consequence of the advance in the price of provisions has been caused by scarcity of food in Great Britain.'[118] The General Irish Relief Committee in New York alluded to this when, in a widely printed public address, they stated:

> The miseries of Ireland are the direct cause of our increasing wealth. Our fellow citizens, generally of the agricultural and commercial classes, are making large gains by the advance in foreign prices. What is death to Ireland is but augmented fortune to America; and we are actually fattening on the starvation of another people.[119]

The appeal for donations was given additional weight by the involvement of the Vice-President, George Mifflin Dallas, who chaired a meeting in Washington on 9 February 1847. This was attended by many wealthy and influential Americans, including a large number of members of the Houses of Congress. The meeting agreed that 'such unexampled calamity and suffering ought to overcome in their regard all considerations of distance, foreign birth and residence'. Letters were read from Ireland depicting the horrors of starvation, including one from the women of Dunmanway in County Cork. Addressed to 'Ladies of America', it read:

> Oh! that our American sisters could see the labourers on our roads, able-bodied men, scarcely clad, famishing with hunger, with despair in their once cheerful faces, staggering at their work … oh! that they could see the dead father, mother or child, lying coffinless, and hear the screams of the survivors around them, caused not by sorrow, but by the agony of hunger.[120]

At the Washington meeting, a committee was formed and representatives were appointed on behalf of each state and territory.

In February 1847, Citizen Crittenden of Kentucky suggested that the federal government give $500,000 to Ireland and Scotland. Although passed by the Senate, it was subsequently thrown out by the Ways and Means Committee. President Polk was personally sympathetic to this gesture but admitted that it would have been unconstitutional to use government money for such a purpose. A few days later, Congress demonstrated its desire to help Ireland when, responding to a request by the Boston Relief Committee, it gave permission for the sloop of war the *Jamestown* and the frigate *Macedonian* to be used to transport supplies to Ireland and, in the case of the *Macedonian*, to Scotland.[121] This was a remarkable gesture in view of the fact that the United States was at war with Mexico, but the relief committees justified the action on the grounds that there was a critical shortage of seaworthy vessels to transport the relief to Ireland.

The voyage of the *Jamestown* caused much excitement and received widespread publicity in Ireland and America. On 17 March 1847 (St Patrick's Day), foodstuffs began to be loaded onto the *Jamestown*, which left Massachusetts on 28 March. The ship was manned by volunteers who slept in hammocks on deck in order to maximise room for supplies. The Captain, Robert Bennett Forbes, was well-respected and had extensive experience, especially in China. In response to criticisms that a government warship was being used for such a purpose, he responded, 'It is not an everyday matter to see a nation starving.'[122]

The *Jamestown* took 15 days and 3 hours to arrive in Cork. There it was greeted by the Liverpool philanthropist, William Rathbone, who had agreed to help oversee the impartial distribution of relief.[123] Forbes was anxious that the distribution be carried out speedily, arguing that if the relief could cross the Atlantic in 15 days, it should not take a further 15 to reach the poor.[124] To Forbes' embarrassment, he was feted on his arrival and two public receptions were held in his honour. He noted with approval that the ladies in Cork 'do shake their hands like men'; their handshake was 'no formal touching of the tip ends of the fingers, chilling the heart, but a regular grip of feeling'.[125] The local newspapers in Cork, whilst rejoicing at the arrival of the *Jamestown*, used its arrival as an opportunity to contrast the response of the British government. One paper suggested that the response of America, 'a Nation which owes us nothing ... [should] be a model to the Nation that owes to us her pre-eminent greatness'.[126] Another article compared the speed of the American response with the tardiness of British relief provision, pointing out that the *Jamestown* had arrived in Ireland 'in less time than it would take to get an intelligible answer from the Board of Works, to comprehend the provisions of one of our bewildering Acts of Parliament, or to take the initiatory steps towards carrying them into execution'.[127] The *Jamestown* stayed in Cork for just over a week. During this time, Forbes was shown the locality by Father Mathew, the leader of the Temperance movement, but refused to visit either Dublin or London to receive the official thanks of the government. The *Jamestown* left Cork on 22 April and took 24 days to complete the homeward journey. The return voyage was spoilt by the loss of the third mate overboard, the only Irish-born member of the crew.[128]

In the summer of 1847, prospects for the harvest appeared favourable as there was little evidence of blight in the country. The crop, however, was small and there was an economic recession in both Britain and Ireland. The British government used the absence of blight as an opportunity to declare the Famine to be 'over' although this proved not to be the case. Nevertheless, this declaration contributed to a fall-off in donations. Even though blight reappeared in 1848 and 1849, the Irish Famine no longer received the attention or the sympathy of people from overseas. A further dimension of this decrease in support was the fact that when Irish paupers began to land in the very countries which had given so generously, sympathy evaporated; they were soon seen as a threat to jobs and public health and a burden on local taxation. With few exceptions, therefore, donations to Ireland reduced sharply following the harvest of 1847.

The scale and diverse nature of private contributions makes them difficult to itemise or quantify. The British Relief Association, for example, calculated that they received over 15,000 individual contributions and the General Central Relief Committee estimated that they had to audit over 70,000 items. Many more donations were sent privately, through emigrants' letters to their families and friends in Ireland. In total, private donations to Ireland amounted to at least £1,000,000 and possibly much more – at least 10 per cent of the amount provided by the British government. Private donations also had the advantage of going directly to the people who required assistance, unhindered by ideological constrictions. Also, most of the work was undertaken by private individuals although, as in the case of the Quakers, this proved to be costly in terms of energy and health. Without the contribution of these and others – the vast majority of whom were invisible and nameless – suffering and mortality during the Famine would have been much greater.

CHAPTER 6

'The Expatriation of a People'

In 1847, the potato blight was less extensive than it had been in the previous two years. This was fortuitous as, from the autumn of that year, a specially extended Poor Law was to be made responsible for both ordinary and extraordinary relief. As a consequence, it was hoped that each Poor Law Union would become financially self-supporting. The object of the government was to implement a policy whereby local resources would have the responsibility for meeting the cost of the local provision of relief.

The hopes of stability and economic recovery proved to be illusory. The 1847 harvest was poor. The crop yield was small due to the disruption caused by the relief works in the previous winter and the shortage of seeds for planting. In addition, the British economy was in the throes of an economic depression which had repercussions in the industrial sector in Ireland, most notably Ulster. The slump mobilised middle-class opinion within Britain to oppose further financial aid to the Irish destitute, especially those who reached the shores of England without skills, capital or good health. The rise in agrarian crime and the murder of a few Irish landlords were viewed as evidence of Ireland's lawlessness. The small and unsuccessful nationalist uprising led by the Young Irelanders in July 1848 was interpreted as compelling confirmation of Ireland's ingratitude to her political partners.

In 1848, starvation and disease were still destroying whole communities in Ireland. A widespread policy of evictions completed the destruction of the potato economies in parts of the south and west. Emigration became an important strategy for survival for those who had the energy or resources to leave the country. In the face of this continuing devastation, the government reluctantly announced that 22 unions were still officially 'distressed'.

Increasingly, 1848 was marked by a series of polarisations. There were divisions between the east and west of the country; between landlords and tenants whose interests were separated by the system of taxation; between those who wanted a repeal of the Union and those who simply wanted food and shelter; within the Whig Party; between relief officials in Ireland who pleaded for more assistance to Ireland and those in London who ignored such demands; and divisions between Ireland and Britain, as the latter no longer believed that it had a duty to finance the Famine in Ireland.

Property Supporting Poverty

In the summer of 1847, Ireland had acquired a new Lord Lieutenant, the Earl of Clarendon, following the premature death of Lord Bessborough. His death and Daniel O'Connell's in May of that year had created a power vacuum in Irish politics. Bessborough, although an ally of Lord John Russell, had become increasingly critical of the role of the Treasury in Famine relief. His loss was made all the more significant by the fact that it coincided with a new and significant shift in policy. From August, the Irish Poor Law was to be made responsible for providing relief to the 'ordinary' destitute and to the victims of the Famine. This new policy marked an important move in the desire to make Irish property support Irish poverty.

Although Clarendon was an experienced politician, he had little direct experience of Ireland beyond overseeing the unification of the English and Irish Boards of Excise in 1827. In the Whig administration of 1846–47, he had been in charge of the Board of Trade. Considered to have a strong personality, he was not afraid of unpopularity.[1] Although he had earlier described the Irish Lord Lieutenancy as akin to being thrown into an 'Irish Bog', he seemed pleased to be appointed.[2] His early communications were optimistic and displayed confidence in his ability to effect positive changes in Ireland. He believed that the main problem of the Irish – landlord and peasant alike – was their willingness to rely on other people, a habit which he hoped to eradicate, by means of the amended Poor Law.

Two days after arriving in Ireland, Clarendon informed Russell that the situation was better than he had expected. At this stage, the Temporary Relief Act was in operation and feeding more than 3 million people daily. This successful relief mechanism had contributed to a reduction in criminal incidences, from 2647 in May to 1672 in June. Clarendon was aware that most of the crimes had been motivated by hunger and might resume when the soup kitchens closed. He was, nevertheless, unsympathetic to the widespread plundering of ships off the west coast of Ireland, as he was convinced that the perpetrators preferred these 'piratical pursuits' to cultivating their land. Echoing a belief which was to be frequently stated in *The Times* in the following twelve months, he declared, 'It is hard to tax the industrious paupers of England for the support of such ruffians.'[3] Overall, his initial impression was that the country was 'tranquil' and he added, 'if it were not for the harassing duty of escorting provisions, the troops would have little to do'.[4]

Clarendon initially believed that the worst of the Famine was over, the view adopted by the majority of the Whig Party after the autumn of 1847. He therefore anticipated that there would be resistance to paying the rates to finance the Poor Law, particularly from landlords and farmers. The government would have to adopt a firm policy and he warned Charles Wood, the Chancellor of the Exchequer, that:

> There will be a good deal of money concealed in the country, the farmers were well off this year having got unusually good prices for cattle and corn; in many places rents were well paid, and the large amounts of silver sent over for payments of people on the public works never reappeared.[5]

In mid-July 1847, a number of cases of potato blight were reported, although the forecast for other crops was good. Clarendon was unconcerned about the reappearance of blight on the grounds that if the crop were a good one, 'both the people and the landlords would rely on them as much as ever, and the experience of last year would go *absolutely for nothing'*.[6] Like many of his colleagues, he believed that the failure of the potato had initiated a social revolution in Ireland which the government needed to ensure was extended and consolidated. He felt that this revolution could be completed only if the government adhered to its policies:

> In the next two years there will be a grand struggle and the government of Ireland will be a painful thankless task, but I am convinced that the failure of the potatoes and the establishment of the Poor Law will eventually be the salvation of the country – the first will prevent the land being used as it hitherto has been.[7]

Despite Clarendon's overall optimism, he was concerned that the closing of the soup kitchens in the middle of August and the transfer to Poor Law relief would create initial hardship. He was also worried about the financial situation in a number of individual Poor Law unions and asked the Treasury to give Edward Twistleton, the Chief Poor Law Commissioner, 'flexible powers to provide food and money'.[8] In government, there was reluctance to deviate in any way from the terms and conditions of the new Poor Law. Increasingly, the relief policy was controlled by a small but powerful clique. The General Election in the summer of 1847 had demonstrated widespread impatience with the affairs of Ireland on the part of the British middle classes. The crisis in the commercial and banking sector had reinforced the demands for retrenchment and cheap government, and Ireland was specifically targeted as an area for reduced spending. Also, by the autumn of 1847, the sympathy which had been evident in the press in the previous two years was being replaced by cultural stereotyping of the Irish character.

All of this served to consolidate the powers of the Chancellor of the Exchequer, Charles Wood, his right-hand man in the Treasury, Charles Trevelyan, and their powerful ally in the Home Office, Sir George Grey. These men, who from the outset had favoured a moralistic interpretation of the blight, viewed it as a crusade, with themselves (but particularly Trevelyan) in the vanguard. The vision and determination of the group contrasted sharply with vacillations of the prime minister and the disinterest of other MPs. The mood in parliament was against future intervention and expenditure on Ireland. Although Lord Russell, supported by the Lord Lieutenant, had attempted to introduce a radical Land Reclamation Scheme at the beginning of 1847, and Lord George Bentinck, the leader of the Protectionist faction, had suggested a massive loan to build railways in Ireland, both these Bills had been comprehensively defeated. Henry Grattan, whilst chairing a meeting of Irish MPs, described the recent policies as arising from the fact that 'the Lord Lieutenant had no power and Downing Street had no heart'.[9]

In October 1847, Trevelyan, acting autonomously and without the prior permission of his superiors, sent a letter to *The Times*, outlining the relief programme for the coming year. He explained how a key purpose of the policy was to herald 'The change from an idle, barbarous isolated potato cultivation, to corn cultivation, which frees industry, and binds together employer and employee in mutually beneficial relations'.[10] Such changes, however, required 'capital and a new class of men'.[11] For Trevelyan, it was necessary to remove not only the potato cultivators from the land, but also many Irish landlords who were regarded as a barrier to modernisation.

The most powerful tool in the transformation of Irish agriculture and Irish society was the amended Poor Law of 1847.[12] In the first two years of shortages, the Poor Law had played a subsidiary role to the specially introduced relief measures. The cost of these measures and, in particular, the ineffectiveness of the public works, had made a change of policy necessary. The existing Poor Law was seen as an advantageous vehicle for the implementation of relief measures and Poor Law taxation (or rates) were viewed as a way of ensuring that the localities bore the cost of their own destitution. At the same time, the Poor Law would force landlords – who had become the scapegoat for the ills of Ireland – to become more interested in their estates and take financial responsibility for them. It was hoped that those who had neither the capital nor the inclination to do so, would sell their land. The introduction in 1849 of an Encumbered Estates Act facilitated this process and, in doing so, removed weaker landlords from their properties.

To enable the Poor Law to provide for all destitution after the autumn of 1847, an Extension Act was passed in June 1847, despite the opposition of many Irish landlords, most notably Lord Monteagle. By 1845, although most of the workhouses were providing relief, many of them only contained small numbers of paupers. The successive failure of the potato blight was to transform this situation. Initially, the government had determined to keep separate 'normal' and 'extraordinary' Famine relief, but such distinctions became impossible to administer as the specially introduced relief measures proved inadequate to cope with the demands being made on them. Also, as the population became increasingly debilitated and evictions became more widespread, many of the destitute required shelter and medical attention rather than food alone. By the end of 1846 many of the workhouses were full and denying relief to additional paupers. Many unions were also greatly in debt as ratepayers defaulted on payments. By 1847, the Poor Law administration was in crisis. None the less, the government imposed upon it the responsibility for providing relief. The amended law also allowed for the swift dismissal of those Boards of Guardians who were believed not to be carrying out their duties, these being interpreted mainly as a failure to collect the level of rates required to finance the new system.

The government now announced that the Famine was 'over' and that no future financial aid from the Treasury could be justified.[13] To provide relief through the mechanism of the Poor Law, a large number of additional workhouses had to be rented and outdoor relief permitted, contrary to the ideological premises upon which the Irish Poor Law had been based. Inevitably, the burden of poor rates increased. Paradoxically, the highest burden fell on those areas which had the least financial resources. In recognition of the lack of resources of a number of unions, 22 were declared to be officially 'distressed' and it was promised that external financial assistance would be made available to them in the coming year. The distressed unions were situated predominantly in the west. They were the Ballina, Ballinrobe, Bantry, Cahirciveen, Carrick-on-Shannon, Castlebar, Castlerea, Clifden, Dingle, Ennistymon, Galway, Glenties, Gort, Kenmare, Kilrush, Mohill, Roscommon, Scariff, Sligo, Swinford, Tuam and Westport unions. Privately, Edward Twistleton estimated that the true number requiring external financial assistance was over twice as many.[14] The Chancellor of the Exchequer justified the parsimony of the relief after 1847 on the grounds that, 'except through a purgatory of misery and starvation, I cannot see how Ireland is to emerge into anything approaching either quiet or prosperity'.[15]

Central to the new law was the introduction of outdoor relief, which had been forbidden by the 1838 legislation. The granting of outdoor relief was, however, subject to various controls and was accompanied by a number of harsh conditions. Able-bodied men (those who were judged to be capable of work), for example, had to work for at least 8 hours a day on a task which was 'as repulsive as possible consistent with humanity'.[16] Furthermore, outdoor relief could only be given with the prior consent of the central Poor Law Commissioners. They, in turn, were answerable to the Treasury, which in reality meant Trevelyan. Significantly, responsibility for appointing Poor Law officers was removed from the Commissioner in Ireland and placed in the hands of the Home Office. Although a separate administrative Poor Law structure had been created in Dublin under Twistleton, in reality most of its power had been removed to London.

The most controversial and callous aspect of the new Extension Act was the Quarter Acre or 'Gregory Clause'. William Gregory, MP for Dublin and landlord in County Galway, introduced an amendment to the Extension Act, which denied relief to any occupier of more than a quarter of an acre of land. This clause became a powerful tool for those landlords wishing to clear their estates of small tenants and evictions rose dramatically following its introduction. It also demonstrated a new rigour and stringency in the terms permitting entitlement to relief. Moreover, it meant that small-holders who had managed to hold on to their plots in the previous two years of shortages now had to face a situation where staying in their homes could result in starvation. This meant that the Famine was removing from the land not just those groups who had previously subsisted on potatoes, but those who, before the blight, had been small farmers. When challenged about this outcome, many Whigs claimed it as a necessity if Ireland was to benefit from the years of Famine. When it was suggested to William Gregory that the provision would destroy the class of small farmers in Ireland, he replied that 'he did not see of what use such small farmers could possibly be'.[17] Lord Palmerston, an influential member of the government and an Irish landlord, stated:

> It is useless to describe the truth that any great improvement in the social system in Ireland must be founded upon an extensive change in the present state of agrarian occupation, and that this change necessarily implies a long, continued and systematic ejectment of small holders and of squatting cottiers.[18]

Opinion within Ireland regarding the Gregory Clause was mixed. A number of landlords saw it as a source of protection within a system where rents were not being paid and taxation was high. Others regarded it as punitive and harsh. However, on a parliamentary division, only nine MPs voted against it. These included William Sharman Crawford and George Poulett Scrope, both of whom had been outspoken critics of the relief policies of the Whig government. A further opponent of the clause was Twistleton, who regarded it as imposing an unfair test of destitution.[19] Canon John O'Rourke, whose account of the Famine was published in 1874, said, 'A more complete engine for the slaughter and expatriation of a people was never designed.'[20] The harshest aspect of the clause was the fact that the families of men who occupied more than a quarter of an acre were also denied relief. A legal opinion which challenged this interpretation found, much to the dismay of the government, that the occupier alone and not the entire family should be refused relief. But already, a process of wholesale evictions was in place and in the interim, further lives had been lost.[21]

In England, the introduction of outdoor relief was welcomed by English Poor Law officials, many of whom had petitioned for the change, believing that if the Irish Poor Law could provide outdoor relief, Irish paupers were less likely to seek refuge in English workhouses.[22] This expectation proved to be unfounded, as Irish paupers in increasing numbers continued to flood into the main British ports. The pleas of the Guardians of Liverpool and Glasgow for this to be regulated by central government was refused. A number of British Boards of Guardians, therefore, invoked the recently introduced Settlement Act, which stipulated that only paupers who had at least five years' 'residency' in an area were eligible for relief.[23] Other Boards of Guardians displayed less concern for the niceties of the English Poor Law. In Cardiff, for example, a committee was established to return Irish paupers to Ireland on their arrival. When it was found that a number of captains were landing their human cargo some distance from port, a reward of £10 was offered for information which could lead to conviction. Many of the paupers abandoned in this way lost their lives in the quicksands off the shore of Cardiff, as they attempted to reach the shore.[24] The overall response to the Irish crisis by Boards of Guardians in Britain demonstrated a widespread concern that Irish paupers were not allowed to become a burden on British taxpayers, thus reinforcing the separateness of the victims of the Famine.

In 1845, following the first appearance of blight in Ireland, the Home Secretary in Peel's government, Sir James Graham, rejected the idea that the Poor Law could cope with a period of extraordinary distress, believing that it would place a financial burden on the system which would be impossible to meet. He cautioned that:

> It could not be expected, that by a compulsory rate, on the basis of the poor rates, introduced suddenly, any large fund could be obtained for the relief of the poor in Ireland during the present scarcity.[25]

This sentiment was echoed by George Nicholls, architect of the Irish Poor Law and first Commissioner in Ireland, who recognised the fragile relationship between a self-financing Poor Law and a period of famine and warned, 'where the land has ceased to be reproductive, the necessary means of relief can no longer be obtained from it, and a Poor Law will no longer be operative'.[26] Yet the Whig government chose to make the Poor Law the main plank of its relief policy after 1847. That the Famine was not over was clearly demonstrated by the fact that 22 unions were declared distressed and others continued to require support. In 1848, 1.5 million people depended on the Poor Law for a scant existence, in spite of the harsh regulations governing the provision of relief.

The Impact of Famine

In August 1847, the soup kitchens closed and all relief became the responsibility of the amended Poor Law. Trevelyan decided that he and his family should have a holiday 'after two years of such continuous hard work as I have never had in my life'.[27] As a third year of Famine commenced in Ireland, he toured France. Within Ireland, the transfer to Poor Law relief entailed changes in both its provision and funding. The conditions of receiving relief had been made more stringent by the introduction of the Gregory Clause, which meant that entitlement to relief was more restricted than at any time in the previous two years. Since 1846, Poor Law taxation had been used as the basis for Famine relief, and after the autumn of 1847, poor rates had to finance not only current relief, but also repay loans for earlier relief systems. As a consequence, Poor Law taxation soared.[28] An amendment to the law in 1843 had placed the onus for paying rates on land that was highly subdivided on the owners themselves. As Poor Law taxation increased, this placed a heavier burden on landlords whose estates were highly subdivided and provided an added incentive to clear their estates of smallholders. Evictions and the sale of property, both of which had been increasing since 1846, gathered momentum, precipitating a social revolution in landholding. Between 1849 and 1854, approximately 250,000 persons were evicted from their homes, officially and permanently.[29] If illegal evictions and voluntary surrender of land are added, the figure is much greater. Evictions varied from region to region, with the largest number occurring in County Clare, followed by Counties Mayo, Galway and Kerry. These four counties alone represented one-third of all evictions.[30]

Within parliament and the British press, evictions were unpopular as they were seen as a means for landlords to place the burden of relieving their tenants onto the state. This was regarded as further

proof of their selfishness. At the same time, many MPs believed
that Irish agriculture could only be modernised if both impoverished
tenants and landlords left. When the Poor Law Commissioner
complained of the hardship resulting from these clearances,
Trevelyan responded by stating that only by continuing this process
would they 'at last arrive at something like a satisfactory settlement
of the country'.[31]

The attitude of individual landlords to eviction varied. A number
believed that the new system of taxation combined with the large
rent arrears had given them little choice but to clear their estates.
In October 1848, the Marquis of Sligo, who had hitherto shown
leniency to his tenants, stated that he was now 'under the necessity
of ejecting or being ejected'.[32] A smaller number of landlords,
including the Edgeworths in County Longford and Henry Moore
in Galway, refused to evict, even though their own incomes were
much diminished. A minority combined a policy of eviction with
emigration, although the conditions of the latter varied considerably.
Lord Lansdowne in County Kerry financed a programme of
emigration which his agent calculated was a cheaper alternative to
tenants becoming a burden on the local poor rates. His emigration
scheme was well co-ordinated and the majority of his tenants
arrived safely at their destinations.[33] A large number of the landed
elite and their agents viewed the social dislocation as an opportunity
to clear their estates without fear of resistance. They regarded the
Famine as an opportunity to impose order and discipline on their
estate management.[34] Lord Lucan in County Mayo evicted 2000
tenants from one parish in Ballinrobe alone. Other proprietors, such
as Major Mahon of Strokestown in County Roscommon, cleared
his estates with the intention of replacing his Catholic tenants with
Protestants, preferably from Scotland.[35]

The way in which evictions were carried out was often ruthless
and added to the pain of displacement and homelessness. James
Hack Tuke, an English Quaker, who observed a number of official
evictions, was shocked by what he saw and described the process
in detail in a series of letters. In Erris, in a remote part of Connaught,
for example, 140 families were evicted. They were, Tuke claimed,
50 miles from the nearest workhouse. A high military presence of
50 armed troops and 40 policemen was on hand. After the notice
to quit had been read, Tuke described how:

> The policemen are commanded to do their duty. Reluctantly
> they proceed, armed with bayonet and muskets, to throw out
> the miserable furniture ... But the tenants make some show of
> resistance – for these hovels have been built by themselves or
> their forefathers who have resided in them for generations past
> – seem inclined to dispute with the bayonets of the police, for

they know truly that, when their hovels are demolished, the nearest ditch must be their dwelling, and that thus exposed, death could not fail to be the lot of their wives and little ones.[36]

Tuke also recorded how, at a dinner party that night, the landlord 'boasted that it was the first time that he had seen his estate or visited his tenants'.[37]

A number of those evicted attempted to create shelter in dug-out holes or build refuges from the remains of their destroyed cabins. These temporary dwellings, known as 'scalps' or 'scalpeens', were often destroyed. Many families were reported to have died by the roadside. Clarendon's response was a mixture of anger at the landlords and fear of a popular uprising. When he learnt of the details of an especially merciless eviction in Kilrush in County Clare, where some 4000 people were evicted within about seven months, he was anxious that this and similar incidents not be made public. In a warning to the Home Secretary, he maintained, 'The case is too shocking for publication if it can be avoided.'[38]

The manner in which evictions were carried out caused an outcry. In parliament, the matter was raised in March 1848 by George Poulett Scrope, with the support of Sir Robert Peel.[39] Whilst the politicians were shocked by what they were told, no legislative changes were made. Clarendon viewed the increase in lawlessness at the end of 1847, especially attacks on landlords, as having roots in the wholesale evictions and demanded more powers to deal with the situation. At the end of 1847, a Crime and Outrage Bill was rushed through parliament and 15,000 additional troops were sent to Ireland. Russell's impatience with the Irish landlords was evident in his statement that 'It is quite true that landlords in England would not like to be shot like hares and partridges ... but neither does any landlord in England turn out fifty persons at one go and burn their houses over their heads, giving them no provision for the future.'[40]

The Poor Law was unable to deal with the considerable demands made for both relief and shelter. It had neither the financial nor the administrative ability to deal with its new role. Both workhouse and outdoor relief had to be greatly extended to cope with the additional requirements upon them and, for many months, demand exceeded supply. In the summer of 1848, a mere nine months after the system had been introduced, 800,000 people were in receipt of outdoor relief alone.[41] The correspondence of the local relief officials in the west and other parts of Ireland to the central Relief Commissioners was full of descriptions of people dying through disease, privation, lack of food or shelter. The harsh winter of 1847–48 increased the suffering of the poor and demands for Poor Law relief intensified. Under such pressure a number of Guardians were unable to cope and they and their officers increasingly became the scapegoats for the failure of the system. In 1847–48, 39 Boards of Guardians were suspended. Many of these, especially the more conscientious, were glad to be relieved of this onerous and difficult duty. They were replaced by paid officials who had to look after as many as three unions and therefore could only devote two days a week to each.[42] The paid Guardians swiftly found themselves facing the same problems as their predecessors, namely the inability to collect rates, inadequate and insufficient workhouse accommodation, no coffins, a high proportion of paupers who were weak or sick, and unreliable supplies of clothing, bedding, food and medicine. A high proportion of workhouse inmates (over 40 per cent) were children who were paupers or had been abandoned, and whose prospects of leaving the workhouses were small.[43] In some unions it was difficult to find workhouse officers who were responsible or honest as the low rates of pay and risk of disease tended to make these jobs particularly unattractive. Doctors employed by the Poor Law considered their remuneration for working in fever hospitals to be unrealistically low and a national memorial was drawn up containing 1500 signatures. The pay of workhouse officers, including that of the doctors, was under the control of the Treasury, who refused to sanction an increase.[44]

Throughout the distressed unions, the level of suffering was comparable to that of the previous year. Confused by the numerous changes in the methods of obtaining relief, people often travelled great distances to their local workhouses, only to be sent home again. On 13 December 1847, the newly appointed paid Guardians described to the Commissioner the scenes which greeted them on their arrival at the workhouse:

> On our arrival at Ballinrobe, on Thursday morning, we found, at least 1,000 individuals at the door of the workhouse claiming admittance and a more wretched or desolate group it would be difficult to imagine; the rain was descending in torrents; accompanied by a severe wind, both sufficient to destroy the whole body ... we engaged in urging the crowd to depart to their homes, with an assurance that they would receive immediate relief ... It was a most harrowing exhibition, and many and great efforts were required to pacify their clamorous appeals.[45]

As had been in the case twelve months before, numerous cases of death from starvation were recorded. In the winter of 1846–47, the Board of the Public Works had often been blamed for such deaths, but the officers of the Poor Law were now held to be responsible. In one such case, in the Kenmare Union in County Kerry, the death of four brothers and sisters was attributed to starvation; when a post-mortem was carried out, 'not a particle of food was there in the stomach or intestines'. The verdict was 'deaths from want of food, in consequence of the neglect of Captain Erasmus Ommanney and the Board of Guardians of the Kenmare Union'.[46] The Knight of Kerry believed that conditions were so bad in the county that an armed uprising was inevitable. He asked the local Lieutenant to 'tell the police to keep a sharp look out for strangers'.[47] His fears were groundless as the people lacked the energy and the will to challenge the local officials or the central government. The Young Ireland uprising in 1848 took place without the knowledge or the support of the vast majority of the people.

For relief officials in Dublin, the deteriorating condition of the local unions was a major source of concern. The most pressing problem was lack of funds and the limited prospect of collecting sufficient rates. The Treasury, which had been made responsible for distributing funds to the distressed unions from the residue of government revenue, believed that it was possible to collect sufficient rates to subsidise widespread distress. The Chancellor of the Exchequer informed Russell, 'There is plenty of money in Ireland ... [yet] we are called upon to support a thoroughly rotten state of things'.[48] Collectors who complained that it was impossible to collect the local taxes were offered the use of a military or police escort.

In Dublin, various relief officials were less sanguine about the ability of Ireland, especially the western unions, to support its own poverty. The gap between how the Famine was perceived in London and how it was seen in Dublin widened. In London the attitude was ideologically and financially motivated, whilst in Dublin it was based on practical and humanitarian considerations. Within a few months of arriving in Ireland as Lord Lieutenant, Clarendon had moved from believing that Ireland must be forced to be self-supporting to acknowledging that the human cost of this policy was too high. He became convinced that poor rates could not be raised in a number of unions and warned that unless further concessions were made, 'the poor unions in the west must close and the inmates starve'.[49] He also feared that these polices were bringing the country closer to revolution. Whilst acknowledging that the tide of public opinion had turned against intervention, he wrote an agitated letter to the prime minister at the end of October 1847 saying that:

> There is one thing I must beg of you to take into serious and immediate consideration, which is, whatever may be the anger of people or parliament in England, whatever may be the state of trade or credit, Ireland *cannot be left to her own resources*, they are manifestly insufficient.[50]

Within a few months, Clarendon's perceptions had been justified as a number of distressed unions were bankrupt and unable to provide relief. The closing of the relief operations by the British Relief Association in the summer of 1848, one of the few charitable organisations still in operation, threw a further burden on local taxes.

The person with ultimate responsibility for the affairs of the local unions was the Chief Poor Law Commissioner, Edward Twistleton. His powers were limited, however, and decisions regarding the amount and manner in which money was to be distributed to the distressed unions lay firmly in Trevelyan's hands. Trevelyan, who had managed to offend the majority of former relief officials, was soon at odds with Twistleton. For Twistleton, the fundamental problem was the fact that the Poor Law could not save lives unless it had access to external financial assistance. The Treasury, on the other hand, was unwilling to provide government money whilst rates remained unpaid. This resulted in a situation in which Twistleton was forced to plead with Trevelyan for money. And Trevelyan would only consent if he believed the failure to comply would result in loss of life. The money advanced to the unions was meagre, piecemeal and issued as a loan to be repaid as quickly as possible. The delay in issuing it also contributed to further anguish and sometimes death. Despite an increase in the number of deaths in the distressed unions in the summer of 1848, Trevelyan accused the Poor Law Commissioners of allowing money to be spent 'lavishly'.[51] For Twistleton, the opposite was true. He feared that if precise details regarding the scantiness of relief were known in England, public opinion 'might say that we are slowly murdering the peasantry by the scantiness of the relief'.[52] In financial terms, the transfer to Poor Law relief after 1847 was successful, as the contribution from the Treasury fell to £300,000 in the 18 months following this. In human terms, it was disastrous as the suffering caused by hunger and disease was matched by the additional misery of homelessness.

The Press and British Public Opinion

The role of the press was influential in shaping public opinion throughout the course of the Famine. Even before the blight, many British newspapers had been critical of the system of agricultural production in Ireland and the alleged laziness of both the cultivators and the landlords. Change on the English model of development was considered necessary, although this was regarded as unlikely whilst the same proprietors owned the land and potato cultivation was still as extensive. Whilst poor people throughout the United Kingdom were looked down upon, the Irish destitute were viewed as being culturally inferior and particularly indolent, violent and cunning. Visual representations of the Irish often depicted them as brutish, a trait which became even more pronounced in the late nineteenth century with the spread of Social Darwinism. This form of cultural stereotyping was long established and was a traditional part of the colonial relationship.[53]

In the early stages of the Famine, British newspapers devoted extensive coverage to events in Ireland. Many papers included letters and eyewitness accounts of the human misery. When the blight appeared in 1845, *The Times* already had a special reporter based in Ireland. He sent back extensive accounts describing the progress of the disease and suggested his own solutions, both to the blight and in regard to Ireland's social condition. At the end of 1846, the *Illustrated London News* sent an artist, James Mahony, to Ireland. He sent back sketches of the devastation, including a number from the Skibbereen area, images which graphically brought the anguish of the Famine into the middle-class homes of England. Yet even these illustrations did not – and could not – capture the full horror of the disease, starvation and death in these areas.[54] The suffering of the Irish was initially greeted with sympathy, which manifested itself in practical efforts to raise money for Ireland. At the same time, this charity was underpinned with a belief that the Irish had brought much of the suffering upon themselves. This increased as the Famine entered its third year. Moreover, as thousands of diseased paupers landed in Britain, threatening public health, taxes and the jobs of the working classes, opinion was increasingly motivated by fear and hostility. The antagonism which greeted the second appeal by the Queen in October 1847 demonstrated that within the space of a few months, sympathy towards the Irish destitute had dissipated.[55]

At the time of the Famine, the British middle classes were a dynamic force within politics. A large number had been enfranchised in 1832. They had been further politicised by two major campaigns in the 1830s and 1840s: the Chartist agitation, which they opposed, and the movement to repeal the Corn Laws, which they generally supported. These events had helped to consolidate class unity and the success of the repeal movement had demonstrated their potential power. The recession of the late 1840s again mobilised this group and sharpened their demand for financial retrenchment in Ireland. The General Election in 1847 was a further victory for middle-class, radical Whigs, whilst it simultaneously weakened Russell's control over his party. The deepening divisions within the Whig Party, and the split within the Tories gave public opinion more influence than it otherwise would have had if the government had been unified.

A shift in public opinion was evident in the wake of the harvest of 1847. The reduction in blight gave credibility to those who had declared the Famine to be over. A wave of agrarian violence in the winter of 1847, especially the much publicised murder of Major Mahon in County Roscommon, diminished sympathy for the Irish destitute.[56] The Young Ireland uprising in July 1848, despite its palpable lack of support, completed this process. Newspapers which had been sympathetic to Ireland only two years earlier saw the insurrection as the ultimate act of betrayal and ingratitude. Those papers which continued to advocate more aid to Ireland, such as the *Illustrated London News* and *The Tablet*, were in a minority and were running against the tide of public opinion. Even the return of the blight and the massive destruction of the crop in 1848, and the consequent mass mortality in 1849, could not rekindle sympathy.

Following the first appearance of blight, the British press had for the most part accepted Peel's programme of relief, viewing both the blight and the need for intervention as being purely short-term. An exception was *The Economist*, which was ideologically committed to free trade and from the outset advocated non-intervention. The second and more devastating failure of the potato in 1846 meant that relief could no longer be seen as a short-term expedient and policy formulation became linked with the need to find a long-term solution to Ireland's problems. Intervention in the food trade was universally disliked, although it was acknowledged that some form of assistance was necessary. Many papers supported the extension of outdoor relief to Ireland as a method of removing the tax burden for Ireland from the British (middle-class) taxpayers. By the end of 1847, there was a widespread demand that those most culpable, namely the Irish landlords, should be forced to pay for the Famine. After 1847, public opinion and the majority of the government agreed that the burden of providing relief should be shifted from the Treasury to Irish landlords and their tenants.

Public opinion in Britain was both articulated in the press and shaped by it. Many government ministers were sensitive to unfavourable press coverage. As the Whig Party became increasingly divided after 1847, public opinion became important in helping to mould policy. At the same time, a number of government ministers recognised that the press was an important tool in the goal of modernising Ireland and a number of influential politicians and civil servants, including Trevelyan, selectively 'fed' stories to the newspapers.[57] By the late 1840s, there were numerous journals being published in Britain. A number of these had been recently established. These included *Punch* (1841), the *Illustrated London News* (1842) and *The Economist* (1843) all of which aimed at promoting and provoking political discourse. Despite this competition, *The Times* was the undoubted market leader and was regarded as being the most politically authoritative paper. Both *Punch* and the *Illustrated London News* combined the written word with visual imagery. The Irish cartoons which appeared in the former under the guise of satire frequently promoted ideas of racial inferiority, especially after the1848 uprising when the Irish were given simian features. The *Illustrated London News* throughout the course of the Famine, however, displayed more sympathy and sensitivity to the Irish destitute.

In addition to having the largest circulation of all of the daily newspapers, *The Times* was frequently quoted by other British newspapers and by the overseas press, which spread its influence even further. It claimed to be non-partisan and to transcend the political divide. Its columns, however, increasingly became a vehicle for those who opposed intervention in Ireland. What *Punch* achieved with its satirical cartoons, *The Times* accomplished with its 'objective' editorials. In addition to being opposed to state expenditure in Ireland, *The Times* was also against private aid and urged the English not to give to what they described as 'so pernicious an expedient'.[58] The paper repeated this point frequently, arguing that Ireland had to be forced to rely on her own resources. This opinion frequently appeared side-by-side with reports of mass mortality. Similar attitudes were evident in many other papers such as the *London News*, the *Morning Chronicle* and the *Manchester Examiner*. They arose out of a consensus that Ireland was rich in resources, but needed to be forced to take advantage of them. At the beginning of 1847, as hundreds of thousands of people were dying in Ireland, *The Times* argued against private relief on the grounds that sufficient was already being done by the state. *The Tablet*, the main Catholic newspaper, robustly disagreed with this viewpoint, saying that 'the reasoning of *The Times* seems to us beyond measure foolish'.[59] In a similar vein, the *Nonconformist*, the leading paper of dissenters, urged its readership to 'Give' and 'Give liberally'.[60]

A frequent theme in the editorials of *The Times* was the claim that Irish poverty lay deep in the Irish character and arose from a moral and biological failing. Such editorials described the Irish as living by the principle that, 'Man shall *not* labour by the sweat of his brow.'[61] England, therefore, was regarded as both the model for, and the saviour of, the Irish nation, one article in *The Times* claiming:

> Before our merciful intervention, the Irish nation were a wretched, indolent, half-starved tribe of savages, ages before Julius Caesar landed on this isle, and that, notwithstanding a gradual improvement upon the naked savagery, they have never approached the standard of the civilised world.[62]

Reports in popular working-class newspapers frequently mirrored the stereotypes evident in the more 'respectable' press. Since the late 1830s, there had been a vigorous Protestant crusade in Britain which was aimed primarily at skilled workers.[63] Protestantism and patriotism became fused at a time when the influx of predominantly Catholic Irish immigrants was perceived as a threat to wages and jobs. A number of newspapers, which included the *Protestant Penny Operative*, the *Family Herald*, *Lloyd's Entertaining Journal* and *Lloyd's Weekly Miscellany*, repeatedly characterised the Irish as 'stupid, lazy, improvident, disruptive and, above all, drunken'.[64]

A number of newspapers viewed Ireland's failings as stemming from the religion of the majority of the population. The more extreme views, however, tended to be confined to papers and journals with relatively small circulations. In a letter to Lord John Russell, the *Protestant Watchman* explained the reason for Ireland's suffering as:

> Six millions of the people of Ireland are chained to a system that excludes, and is found to exclude, them from the true knowledge of the true God ... You must endeavour to bring the knowledge of God to every cabin in Ireland. To do this you must use your endeavours to have the word of God taught and preached in every village in Ireland; and when you thus honour God by honouring His word, you may expect redemption in Ireland.[65]

Whilst such articles may not have had the impact and influence of the frequent editorials and letters in *The Times*, they indicate the extent to which the Irish Famine was being debated within the public domain. They also reflect the general consensus that Ireland *had* to change, and that the Famine was the ideal opportunity for this to occur. *The Times*, like many other papers, saw the system of landholding in Ireland as a barrier to progress. More importantly, it believed that, until Ireland modernised, the country would continue to be a burden on the English taxpayers. Irish landlords were blamed for both these failings. As long as they provided a convenient scapegoat, people in England did not have to question their own role in the poverty and suffering of Ireland and their responsibilities under the Act of Union. In February1849, Parliament issued a small grant of £50,000 to Ireland. *The Times* described this money as 'breaking the back' of English benevolence.[66] Nevertheless, despite this belief, the paper recognised that given the high mortality in the country more state intervention might be necessary.[67] By this stage, it was too late. Parliament and public opinion had long been convinced that Ireland could and should be forced to depend upon her own resources.

CHAPTER 7

'A Policy of Extermination'

Despite the widespread destruction of the potato crop in 1848, there were signs that parts of Ireland were beginning to emerge from the most severe impact of the Famine. This was due largely to the fact that commerce, especially the linen industry, had begun to revive from the depression of the previous year. Moreover, three consecutive years of shortages had meant that many of the most vulnerable members of society were already dead or had fled from their homes, with little expectation of return.

The Famine, however, was far from over. The potato crop failed extensively in 1848 and losses in the west equalled those of 1846. Blight returned in 1849, 1850 and 1851, although increasingly in a more localised form. The disease was most concentrated in those areas which had the fewest resources to combat its effects. Evictions, emigration, disease and death rates remained high. The appearance of cholera in parts of Ireland in 1849 claimed many lives. In that year, mortality was as high in some places as it had been in 'Black '47'. The years of low income and high taxation had also taken their toll on a number of landlords. Assisted by government legislation, many large estates were sold, resulting in a social revolution amongst the landowning classes. Other landlords resorted to a policy of wholesale eviction. As a consequence, after 1848, homelessness became as much of a problem for the Irish poor as hunger.

Despite evidence of suffering, the government was anxious to promote the idea that the Famine was over, partly in an attempt to attract foreign capital to Ireland. To this end, in August 1849 Queen Victoria made her first visit to the Ireland. However, financing Irish relief continued to be a problem for the British government which was increasingly committed to a policy of financial retrenchment. Although the contribution of the British Treasury to Ireland had decreased dramatically since 1847, both within parliament and in Britain generally, the expenditure was still regarded as being too high. This resulted in a further change of policy in 1849. The Rate-in-Aid Act, introduced in that year, imposed an additional tax on the wealthier eastern unions for redistribution to the poorer unions in the west. This new financial burden was unpopular in Ireland. It resulted in the resignation of the Chief Poor Law Commissioner, Edward Twistleton. Moreover, the Rate-in-Aid Act implied that, despite the Act of Union and all that it signified, Ireland was to be left to her own resources.

The Prodigal Son

In 1848 over 50 per cent of the total potato crop was lost. In the west, the crop was almost totally destroyed. Heavy rainfall had damaged the corn and wheat crop and the shortfall in food supplies was comparable to what it had been in the catastrophic winter of 1846–47.[1] For the local population, the fourth successive year of shortages left them without resources. The return of the blight did not result in any new relief policies, even of a temporary nature. Instead, the already overstretched Poor Law was expected to alleviate all the distress. Lord John Russell was aware that neither parliament nor the people would support any further intervention in Ireland, regardless of the extent of the suffering. He warned Clarendon, his representative in Ireland, that, 'The course of English benevolence is frozen by insult, calumny and rebellion'.[2]

After 1848 the distance between attitudes to relief in Dublin and London became even more divergent. Within London, relief provision had become the exclusive preserve of Wood and Trevelyan and their powerful allies within the Cabinet. The frequent demands from Ireland for more assistance were regarded with impatience and disdain. A deterioration in relations was particularly apparent between Trevelyan and Twistleton. In 1848 and the early months of 1849, an ideological battle was fought between the Treasury in London and the Poor Law Commission in Dublin over the scale and nature of the relief provision. The latter believed that deaths from starvation and disease were inevitable if the government continued to insist that local resources alone were to support all destitution. Trevelyan, however, regarded the assertions of Twistleton as exaggerated and reprimanded him for being 'lavish' in his provision of relief. Twistleton tartly pointed out that the high level of mortality in many unions was painful evidence of the parsimony of the relief provision.[3] He also asked Trevelyan to refrain from casting further public 'slurs' on the work of the Poor Law Commission without first checking the accuracy of his information.[4]

By the beginning of 1849, mortality in the western workhouses was proportionally as high as it had been in the winter of 1846–47, reaching 2500 deaths per week. It was not only the 22 distressed unions which were still experiencing famine conditions, but a further 30 unions were also in financial difficulties.[5] Even if poor rates had been paid, they were insufficient to finance both current expenses and the accumulated debts of four years of crisis.

Consequently, a high proportion of unions found themselves with mounting debts. The number of people in receipt of Poor Law relief peaked in July 1849 when it reached over 1 million, three-quarters of whom were in receipt of outdoor relief.[6] This meant that approximately one person in six was supported by the Poor Law in Ireland.

Reports of suffering in the west of the country paralleled those from the winter of 1846–47. A report sent from the unions of Ballina, Ballinasloe, Ballinrobe, Castlebar and Tuam to *The Times* in June 1849 described the peasantry as having 'famine unmistakably marked on their brows'.[7] Although the writer praised the vice-guardians for their hard work and dedication, he felt that they were labouring against insuperable odds. The workhouses were overcrowded and many of the rented buildings lacked drainage or ventilation and were particularly inappropriate for sick people. Moreover, the amount of relief given was not sufficient 'in quantity or quality' to support life.[8] The writer described the scene in one shelter which had been made from the remains of a tumbled-down house. In it, he found:

> a mother and some small children; the latter some of them quite naked, mere skeletons, but with that enlargement of the abdomen now so common amongst them. A thing of mere bone, of about two years old, lay on an old red petticoat, looking nearly as near death as I could have wished it. I gave the woman a loaf of bread; in one moment she had torn a piece out of it and placed it in her own mouth; I was just about to point to her to give some to the children when, with a look I shall never forget, she placed her finger in her mouth, drew out the moistened bread and at once began to place it between the child's lips.[9]

In the same month, reports of alleged cannibalism in Clifden, County Mayo further shocked public opinion in Britain.[10]

The closing of the operations of the British Relief Association in the summer of 1848 left a large gap in relief provision, not only financially but because it meant the loss of the energy and personal commitment of their agent, Count Strzelecki. This was especially true in regard to a project devised by Strzelecki for feeding children in the most distressed unions through the schools. In July 1848, 200,000 children were being fed under this scheme at relatively little cost. Strzelecki had estimated that the cost of feeding each child was only one-third of a penny each day.[11] Russell personally promised that the scheme would continue even after Count Strzelecki had left Ireland.[12] The promise was not kept and relief provision was further centralised in the already overburdened Poor Law.

In private, Trevelyan admitted that the situation in the western unions was critical. He accepted that unless there was more government intervention, 'the deaths would shock the world and be an eternal blot on the nation and the government will be blamed'.[13] Again, Trevelyan viewed events in Ireland through a moral and providentialist prism. Comparing the Irish poor to the 'prodigal son' in the Bible, he said that they could not be turned away. At the same time, they were not to be given a 'fatted calf' but 'the workhouse and one pound of meal per day'.[14] By this stage, so many of the distressed unions were insolvent that even a pound of meal daily was no longer possible. By June 1849, the debts of the unions had risen to almost £500,000 and the mechanisms of relief had broken down in a number of western unions. In desperation, the amount of relief given to paupers on outdoor relief was reduced to half a pound of meal per day.[15] The relief being provided was far from being a 'fatted calf'.

Early in December 1848, Clarendon had warned the government of the possibility of wholesale starvation, which, he cautioned, 'would not only be shocking but bring deep disgrace on the government'.[16] By the end of the month, when his demands for additional aid had failed to elicit any response, he admitted that he was at his 'wits' end' to know how the poorest unions were to survive the following six months.[17] By the beginning of 1849, Clarendon was becoming more overtly exasperated with the relief policies of his colleagues in Westminster. He was increasingly critical of Russell for having lost authority over his Cabinet. However, Clarendon felt that the greater fault lay with Charles Wood, Charles Trevelyan and George Grey. In a withering attack, he declared that:

> C. Wood, backed by Grey, and relying upon arguments (or rather Trevelyanisms) that are no more applicable to Ireland than to Loo Choo, affirmed that the right thing to do was to do nothing – they have prevailed and you see what a fix we are in.[18]

Clarendon also believed that Ireland was being sacrificed to a misguided faith in 'natural causes' and that no matter what he and his colleagues in Ireland said or did, 'the doctrinaire policy of Trevelyan, reflected through C. Wood, and supported by Grey, would prevail'.[19] He judged such policies to be especially harsh given the widespread existence of cholera in some unions. Clarendon confided to Russell that the situation 'is enough to drive one mad' and asked the prime minister:

> Surely this is a state of things to justify you asking the House of Commons for an advance, for I don't think there is another legislature in Europe that would disregard such suffering as now exists in the west of Ireland, or coldly persist in a policy of extermination.[20]

In addition to the parsimony of the government, a number of factors contributed to the growing destitution and mortality in 1849. The increase in evictions meant that relief in food alone was no longer sufficient as thousands of people were left without lodgings. Following the cessation of the operations of the British Relief Association, the Society of Friends also wound up their operations in June 1849. The cumulative effect of five years of shortages had left the people without capital or resources. Finally, and cruelly, a cholera epidemic arrived in Ireland at the end of 1848 and the need for containment and treatment was a further drain on Poor Law finances. The people who were most vulnerable, the destitute, had the least resistance and mortality was heaviest in the western unions. Although cholera had virtually disappeared by the summer of 1849, it had claimed thousands of lives.[21] In February 1849 parliament had voted, in the teeth of much opposition, an inadequate grant of £50,000 for Irish distress. Within two months this money had been spent. The financial collapse of a number of unions in the west forced parliament to release a small sum of £6000 to the Treasury in the expectation that the new Rate-in-Aid tax would end the need for further contributions from Britain. This amount was a third less than the Commissioners had estimated to be the necessary minimum.[22] It demonstrated that the opinion of the relief officials in Ireland had become irrelevant to policy decisions made in London.

In the summer of 1849 reports of destitution in Ireland had become so appalling that emergency relief was provided, mostly from privately raised subscriptions. In May, the General Relief Committee was re-established in Dublin. They believed that 'the year 1849 is likely to be the most memorable epoch in the annals of British misery'.[23] At a public meeting held in Dublin, they decided to send a delegation 'to lay the condition of the people and of the country before the Minister and, if needs be, the Throne'.[24] In June, a private subscription was initiated by members of the government, each Minister giving £100 and the Queen, £500. Count Strzelecki, formerly of the British Relief Association, agreed to return to Ireland and oversee its distribution.[25] Trevelyan tried to persuade the Society of Friends to re-engage in the provision of relief by offering them £100 to do so. They refused on the grounds that the support that Ireland needed was 'Far beyond the reach of private exertion, the government alone could raise the funds and carry out the measures necessary in many districts to save the lives of the people'.[26] In the midst of the scrambling for money for Ireland, it was announced that the Queen was to visit the country.

Victoria's visit had originally been planned for 1846 but had been postponed due to the appearance of blight and the Queen's own reluctance to visit the country. It was the first royal visit to Ireland since 1821. The visit was viewed as an opportunity by the British government to demonstrate that the Famine was truly over. At the same time, they hoped that the visit would encourage English and Scottish capitalists to invest in the country. Victoria, Albert and four of their children visited Cork, Dublin and Belfast. The Queen first landed in Cobh, near Cork, which was renamed Queenstown in her honour. The areas of the country still in the grips of the Famine were ignored.

Victoria's visit appeared to be a success, which the authorities attributed partly to the good weather and also to Victoria's delight at being in Ireland.[27] Victoria herself seemed to be pleased with her Irish subjects, commenting on the handsomeness of the Irish women – 'such beautiful black eyes and hair, and such fine colours and teeth'.[28] She observed their rags, but attributed this to the fact that 'they never mend anything'.[29] There were, however, a few notes of discord beneath the surface. The visit caused dissent amongst the hierarchy of the Catholic Church. Archbishop Murray's warm welcome address offended a number of bishops, especially John MacHale, Archbishop of Tuam. He refused to sign the address saying, 'I find no allusion whatever to the sufferings of the people, or the causes under the control of the legislative enactment by which their sufferings are still aggravated.'[30] MacHale drew up an alternative text in which he drew attention to the fact that mortality 'has in several parts of Ireland, diminished your Majesty's subjects by a fourth, in some by a half'.[31] Michael Slattery, the Catholic Archbishop of Cashel, refused to attend the Queen's levée and also criticised her apparent indifference to the Famine.[32] On the streets of Ireland they sang the ditty:

> Arise ye dead of Skibbereen
> And come to Cork to see the Queen.[33]

Behind the pomp and ceremony and the veil of normality that attended Victoria' s visit, parts of Ireland was still undergoing famine and mourning their dead. The blight struck again in 1849 and 1850, although its impact was increasingly more localised. Even unions where blight had not appeared were still in financial straits, resulting in the introduction of a second Rate-in-Aid tax of 2d in the pound. At the instigation of Russell, a loan of £300,000 was provided for Irish relief. The debts of many unions were consolidated and rescheduled. But in 1849, evictions became more widespread and unrelenting. Some of the most ruthless evictions occurred on land that did not contain the poorest tenants, but was fertile and therefore highly desirable. A number of tenants resisted, but opposition was fragmented and generally unsuccessful. In 1849, however, two priests in County Kilkenny organised the first successful Tenant Protection Society, which developed into the Tenant League.[34]

After 1849, the impact of blight was severest in Counties Clare, Kerry and Tipperary. In parts of County Clare it combined with widespread evictions, the local Poor Law Inspector estimating that approximately 300 people were being evicted daily. In May 1849, 1200 people were evicted in the space of just two weeks.[35] As a consequence, mortality was as high as at any time since the first appearance of blight and the small union of Kilrush in County Clare began to attract similar notoriety to Skibbereen. In 1850, at the insistence of George Poulett Scrope, a select committee was appointed to enquire into the local administration of relief in the Kilrush Union. The committee was critical of the actions of local landlords, the administration of the Poor Law and the role of the British government. It concluded by drawing attention to the fact that Ireland was not treated as an equal partner in the Union, stating:

> Whether as regards the plain principles of humanity, or the literal text and admitted principle of the Poor Law of 1847, a neglect of public duty has occurred and has occasioned a state of things disgraceful to a civilised age and country, for which some authority ought to be held responsible, and would long since have been held responsible had these things occurred in any union in England.[36]

'An Army of Beggars'. The Rate-in-Aid Issue

The continuation of Famine in the wake of the reappearance of blight in 1848 meant that the western unions continued to be dependent on external funds to provide even a minimum level of relief. By this stage, middle-class opinion, marshalled and given an outlet by *The Times*, was opposed to further financial intervention in Ireland. Recession in Britain and the uprising in Ireland in 1848 had hardened hearts against Irish suffering. Moreover, the sight of impoverished and disease-ridden paupers from Ireland disembarking in the ports of Britain meant that the Irish were increasingly perceived as a double burden on British taxpayers. Taxation was a particularly sensitive issue because, unlike Britain, Ireland was not subject to income tax. The calls by Wood and Trevelyan for financial retrenchment and cheap government, therefore, fell on receptive ears.

The unpopularity of giving money to Ireland was demonstrated in February 1849 when the decision to provide a small grant of £50,000 resulted in a public outcry. The more moderate members of the Cabinet viewed this as marking an end to aid in Ireland, irrespective of the situation there. Clarendon, who had become increasingly despondent about his colleagues' response to Irish suffering, confided to Lord Monteagle, 'I am sadly out of spirits. If I ever allowed myself to despair about *anything* I would be inclined to do so about Ireland.'[37]

At the beginning of 1849, the government was devising a new policy for providing funds to the 'distressed unions' without incurring a further burden on the Treasury. This policy, known as the Rate-in-Aid, was a new tax. It was to be levied on the more prosperous unions in the country and redistributed to the poorest unions in the west. The rationale underpinning this policy was that Irish distress was now to be regarded as an exclusively Irish problem, not a British nor even an Imperial issue. Regardless of the Act of Union and despite the on-going crisis, Ireland was to be left to her own devices.

The introduction of this Bill proved to be controversial. It was opposed by many Irish landlords who, since 1847, had borne most of the financial burden of Irish distress. A national petition was drawn up opposing its introduction and was signed by Lord Lucan of County Mayo, Lord Manchester of County Down and Lord Monteagle of Brandon, amongst others. They argued that the Bill, if passed, would be a burden on areas where the Poor Law had been successfully administered and rates had been 'most cheerfully paid'.[38] Whilst the Rate-in-Aid proposal was generally unpopular, it was Protestant landlords in Ulster who opposed it most vociferously. A number of mass rallies were held in eastern Ulster and a delegation from Belfast met with Lord John Russell in London, but without success. It was argued that the imposition of this additional financial burden on the people of Ulster had already resulted in an increase in the emigration of wealthier farmers who were unwilling to pay another tax.[39] A suggestion by Russell that income tax could possibly be extended to Ireland in lieu of the Rate-in-Aid was regarded as even less desirable.[40]

At times the protest gave vent to sectarian rhetoric.[41] It was argued that the well-administered unions in the north were being forced to subsidise the badly managed unions in the west and south of the country. This was viewed as especially harsh given that northern unions had generally remained self-financing and received relatively little money from the government for relief measures. One Ulster newspaper drew a clear geographic distinction between the indolence of the distressed areas compared with the industriousness of the north and declared:

> It is true that the potato has failed in Connaught and Munster; but it has failed just as much in Ulster; therefore, if the failure of the potato has produced all the distress in the South and West, why has it not caused the same misery here? It is because we

are a painstaking, industrious, laborious people, who desire to work and pay our just debts, and the blessing of the Almighty is upon our labour. If the people of the South had been equally industrious with those of the North, they would not have so much misery among them.[42]

The probity of Ulster versus the sloth of Connaught was an interpretation that was invoked frequently. Edward Senior, Assistant Poor Law Commissioner in the north, described the tax as a subsidy to the 'indolence' of the west.[43] Joseph Napier MP argued that the only achievement of the Bill would be in 'keeping up an army of beggars, fed out of the industry of Ulster'.[44]

The Rate-in-Aid was also seen as calling into question the sanctity of the Union between Britain and Ireland. This argument was presented forcibly in a number of local newspapers, which described it as an 'anti-Union scheme' and warned that 'Antrim, Armagh and Down are to be made the preserves for the paupers of Connaught to graze on'.[45] *The Banner of Ulster* suggested that if the Bill were passed against the wishes of the Irish people, it might become

fatally wrested into an argument against the connection between the two countries and against the trust which ought to be placed in the impartiality and justice of the Imperial Legislature. It is, therefore, dangerous to the stability of that Union on which the safety of the British Empire depends.[46]

The radical MP William Sharman Crawford, who owned estates in County Down, criticised the Bill on the grounds that it was both unjust and unconstitutional. As Irish taxes, he argued, were paid into 'an Imperial Treasury and placed at the disposal of an Imperial Legislature for the general purposes of the United Kingdom', it followed that expenditure for Irish distress should come out of the same coffers and not just from one portion of the United Kingdom.[47]

Despite the opposition to the Bill, most of the Poor Law guardians and ratepayers were not willing to resort to violence. Representatives from the unions of Armagh, Belfast, Cookstown, Derry, Downpatrick, Kilkeel, Larne, Lisburn, Lurgan and Newtownards attended a mass meeting in May 1849. They unanimously agreed that they did not want to encourage 'active opposition' to the Bill, but suggested passive resistance should be used as far as possible.[48] The unwillingness of the Ulster ratepayers to engage in more forceful methods to oppose the Rate-in-Aid led a London newspaper to declare that the agitation had ended in a 'battle of smoke', to which an Ulster newspaper replied that smoke was better than blood.[49]

Whilst the debate was raging, the Rate-in-Aid Bill passed relatively easily through the House of Commons in March by 206 votes to 34. Although it had a more difficult passage in the House of Lords, the Bill became law in May 1849.[50] In fact, only a minority of Irish MPs voted against it, the general feeling being that a continuation of financial assistance to Ireland would result in a culture of dependency. There was also a fear that if income tax were extended to Ireland, it would become permanent, whereas the Rate-in-Aid was simply a temporary measure. The Act provided for a sum, not exceeding 6d in the pound, to be collected, based on the annual valuation of the union. It was to remain operative until 31 December 1850.

To a large extent, the protests of the Ulster ratepayers derived more from propaganda than from the reality of the legislation. The amount of additional rates to be paid by the Ulster unions was proportionately less than in any of the other three provinces, with Connaught paying the highest level for the new tax.[51] The resistance of the Ulster ratepayers appeared to dissolve following the passage of the Act, but the opposition was manifested in a more subtle and effective way. By 1851, the province of Ulster had the highest amount of rate uncollected. Its arrears were 16 per cent, compared with 4 per cent in Leinster, 6 per cent in Munster and 9 per cent in Connaught.[52]

Many ministers and Poor Law officials were also opposed to the legislation. Lord Clarendon viewed the Bill as contrary to the idea of a *United* Kingdom and feared that it could lead to further rebellion in Ireland.[53] The Rate-in-Aid was also condemned by the doyen of Poor Law legislation, George Nicholls, who had framed the 1838 Irish Poor Law. He described the Bill as an 'alarmist response' to the situation in Ireland and considered that the potato blight should be treated as an 'imperial calamity'.[54] The most vehement opposition to the Bill, however, came from the man who was expected to implement it, Edward Twistleton, the Chief Poor Law Commissioner in Ireland. The Rate-in-Aid led to a further – and final – confrontation between Trevelyan and Twistleton, which resulted in the resignation of the latter. Trevelyan viewed the new tax as a way of protecting British taxpayers from 'the great injustice of the burden which belongs to the rate-payers of each [Irish] union being unnecessarily transferred to the tax-payers of the United Kingdom'.[55] For Twistleton, the Rate-in-Aid was the final straw in what he regarded as an abandonment of Ireland. By April 1849, he had no funds, even for distribution to the 'distressed unions'. The £50,000 given to Ireland at the beginning of 1849 was exhausted and the British Relief Association had made their final donation of £1000 the previous month. Despite increasing mortality and the outbreak of cholera, the Poor Law Commissioner had no access to additional funding. The Treasury's failure to heed Twistleton's repeated pleas for emergency funding led him to declare that he considered he and his colleagues were 'absolved from any responsibility on account of deaths which may take place in consequence of those privations'.[56]

Twistleton opposed the Rate-in-Aid on the grounds that it was the duty of the state and the national Treasury to provide for the areas still suffering from the Famine. He also felt that insufficient account had been taken in Britain of the extent of taxation already raised in Ireland for Famine relief. He viewed this new policy as an abdication of the responsibilities imposed by the Act of Union and tendered his resignation, declaring that he could not implement the legislation 'with honour'.[57] Following his resignation, Twistleton made a number of public statements in which he unwaveringly criticised the failure of the government to prevent the suffering and starvation in Ireland. He no longer viewed the distress as being inevitable, but saw it as the result of a political and ideological refusal to give adequate financial assistance to the destitute of Ireland. In his opinion, the failure of provision had brought lasting shame on Britain. He stressed that providing relief to Ireland would not be expensive but could be achieved for a 'comparatively trifling sum'. This, he believed, would enable Britain

> to spare itself the deep disgrace of permitting any of our miserable fellow subjects in the Distressed Unions to die of starvation. I wish to leave distinctly on record that, from want of sufficient food, many persons in these Unions are at present dying or wasting away; and, at the same time, it is quite possible for this country to prevent the occurrence there of any death from starvation, by the advance of a few hundred pounds.[58]

An endorsement of Twistleton's sentiments and his decision to resign was made privately by Clarendon, who was also increasingly critical of the policy decisions made by his party. He explained to Russell that Twistleton's action had been motivated by the fact that: 'He thinks that the destitution here is so horrible, and the indifference of the House of Commons to it so manifest, that he is an unfit agent of a policy that must be one of extermination.'[59]

The introduction of the Rate-in-Aid demonstrated clearly the British government's determination to sever financial links with Irish distress. Opposition to the Bill was extensive. In Ireland, much of the criticism was motivated by financial considerations. The policy was also condemned by relief administrators in Ireland who felt that the decision to leave the country to her own resources was both constitutionally and morally wrong. Despite this sizeable opposition, policy was increasingly controlled by a small government clique who were both geographically and intellectually distant from the distressed unions in Ireland.

The Flight from Ireland: Emigration

Even before the Famine, there had been large-scale emigration from Ireland. The flight from Ireland during the years 1846–54 was, however, unprecedented in its scale. Nor did the exodus end when the Famine was over. Emigration was higher in the five years after 1850 than it had been in the preceding five. The composition of the emigrants also made Famine emigration unusual. Before 1845, the emigrants had predominantly come from the better-off eastern counties, and emigration represented economic opportunity to the most ambitious members of society. Although the poorest and least skilled emigrants were the largest group and rendered more visible by their poverty, emigration during the Famine cut across all social classes. After the Famine, more emigrants were drawn from the poorer provinces of Connaught and Munster. Whereas before 1845 many of the emigrants were either family groups or unmarried men, during the Famine the emigration of single women in equal numbers to single men became more common.[60] This was a unique feature of Irish emigration.

Even more remarkable was the fact that such large-scale emigration was achieved so cheaply. Before the Famine, social commentators, including Thomas Malthus and Archbishop Whately, had seen emigration as a solution to Ireland's high population and economic underdevelopment. The government, however, had been reluctant to finance an emigration policy, fearing that if they did so the most enterprising people would leave the country. During the Famine, emigration and mortality cleared the poorest counties of a large proportion of their populations at no expense to the government. The majority of the emigration was self-financed, assisted emigration accounting for only about 5 per cent of the whole process. A scheme which assisted over 4000 female orphans to emigrate to Australia was paid for by the Australian government.[61] The fact that a large proportion of the emigrants were Catholic was a source of concern to the Church hierarchy. Many members of the government by contrast viewed this fact as desirable, especially if they could be replaced with Protestant settlers from Britain. Even Clarendon who had been increasingly sympathetic to the victims of the Famine, viewed the disappearance of so many Catholics as a hopeful sign for the future of Ireland. He stated that, 'the departure of thousands of papists Celts must be a blessing to the country they quit' and he was particularly pleased to note that 'Some English and Scottish settlers have arrived.'[62]

Before the Famine most of the emigration had been to Britain, but increasingly America became the destination of choice of emigrants. This was partly to do with the coincidence of a trade depression in Britain in the most critical years of the Famine. As hundreds of thousands of British workers were thrown out of work, Britain became less attractive as a place to settle. In Britain also, despite the Act of Union, a provision under both the English and the Scottish Poor Laws meant that Irish immigrants could be 'removed' back to Ireland unless they could prove five years' residence in the country. The existence of this law probably acted as a deterrent to newly arrived immigrants applying for Poor Law relief. The law also demonstrated that Irish paupers were not given equal rights with other paupers in the United Kingdom. The attraction of America as a destination was helped by developments in shipping which made the journey cheaper, safer and more rapid. More important, though, was the tendency of new emigrants to send remittances to Ireland to finance further emigration. This contributed to chain migration and the creation of Irish clusters or communities.

Because passenger travel was subject to very few regulations, the journey was generally unpleasant and fraught with danger. The emigrants were expected to take sufficient provision for the crossing which, on the journey to America, could take 40 days. Hygiene on board the ships was usually inadequate and was exacerbated by the generally poor health of the emigrants. Seasickness and diarrhoea were commonplace. The high mortality on board the ships and the unseaworthy condition of a number of the vessels, led to the description of 'coffin-ships'. Though the vast majority of the Famine emigrants did reach their final destination, their lifespan in their adopted country was often short. Arriving in a new country did not mark an end to the horrors of migration; anti-Irish prejudice and fear of disease made the Irish emigrants universally unpopular.[63]

In many of the places where the Irish immigrants settled, they were despised by the native population who viewed them as carriers of disease, competition for employment, or a further burden on taxation. At the same time, emigration was viewed as a means by which Irish landlords exported Irish poverty to England. Again, *The Times* led the attack on both landlords and immigrants. At the beginning of 1847 it warned that 'the anticipated invasion of Irish pauperism had commenced, 15,000 have already, within the last three months, landed in Liverpool and block up her thoroughfare with masses of misery'.[64] The port of Liverpool, where the bulk of Irish immigrants arrived, appealed unsuccessfully to the central government to assist them in looking after the Irish immigrants. The Irish people who settled in Liverpool, either by design or accident, were generally drawn from the poorest sections of all the emigrant groups and, inevitably, had little capital and few skills. Within Liverpool, the paupers were increasingly regarded as a tax burden and local newspapers frequently referred to the cultural inferiority of the Irish people. The *Liverpool Mail* blamed the influx of Irish on 'idleness on the part of the peasantry and ignorance and extravagance on the part of the gentry'.[65] The *Liverpool Mercury*, in what was becoming a stereotypical representation, described the character of the Irish people as being 'slothful, improvident and reckless'.[66]

Although there was a concern that farmers might leave Ireland taking their capital with them, the government was generally pleased that so many poor Catholic peasants left Ireland. In parts of the west, whole communities emigrated. When Twistleton brought this to the attention of Trevelyan, the latter, in an official reply, informed him:

> I do not know how farms are to be consolidated if small farmers do not emigrate, and by acting for the purpose of keeping them at home, we should be defaulting at our own object. We must not complain of what we really want to obtain. If small farmers go, and their landlords are reduced to sell portions of their estates to persons who will invest capital, we shall at last arrive at something like a satisfactory settlement of the country.[67]

The scale of emigration led *The Times* to comment, 'in a few years more a Celtic Irishman will be as rare in Connemara as is the Red Indian on the shores of Manhattan'.[68] Whilst the prediction proved to be incorrect, the haemorrhage of people from Ireland continued into the late nineteenth century. The creation of an Irish diaspora not only changed Irish society but made an indelible mark on the countries in which the emigrants settled.

The Cost of the Famine

The Irish Famine was one of the greatest social catastrophes in modern European history. Whilst no part of Ireland emerged unscathed, the devastation was geographically focused and concentrated on the poorest groups in society. Areas which had traditionally been dependent on the potato suffered the highest losses of population. In total, over one million people died. A further million emigrated.

The mortality rate was particularly high amongst children under 5 and adults (especially men) over 40.[69] However, one of the features of the Famine was not only the scale of mortality, but the painful and undignified circumstances in which many people died and were buried. Throughout these years, the British government did not keep a record of the number of deaths. This fact provoked Lord George Bentinck, the leader of the parliamentary opposition, to say:

> The time will come when we shall know what the amount of mortality has been, and though you may groan, and try to keep the truth down, it shall be known, and the time will come when the public and the world will be able to estimate, at its proper value, your management of the affairs of Ireland.[70]

The financing of the Famine was inadequate given the scale of the tragedy. Approximately £10 million was provided by the British government during the Famine period. This represented $\frac{1}{2}$ per cent of Britain's GNP. Most of this money was issued as a loan, which had to be repaid even as the Famine continued. Moreover, over half of it was provided in the winter of 1846–47 – ironically, the period of highest mortality, during the public works phase. After 1847, government spending fell dramatically as ideology triumphed over compassion and Irish property was expected to support Irish destitution. Although Irish landlords contributed in the region of £9 million to Famine relief, both government and British public opinion perceived them not to have done enough.

The management of the relief measures was increasingly controlled by a small group of politicians and civil servants within Westminster and Whitehall. The food shortages were regarded by these men as an opportunity to modernise Ireland. To make this possible, humanitarianism was repeatedly subsumed beneath ideological and financial considerations. After 1847, relief measures became a tool for enforcing a social revolution in Ireland.

In view of the parsimony of the government, the role played by philanthropy was particularly important. Over £1 million was raised privately for Ireland, large portions of it being subscribed by people who had no connection with the country. Moreover, private relief was generally given without the controls and checks associated with government relief, and in such a way as to maintain, not destroy, human dignity.

The Irish Famine occurred within the jurisdiction and at the heart of the richest and most industrially advanced Empire in the world. In spite of the Act of Union, Ireland was not treated as an equal partner within the United Kingdom. This was made clear by the use of the Law of Removal and the introduction of the Rate-in-Aid in 1849. The parsimony of the government towards Ireland was criticised by a number of contemporaries. Archbishop MacHale, amongst others, drew an unfavourable comparison with the state's

generosity only a decade earlier to slave-owners, who were given
£22 million compensation for the abolition of slavery.[71]

Key members of the British government were in no doubt about
the scale of the tragedy that was unfolding on their doorstep. For
a variety of reasons, they chose to allow it to continue, arguing that
the changes ultimately would benefit Ireland . For many people,
these benefits were ephemeral. And, in the short term, the social
and human cost of this approach was beyond measure.

'The Famine Killed Everything'

In the decade 1841–51, Ireland changed radically.[1] The most
visible and easily quantifiable change was a dramatic reduction in
population. Within a few years, over two million people had
disappeared: one million had died, and a further one million had
emigrated. The population continued to fall throughout the
remainder of the century, a combination of emigration, delayed
marriages and celibacy.[2] By 1900, it had fallen to approximately
half of its pre-Famine level. The population decline did not finally
reverse until the 1960s. This demographic decline made Ireland
unique within Europe. It was also an indication that the changes
wrought by the Famine were long-term rather than short-term.

Most of the Famine deaths were geographically and socially
specific. Those who had died as a result of disease, starvation or
exhaustion were mostly from the west of the country. Complete
families and whole communities who had subsisted on potatoes prior
to 1845 were wiped out. The fact that many of them had been Irish-
speaking weakened the use of the Irish language. By 1851, the
number of Irish-speakers had halved. The commercialisation of the
Irish economy, the spread of literacy and large-scale emigration
weakened it further. In post-Famine society, the Irish language was
associated with rural poverty and was viewed as backward, especially
by those whose ambitions lay outside of the country.

Although 1851 marked the disappearance of blight, the effects
of Famine continued to be felt. The destruction and devastation
of the Famine was far from over. Disease, destitution, debilitation
and mortality remained above their pre-Famine levels. The years
of food shortages, stress and physical deprivations had taken their
toll on those who survived the Famine and their descendants
suffered a high incidence of mental illness and poor health. This
further demonstrated that recovery from the Famine was slow
and painful.

Emigration also continued to increase. Approximately one million
people had left the country between 1846 and 1850, but this figure
was even higher in the following four years. Emigration peaked in
1854, but thereafter it was irreversibly established as part of the
lifecycle of late nineteenth-century Ireland. Emigrants were drawn
from a more diverse economic and social mix than those who died
during the Famine. Paupers, ruined farmers and disillusioned

businessmen alike sought their future outside Ireland. The majority of them were never to return.

The economic impact of emigration on those who remained in Ireland was positive. Those who were left behind faced less competition for employment, whilst 'remittances' received from overseas acted as subsidies and allowed uneconomic farms in the west of the country to survive. By the late 1860s, there were an estimated 2 million Irish-born in America who were sending £1 million to Ireland annually. Whilst emigration may have been economically beneficial, the social cost was high. The loss of so many young people meant that Irish society was comprised disproportionately of the old and the very young. This contributed to the growth of the social conservatism and torpor associated with post-Famine Ireland. The growth of a culture of exile became more evident and banishment and dispossession became recurring themes in songs, stories and oral tradition. A number of emigrants included anti-British sentiment as part of their ideological baggage. The legacy of such attitudes was to ensure that Irish politics was placed on an international agenda and was no longer viewed as a domestic issue for the British government to resolve.

Many of the people who were lost during the Famine were Catholic, except in parts of east Ulster. The fact that the Famine was widely regarded as a judgment of God, even by those groups who suffered most, did not appear to weaken their faith in the Almighty. Nor did the failure of the Church hierarchy to forge a coherent response to the Famine undermine the hold of His representatives on earth. In the post-Famine decades, the position of the Catholic Church within Ireland was strengthened. The Catholic Church internationally, under the long pontificate of Pius IX, became more conservative. After the Famine, there was a shift away from traditional religious practices, which had combined elements of pagan rituals with superstition. They were replaced by a more orthodox and disciplined approach to religion. Moreover, as the population fell, the proportion of priests to people rose, resulting in greater clerical control. The involvement of the religious orders in education helped to consolidate the position of the Church. The Church also became more authoritarian and thus helped to impose a new social discipline on the lower classes. The spread of devotional conformity may have helped to redress the cultural impoverishment of the post-Famine years. Catholicism was not the only religion to undergo this form of 'devotional revolution' as there was a general revival in religious practices and a shift to a moral Puritanism evident in many denominations.[3] In parts of Ulster, this contributed to an increase in religious tensions and a growth in sectarianism, especially between poor Catholics and poor Protestants.

The position of women also changed. The decline in domestic industry, the shift from tillage to pasture and the move to male primogeniture all undermined the position of women in society. Irish women without the advantage of a dowry were increasingly doomed to spinsterhood if they remained in Ireland. The importance of a dowry permeated Irish sayings and literature, even into the twentieth century.[4] In addition, the growth in influence of the Catholic Church contributed to the growth of a more patriarchal society than had existed previously. This led many women to seek opportunities outside Ireland, and Irish emigration was unique for the fact that so many of the emigrants were single women.[5]

The structure of Irish agriculture also changed significantly. During the Famine decade, approximately one in every four agricultural holdings disappeared, the majority being farms of less than 15 acres. The consolidation of holdings had been one of the structural changes desired by the British government. However, the 'Anglicisation' of Irish agriculture which they expected to follow never occurred. For landowners and large farmers who survived the Famine years, the following decades were marked by increasing prosperity, especially for those who were able to take advantage of the large profits to be made from livestock. A more commercial ethos became evident, especially amongst 'strong farmers' whose treatment of their tenants reflected these new economic values. The move from tillage to livestock intensified as Irish agriculture adjusted to a vastly reduced workforce, a streamlined system of landholding and lack of protection for Irish corn. The decline of tillage became further marked following the agricultural depression of the early 1860s when Ireland found itself unable to compete with growing international competition.[6]

For the poorest groups in society, the standard of living remained low. In the west, many of them continued to subsist on potatoes. Crop yields, however, dropped drastically. This was due to a less intensive use of fertiliser, an increase in the amount of waste land and the intermittent appearance of blight. The prolific lumper potatoes also stopped being grown so extensively. In the second half of the nineteenth century, whilst the number of cattle rose by one-third, the acreage under potatoes and grain halved. Overall, the livestock trade in Ireland was one of the major achievements of Irish agriculture after the Famine.[7]

The diet of the poor labourers slowly became more diverse, helped by the spread of railways and the growth of a market economy. Much of their income came from external sources, either from seasonal migrant labour or remittances sent from abroad. The vulnerability of these groups was indicated by the persistence of food shortages and famine in the second half of the nineteenth century. The shortages were especially severe in 1859–60, 1879,

1890, 1894 and 1897, although death from starvation was rare.[8]
The fact that little of the new prosperity of the large farmers was
distributed to the labourers was a source of resentment and social
division in the late nineteenth century. The memory of the Famine
provided an additional sense of injustice against landowners and,
increasingly, the British state. In the 1880s, Michael Davitt and
Charles Stewart Parnell harnessed this resentment into a powerful
machine for demanding land reform. Overall, 'The fear of Famine,
or rather of having to choose between starvation and evictions was
the great underlying political reality of the late seventies and early
eighties of the nineteenth century in Ireland.'[9]

The Famine had also changed Ireland in ways that were difficult
to quantify. Behind the aggregate numbers of people who died lay
individual stories of human tragedy. For those people who had
survived the Famine years, life had changed dramatically. This was
particularly the case where the losses had been greatest, although
no part of Ireland emerged unscathed. The psychological scars and
legacy of the Famine are difficult to measure, especially as for a
long period silence surrounded these years. The legacy of the
Famine was also evident in the literary sources and the oral
tradition of the late nineteenth century. They suggested that the
cultural richness associated with pre-Famine Ireland had disappeared
and been replaced with values based on commercialism and
respectability. This change was apparent in the writings of a
number of late nineteenth-century commentators. The Famine had
changed Irish society even in areas where the impact of the Famine
was less severe and recovery faster. Newtownards in County Down,
for example, was one of only three unions (out of 130) not to have
to rely on government assistance in 1847. Nevertheless, suffering
had been both harsh and extensive, even for those who derived
additional income from weaving. Twenty-five years later, the local
newspaper recalled:

> The weavers after the Famine were not the same men they were
> before it. Saturday night squabbling had ceased; the public
> houses might as well have been closed for all the business done;
> prayer meetings were established in different localities, in out-
> of-the-way places where cock-fighting, dog-fighting and
> rat-hunting-on-Sunday characters had lived; and a tone of
> seriousness pervaded the people. Many of them felt they had
> something else to live for than to eat, drink and be merry.
> Numbers of old Bibles, hymn books and Psalm books were fished
> up from all sort of places.[10]

In the Rosses in County Donegal an even more poignant description
was provided of post-Famine Ireland:

Tháinig blianta an ghorta agus an droch shaoghal agus an t-ocras agus bhris sin neart agus spiorad na ndaoini. Ní rabh ann ach achan nduine ag iarraidh bheith beo. Chaill siad a' dáimh le chéile. Ba chuma cé a bhí gaolmhar duit, ba do charaid an t-é a bhéarfadh greim duit le chur in do bhéal. D'imthigh an spórt agus a' caitheamh aimsire. Stad an fhilidheacht agus a' ceol agus damhsa. Chaill siad agus rinne siad dearmad den iomlán agus nuair a bhisigh an saoghal ar dhóigheannaí eile ní tháinig na rudaí seo ariamh arais mar a bhí siad. Mharbh an gorta achan rud.[11]

[The years of the Famine, of the bad life and of the hunger, arrived and broke the spirit and strength of the community. People simply wanted to survive. Their spirit of comradeship was lost. It didn't matter what ties or relations you had; you considered that person to be your friend who gave you food to put in your mouth. Recreation and leisure ceased. Poetry, music and dancing died. These things were lost and completely forgotten. When life improved in other ways, these pursuits never returned as they had been. The Famine killed everything.]

Note on Further Reading

Until recently, the two standard works on the Famine were R. Dudley Edwards and T. Desmond Williams (eds), *The Great Famine. Studies in Irish History* (Dublin, 1956) and Cecil Woodham-Smith's *The Great Hunger* (London, 1962). The former was specially commissioned for the anniversary of the appearance of blight, but ultimately it proved to be a narrow and uneven account of the Famine years. The latter was criticised following its publication by the academic establishment in Ireland for its emotive description of the Famine and its castigation of Charles Trevelyan as the villain of the piece. Despite this, the book was an international best-seller. More recently, academics have acknowledged that Woodham-Smith's book was ground-breaking in its use of sources. Recent publications on the Famine have come closer to agreeing with many of her conclusions.

More recent works on the Famine include a collection of P.M. Austin-Bourke's ground-breaking work, *The Visitation of God? The Potato and the Great Irish Famine* (Dublin, 1993) which examines the role of the potato and potato blight in Ireland.

Christine Kinealy's *This Great Calamity. The Irish Famine 1845–52* (Dublin, 1994) reassesses the pivotal role of the government during the Famine years, and demonstrates how the impact of the catastrophe varied from locality to locality. Donal Kerr's *A Nation of Beggars? Priests, People and Politics in Famine Ireland 1846–52* (Oxford, 1994) examines the role of the Catholic Church during the Famine, with special reference to the attitude of Lord John Russell.

The 150th anniversary of the blight has resulted in a large amount of literature of varying quality. Amongst the best are Noel Kissane, *The Irish Famine. A Documentary History* (Dublin, 1995), which is based on documents held by the National Library in Ireland; Cathal Pórtéir's compilations *The Great Irish Famine* (Cork, 1995) and *Famine Memories* (Dublin, 1995) which accompanied the radio series of the same name produced by RTE in Dublin; and *The Famine Decade. Contemporary Accounts 1841–51* (Belfast, 1991) by John Killen, a collection of contemporary newspaper accounts and other reports. Cork Archives Institute produced a facsimile pack based on local archival and library holdings, entitled *Great Famine Facsimile Pack. The Irish Famine* by Peter Gray (New

Horizons, 1995), which provides a collection of contemporary images of the Famine. In *The Meaning of the Famine* (Leicester, 1996) Patrick O'Sullivan (ed.) brings together authors from a diverse range of backgrounds to examine both the history and theory of Famine relief.

To view the Famine in its wider context, Cormac Ó Gráda's *Ireland Before and After the Famine: Explorations in Economic History* (Manchester, 1988) and *Ireland. A New Economic History 1780–1925* (Oxford, 1994) give an overview of the nineteenth-century Irish economy. A specialist account of the pre-Famine economy is provided by Joel Mokyr, *Why Ireland Starved: A Quantitative and Analytical History of the Irish Economy* (London, 1983). A more general history of the nineteenth century is available in W.E. Vaughan (ed.), *A New History of Ireland, Ireland under the Union, 1801–70*, vol. v (Oxford, 1989).

Notes

1 The Great Hunger in Ireland. Ideologies and Interpretations

1. Niall Ó Ciosáin, 'Was there "Silence" about the Famine?', *Irish Studies Review* 13 (Winter 1995–96) pp. 7–10.
2. Canon John O'Rourke, *The Great Irish Famine* (first published in 1874, republished Dublin, 1989). It appeared to be part of the Victorian psyche to use euphemisms, e.g. 'outrage' to describe maimings and assassination; 'coercion' for suspension of legal rights.
3. Michael Davitt, *Fall of Feudalism* (New York, 1904) p. 50.
4. Although the absolute number of deaths in other famines may have been higher, e.g. in the Ukraine Famine of 1932–33 and the Bengali Famine of 1940–43, in relation to the size of the base populations Ireland's losses were greater.
5. I am grateful to Aine Grealy and Rona Fields for their insights into the area of post-traumatic stress and the legacy of colonialism. In regard to the former, they have both drawn valuable lessons from the survivors of the Holocaust.
6. See, for example, D. George Boyce and Alan O'Day, *The Making of Modern Irish History. Revisionism and the Revisionist Controversy* (London, 1996).
7. See, for example, Christine Kinealy, 'Beyond Revisionism. Reassessing the Irish Famine', *History Ireland* (Winter 1995); Willy Maley, 'Varieties of Nationalism: post-Revisionist Irish Studies', *Irish Studies Review* (Summer 1996).
8. Maley, p. 37.
9. For more on this, see Christine Kinealy, *This Great Calamity. The Irish Famine 1845–52* (Dublin, 1994) pp. xv–xxi.
10. Daltún Ó Ceallaigh (ed.), *Reconsiderations of Irish History and Culture* (Dublin, 1994) pp. 12–13.
11. Brendan Bradshaw, *Irish Historical Studies*, vol. xxvi, no. 104 (November, 1989) pp. 329–51.
12. This was evident, for example, in the Irish press during the 1995 commemorations. In the *Irish Times* much of the debate centred on John Waters (an anti-revisionist) and Kevin Myers (who adopted an ultra-revisionist stance).
13. Brendan Bradshaw, 'Revising Irish History', in Ó Ceallaigh, pp. 27–41.
14. Charles Trevelyan, *The Irish Crisis* (London, 1848). This essay was first published anonymously in the *Edinburgh Review*.

15. Lord Clarendon, who was appointed Lord Lieutenant in 1847, became increasingly disillusioned with the policies of Charles Wood, the Chancellor of the Exchequer, and Charles Trevelyan. He coined the phrase 'Trevelyanisms' to describe what he viewed as misdirected policies. Clarendon to Earl of Bedford, Clarendon Papers, Bodleian Library, 16 February 1849.

16. George Poulett Scrope, quoted in George O'Brien, *The Economic History of Ireland from the Union* (London, 1921), p. 261. An opposite view of the role of Trevelyan has been presented by P.M. Austin-Bourke, 'Apologia for a Dead Civil Servant', in Jacqueline Hill and Cormac Ó Gráda (eds), *The Visitation of God?* (Dublin, 1994) pp. 170–7.

17. G.M. Trevelyan, *English Social History. Chaucer to Queen Victoria* (London, 1944) p. 372.

18. Peter Mathias, *The First Industrial Nation. The Economic History of Britain 1700–1914*, (London, 1990, 2nd edition) p. 177.

19. Roy Foster, *Modern Ireland, 1600–1972* (Harmondsworth, 1988) p. 318. This book is sometimes viewed as being the most comprehensive statement of the revisionist viewpoint.

20. There are few mentions of Ireland in Malthus's classical work *An Essay on the Principle of Population* (first published in 1798 and frequently reprinted). Malthus did contribute an anonymous article to the *Edinburgh Review* in 1808 in which he refers to Ireland.

21. Thomas A. Boylan and Timothy P. Foley, 'A Nation Perishing of Political Economy', in Chris Morash and Richard Hayes (eds), *'Fearful Realities'. New Perspectives on the Famine* (Dublin, 1996) pp. 142–4.

22. Ibid., p. 143.

23. Review of *The Great Hunger*, by F.S. L. Lyons, in *Irish Historical Studies* (1964–65) pp. 76–9.

24. This incident was refered to in Cormac Ó Gráda, *The Irish Famine* (Dublin, 1989), p. 11.

25. Roy Foster, 'We are all Revisionists Now', in *Irish Review* (Cork, 1986) pp. 1–6. In an interview with *History Ireland*, vol. 1, no. 3 (Autumn 1993), Foster broadened (and softened) his defence of revisionism, although he did state: 'I think there is very often an agenda behind this so-called anti-revisionism.'

26. John Mitchel, *The Last Conquest of Ireland (Perhaps)* (first published New York, 1860).

27. *Report of the Select Committee Appointed to Enquire into the Administration of the Poor Law in the Kilrush Union since 19 September 1848*, 1850 [613] p. xiii.

28. Mary Daly, *The Famine in Ireland* (Dublin, 1986) p. 113.

29. Ibid.

30. These restrictions were temporarily suspended in February 1847, although this was too late to save the lives lost in the disastrous winter of 1846–47.

31. James Kelly, 'Scarcity and Poor Relief in Eighteenth-century Ireland: The Subsistence Crisis of 1782–84', *Irish Historical Studies*, vol. xxviii, no. 109 (May 1992).

32. The summaries of the grain trade provided by Austin-Bourke are frequently quoted to demonstrate the surplus of grain imports over grain exports in 1847. See P.M. Austin-Bourke, *The Visitation of God? The Potato and the Great Irish Famine*, ed. Jacqueline Hill and Cormac Ó Gráda (Dublin, 1993) pp. 168–9.

33. For example, James Donnelly and Christine Kinealy were born outside Ireland, and Cormac Ó Gráda and Joel Mokyr are econometricians rather than historians.

34. For more on this, see Kinealy, 'Beyond Revisionism'.

35. Raymond Crotty's books, including *Irish Agricultural Production: Its Volume and Structure* (Cork, 1966), through to Roy Foster's widely read *Modern Ireland 1600–1972*, were influential in side-tracking the impact of the Famine on the development of modern Ireland.

36. For example, Eoghan Harris, a political commentator, suggested on the 'Davis' programme, broadcast by RTE (Dublin) in February 1995, that the IRA had lost the military war and were using the Famine to incite anti-British feeling. Conor Cruise O'Brien made a similar suggestion on 'Newsnight' (BBC 2) in June 1995.

37. Woodham-Smith's comprehensive study, for example, hardly refers to events in Ulster.

38. Gerard MacAtasney, 'Challenging an Orthodoxy. The Famine in Lurgan 1845–47' unpublished MA thesis (Queen's University, Belfast, 1995).

39. *Hansard's Parliamentary Debates*, col. 62, 1 March 1849.

40. R.D. Edwards and T.D Williams, *The Great Famine. Studies in Irish History* (Dublin, 1956).

41. For more on this fascinating episode, see Cormac Ó Gráda, 'Making History in Ireland in the 1940s and 1950s: The Saga of the Great Famine', *The Irish Review* (1992) pp. 87–107.

42. Ibid., p. 95.

43. Ibid., quote by Edwards, p. 101.

44. Paper delivered by Professor James Donnelly in Cambridge University, March 1996, entitled *The Construction of the Memory of the Famine in Ireland and the Irish Diaspora, 1850–1900*.

45. T.K. Hoppen, *Ireland since 1800: Conflict and Conformity* (London, 1989) p. 29.

46. John Mitchel, *Jail Journal* (originally published 1854) p. xix.

47. See, for example, Davitt, p. 50.

48. Mitchel, p. 112.

49. Boylan and Foley, p. 143.

50. Cathal Póirtéir, *Famine Echoes* (Dublin, 1995) . Also, to mark the 100th anniversary of the Famine in 1845, a questionnaire on the Great Famine was distributed throughout Ireland and manuscript replies are held in the Department of Irish Folklore in University College, Dublin. Roger McHugh, who contributed a chapter to the Edwards and Williams publication, made some use of this archive.

51. Rossa, p. 196; Davitt, p. 50.

52. Irene Whelan, 'The Stigma of Souperism', in Cathal Póirtéir, *The Great Irish Famine* (Cork, 1995) pp. 135–54.

53. Donnelly, *Construction of Memory*.

2 'A State of Degradation'. Pre-Famine Ireland

1. David Walker, *The Normans in Britain* (Oxford, 1995) pp. 94–115.
2. I am grateful to Dr Seán Egan for his advice on this section.
3. The wars between James and William were, in fact, part of a wider European power struggle of which Ireland was only a minor part. Liz Curtis, *The Cause of Ireland. From the United Irishmen to Partition* (Belfast, 1994) pp. 1–3. For an excellent general introduction to this period, see Eileen Black (ed.), *Kings in Conflict: Ireland in the 1690s* (Belfast, 1990).
4. J.G. Simms, 'The Establishment of Protestant Ascendancy, 1691–1714', in *A New History of Ireland. Eighteenth-Century Ireland 1691–1800*, vol. IV, ed. T.W. Moody and W.E. Vaughan (Oxford, 1986) pp. 16–19.
5. Brian T. McClintock, 'The 1844 Marriage Act: Politico-Religious Agitation and its Consequences for Ulster Genealogy', *Familia. Ulster Genealogical Review* (Belfast, 1986) pp. 33–58; Christine Kinealy, 'Presbyterian Church Records', *Irish Church Records*, ed. James G. Ryan (Dublin, 1992) pp. 69–106.
6. R.J. Dickson, *Ulster Emigration to Colonial America 1718–1775* (Belfast, 1986).
7. See, for example, William Molyneux's, *The Case of Ireland's being Bound by Acts of Parliament in England, Stated* (Dublin, 1698), and Jonathan Swift's *Drapier's Letters*, in 1724, and the same author's *A Modest Proposal*, in 1729. For more on this debate, see J.L. McCracken, 'The Protestant Ascendancy and the Rise of Colonial Nationalism, 1714-60' *A New History*, pp. 104–122; J.C. Beckett, 'Literature in English' ibid., pp. 456–60; and Robert Mahoney, 'Jonathan Swift as the Patriot Dean', *History Ireland*, vol. 3, no. 4 (Winter 1995) pp. 23–7.
8. As a consequence of the political Act of Union between England and Scotland in 1707, it is probably more correct to talk about a 'British' rather than an 'English' parliament after this date.
9. Two more pieces of restrictive legislation were removed – Poynings' Law, named after Sir Edward Poyning who was sent to Ireland in 1494 and introduced a law stipulating that Irish parliaments could not sit or make legislation without the prior approval of the king, and the repeal of 'Sixth of George I', an Act of 1720, which had defined the position of the Dublin parliament as subordinate to the British legislature.
10. R.B. McDowell, 'Parliamentary Independence, 1882–9', *A New History*, pp. 269–72.
11. For varying interpretations on the role of Wolfe Tone, see William Theobald Wolfe Tone, *Memoirs of Theobald Wolfe Tone* (London, 1927); and Marianne Elliott, *Wolfe Tone: Prophet of Irish Independence* (London, 1989).
12. Quoted in Curtis, p. 7.
13. Flann Campbell, *The Dissenting Voice. Protestant Democracy in Ulster from Plantation to Partition* (Belfast, 1991) p. 52.

14. Jim Smyth, 'The Men of No Popery. The origins of the Orange Order', *History Ireland,* vol. 3 (Autumn 1995) p. 50.
15. Thomas Know, 13 August 1796, quoted in Curtis, p. 9.
16. R.B. McDowell, 'The Age of the United Irishmen: Revolution and the Union, 1794–1800', *A New History,* pp. 354–7.
17. K. Theodore Hoppen, *Elections, Politics and Society in Ireland 1832–1885* (Oxford, 1984); D.G. Wright, *Democracy and Reform 1815–85* (London, n.d.) pp. 50–1.
18. Jonathan Bardon, *A History of Ulster* (Belfast, 1992).
19. J.L. Porter, *The Life and Times of Henry Cooke* (London, 1871) p. 412.
20. Eric J. Evans, *Sir Robert Peel. Statesmanship, Power and Party* (London, 1994), pp. 22–5. The title 'Orange Peel' is generally thought to have been first used by O'Connell to describe Peel.
21. The alliance between the Whigs, the British Radicals and the O'Connellites was formalised in 1835 as the 'Lichfield House Compact'.
22. Sir Robert Peel, 9 May 1843, quoted in J.H. White, 'The Age of Daniel O'Connell' in *The Course of Irish History,* T.W. Moody and F. X. Martin (eds) (Cork, 1984); see also Sir Robert Peel to Lord de Grey, 9 May 1843, in Charles S. Parker (ed.), *Sir Robert Peel from His Private Papers,* vol. III (London, 1899) pp. 47–8.
23. *Report from Her Majesty's Commissioners of Inquiry into the State of the law and Practice in relation to the Occupation of Land in Ireland,* 1845, vols xix–xxii.
24. S.J. Connolly, 'The Great Famine and Irish Politics', in Cathal Póirtéir, *The Great Irish Famine* (Cork, 1995) p. 45.
25. Arthur Young, *A Tour in Ireland,* 2 vols (London, 1780).
26. Keith Jeffrey (ed.), *An Irish Empire? Aspects of Ireland and the British Empire* (Manchester, 1996).
27. Thomas Malthus, quoted in Brian Inglis, *Poverty and the Industrial Revolution* (London, 1971) p. 235.
28. Philip Ollerenshaw, 'Industry, 1820–1914', in Liam Kennedy and Philip Ollerenshaw, *An Economic History of Ulster 1820–1939* (Manchester, 1985) pp. 66–76.
29. Frank Geary, 'The Act of Union, British–Irish Trade, and pre-Famine Deindustrialisation', *Economic History Review,* vol. XLVIII, no. 1 (1995) pp. 68–71, 86–8.
30. Mr and Mrs S.C. Hall, *Ireland, its Scenery, Character etc.,* 3 vols (first published London, 1841–3; London, 1984) p. 406.
31. Cormac Ó Gráda, *Ireland: A New Economic History* (Oxford, 1994) p. 120.
32. Peter Gray, 'British Politics and the Irish Land Question 1843–50', unpublished PhD thesis (University of Cambridge, 1992).
33. Gustave de Beaumont, *Ireland: Social, Political and Religious* (London, 1839); William Thackeray, *The Irish Sketchbook* (London, 1843).
34. Hall and Hall, p. xviii.
35. Lord George Hill, *Facts from Gweedore,* 3rd edition (Dublin, 1853).
36. Maureen Wall, 'The Age of the Penal Laws', in Moody and Martin, p. 229.

37. Speech by Earl Grey in the House of Lords, *Hansard (H of L)*, cols 1345–6, 23 March 1846.
38. *Report from Her Majesty's Commissioners of Inquiry into the State of the Law and Practice in Respect of the Occupation of Land in Ireland*, PP 1845, vols XIX–XXII.
39. T.R. Malthus, *An Essay on the Principle of Population*, ed. Donald Winch (first published in 1798; Cambridge, 1992).
40. J.D. Marshall, *The Old Poor Law 1795-1834* (London, 1973).
41. Malthus was persuaded by the *Edinburgh Review* to turn his attention to Ireland for payment of a fee.
42. E. M. Crawford, 'Subsistence Crises and Famines in Ireland: A Nutritionist's View', in E. Margaret Crawford (ed.), *Famine: the Irish Experience 900–1900* (Edinburgh, 1989).
43. R. Floud, K. Watcher and A. Gregory, *Height, Health and History: Nutritional Status in the United Kingdom, 1750–1980* (Cambridge, 1990).
44. For more on this, see Christine Kinealy, *This Great Calamity. The Irish Famine 1845–52* (Dublin, 1994) pp. 18–20.
45. *Third Report of His Majesty's Commissioners for Inquiring into the Condition of the Poorer Classes in Ireland, with appendix and supplement*, 1836 [43] xxx.
46. Kinealy, *This Great Calamity*, pp. 23–6.

3   Rotten Potatoes and the Politics of Relief

1. *The Census for Ireland for the Year 1851*, Part V, Tables of Deaths, vol. 1, PP 1856 [2087] xxix, p. 2.
2. 'William Wilde's Table of Irish Famines, 900–1850', in E. Margaret Crawford (ed.), *Famine: The Irish Experience* (Edinburgh, 1989) p. 3.
3. Ibid., L.M. Clarkson, 'Famine and Irish History', pp. 225–6.
4. For insights on early famines, see ibid., Mary C. Lyons, 'Weather, Famine, Pestilence and Plague in Ireland, 900–1500' pp. 31–74; and Raymond Gillespie, 'Meal and Money: The Harvest Crisis of 1621–4 and the Irish Economy', pp. 75–95.
5. James Kelly, *Famine and Harvest Crisis in Ireland before the Great Famine* (unpublished paper, 1995). I am grateful to Dr Kelly for allowing me to quote from this paper.
6. James Kelly, 'Harvests and Hardships: Famine and Scarcity in Ireland in the late 1720s' in *Studia Hibernica*, vol. XXVI (1991–92) pp. 87–93.
7. Wilde, p. 13.
8. David Dickson, 'The Other Great Irish Famine' in Crawford, pp. 57–8.
9. Wilde (p. 13) estimated that 300,000 died in 1740 alone; see also John D. Post, *Food Shortage, Climatic Variability, and Epidemic Disease in Pre-Industrial Europe. The Mortality Peak in the early 1740s* (London, 1985).
10. This term was used by the great Irish demographer, K.H. Connell, *The Population of Ireland 1750-1845* (Oxford, 1951) p. 144.

11. In England, the significance of the 'moral economy' in alleviating food shortages has been identified as important, although by the nineteenth century it was replaced by the more impersonal philosophy of 'political economy'. See E.P. Thompson, 'The Moral Economy and the English Crowd', *Past and Present*, vol. 50 (1971) pp. 79–126. Less research has been undertaken on this area in Ireland.

12. Kelly, *Famine and Harvest Crisis*.

13. Kelly, *Scarcity and Poor Relief.*

14. Wilde, p. 15.

15. Kelly, *Famine and Harvest Crisis*.

16. Ibid.

17. Wilde, p. 16.

18. Post.

19. Timothy P. O'Neill, 'The state, poverty and distress in Ireland, 1815–45', unpublished PhD thesis (University College, Dublin, 1971) Chapter I.

20. Quoted in Kelly, *Famine and Harvest Crisis* (Peel acquired the title 'Sir' in 1830 on the death of his father).

21. Ibid.; Timothy O'Neill, 'The Famine of 1822', unpublished MA thesis (University College, Dublin, 1966).

22. Wilde, p. 19.

23. Ibid., p. 18.

24. Canon O'Rourke, *The Great Irish Famine* (Dublin, 1989) p. 18.

25. O'Neill, p. 133.

26. Kinealy, *This Great Calamity*, pp. 61–4.

27. Ibid.

28. Austin-Bourke, an authority on Irish potatoes, identified four main phases of potato cultivation in Ireland: Phase 1 (1590–1675) a supplementary food; Phase 2 (1675–1750) a winter food; Phase 3 (1750-1810) staple diet; Phase 4 (1800–45) decline and distress; in P.M. Austin-Bourke, *The Visitation of God? The Potato and the Great Irish Famine*, ed. Jacqueline Hill and Cormac Ó Gráda (Dublin, 1993) pp. 11–25.

29. David Thomson with Moyra McGusty (eds), *The Irish Journals of Elizabeth Smith 1840–1850* (Oxford, 1980) 22 September 1846, p. 101.

30. Adam Smith, *The Wealth of Nations*, Book I, quoted in Peter Mathias, *The First Industrial Nation. The Economic History of Britain 1700–1914* (London, 1990), p. 174.

31. Austin-Bourke, p. 65.

32. The question of potato exports was only discussed during periods of scarcity. By the 1840s, exports of potatoes were over 100,000 tons per year, although some estimates have suggested that it may have been as high as 250,000 tons a year, see Austin-Bourke pp. 105–7.

33. 'Improving' landlords, based on the English model, were relatively rare in pre-Famine Ireland. Those who attempted to modernise their estates and interfere with the traditional way of life in rural areas were often strongly resisted; see, for example, Lord George Hill, *Facts from Gweedore*, (Dublin, 1853, 3rd edn), although, especially in the east, there was more evidence of 'progressive farming' especially

amongst large farmers, see Cormac Ó Gráda, *Ireland. New Economic History. 1780–1939* (Oxford, 1994) p. 31.

34. Elizabeth Smith, *Irish Journals*, 22 September 1846, p. 101.
35. Sir Randolph Routh to Charles Trevelyan, 1 April 1846, *Correspondence Explanatory of the measures adopted by Her Majesty's Government for the relief of distress arising from the failure of the potato crop in Ireland* , 1846 [735] p. 139.
36. Austin-Bourke, p. 21.
37. In 1996 I grew my own lumper potatoes from a potato supplied by the Botanic Gardens in Dublin, They were very easy to grow, prolific (from one potato, I obtained over 130 medium-sized potatoes) and, contrary to their reputation, they were flavoursome and delicious.
38. Douglas C. Daly, 'The Leaf That Launched a Thousand Ships', in *Natural History*, vol. 1. (New York, 1996) p. 27.
39. Ibid.
40. Descriptions of the offensive smell emerge very clearly in folk tradition. See, for example, Póirtéir, p. 36.
41. E. Charles Nelson, *The Cause of the Calamity. Potato Blight in Ireland 1845–47, and the role of the National Botanic Gardens, Glasnevin*, (Dublin, 1995) p. 5.
42. *Gardener's Chronicle and Horticultural Gazette* ,16 September 1845.
43. Austin-Bourke, pp. 27–9.
44. Many poor people believed that God was punishing them for having wasted the plentiful potato crop in 1845, see Póirtéir, pp. 37–40.
45. Sir Robert Peel to the Duke of Wellington, 21 October 1845, *Report of the Commissioners of Inquiry into Matters Connected with the Failure of the Potato Crop*, 1846 [33] xxxvii, p. 223.
46. *Copy of the Report of Dr Playfair and Mr Lindley on the Present State of the Irish Potato Crop, and on the prospect of the Approaching Scarcity*, 1846 [28] xxxviii.
47. The use of biblical imagery and the language of judgment and atonement were extremely prevalent throughout the Famine period. This was particularly evident, for example, in the writings of James Graham (Home Secretary under Peel) and of Charles Wood and Charles Trevelyan, both of whom served under Lord John Russell. For more on the impact of evangelicalism on political decision-making, see Boyd Hilton, *The Age of Atonement; the Influence of Evangelicalism on Social and Economic Thought* (Oxford, 1988).
48. Eric J. Evans, *Sir Robert Peel: Statesmanship, Power and Party* (London, 1994) p. 8.
49. Ibid., p. 7.
50. Quoted in Norman Gash, *Mr Secretary Peel: The Life of Sir Robert Peel to 1830* (London, 1961) p. 22.
51. Norman Gash, *Sir Robert Peel. The Life of Sir Robert Peel after 1830* (Harlow, 1986) pp. 411–12, 642–3.
52. Peel to J. Graham, 13 October 1845, Lord Mahon and Right Hon. Edward Cardwell (eds), *Memoirs by the Right Honourable Sir Robert Peel* (London, 1857) p. 114.
53. Lord Heytesbury to Peel, 17 October 1845, in Mahon, p. 125; ibid., Sir J. Graham to Peel, 19 October 1845, pp. 126–7.

54. Ibid., Extract from Letter of Lord Lieutenant, 27 October 1845, p. 138.

55. Rourke, *Great Irish Famine*, pp. 32–4; *Freeman's Journal*, 4 November 1845.

56. *Belfast Vindicator*, 1 November 1845.

57. Mahon, p. 117.

58. Dr Lyon Playfair to Peel, 26 October 1846, *Report of the Commissioners of Inquiry into Matters connected with the Failure of the Potato Crop, 6 February 1846* [33] xxxvii, p. 225.

59. *Dictionary of National Biography*, vol. xvii, p. 326.

60. This calculation was made by Henry Goulburn, the Chancellor of the Exchequer under Peel; see Gash, p. 543.

61. Cabinet Memorandum, 1 November 1845, Mahon, pp. 141–5.

62. Gash, pp. 554–61.

63. Susan Fairlie, 'The Nineteenth-Century Corn Laws Reconsidered', *Economic History Review*, vol. xviii (1965) pp. 562–75.

64. Quoted in L. J. Cootes, *Britain since 1800* (London, 1968) p. 165.

65. Gash, p. 578.

66. Quoted in Cormac Ó Gráda, *Ireland before and after the Famine. Explorations in Economic History* (Manchester, 1993, 2nd edn), p. 78.

67. Sir Robert Peel, *Speeches*, vol. iv, pp. 589–91.

68. Gash, pp. 628–32.

69. Peel to Sir Henry Hardinge (marked secret),16 December 1845, C.S. Parker, *Sir Robert Peel from His Private Letters* (London, 1899) p. 280.

70. For more on analysis of data, see Kinealy, *This Great Calamity*, Appendix 1, Analysis of Potato Crop Lost in 1845–46, pp. 360–2.

71. Boyd Hilton, *The Age of Atonement: The Influence of Evangelicism on Social and Economic Thought, 1785–1865* (Oxford, 1988); P.H. Gray, 'British Politics and the Irish Land Question, 1843–1850', unpublished PhD thesis (University of Cambridge, 1992).

72. For an example of contemporary providentialist writings, see Hugh McNeile, *The Famine a Rod of God; its Provoking Cause, its Merciful Design* (Liverpool, 1847).

73. Graham to Peel, 18 October 1845, Mahon, p. 125.

74. For example, these measures asked by Dublin, Cork, Belfast, Limerick and Londonderry corporations. Daniel O'Connell suggested that the embargo on exports should not be applied to England, for which he was criticised by radical nationalists.

75. *The Times*, 17 April 1846.

76. Kinealy, *This Great Calamity*, pp. 46–9.

77. *Instructions to Committees of Relief Districts, extracted from Minutes of the Proceedings of the Commissioners appointed in reference to the apprehended scarcity*, PP 1846 [171] xxxvii; Kinealy, *This Great Calamity*, pp. 41–6.

78. Routh to Trevelyan, 31 July 1846, *Correspondence Explanatory of the Measures adopted by Her Majesty's government for the relief of the distress arising from the failure of the Potato Crop in Ireland*, PP 1846 [736] xxxvii, p. 218.

79. Kinealy, *This Great Calamity*, pp. 43–4.

80. C. Trevelyan, 'Report on Public Works for the relief of scarcity in Ireland' in *Correspondence Explanatory*, 8 March 1846, p. 355.
81. A.R. Griffiths, 'The Irish Board of Works during the Famine Years', *Historical Journal*, vol. xiii, no. 4 (1970).
82. For more on this, see Christine Kinealy, 'The Poor Law During the Great Famine; An Administration in Crisis', in Crawford, pp. 157–75.
83. *Dublin Evening Post*, 6 June 1846.
84. Routh to Trevelyan, 31 July 1846, *Correspondence Explanatory*, p. 218.
85. Tickets issued by Pawnbrokers, PP Famine Volume (Dublin, 1985), vol. iv, pp. 406–7.
86. S.J. Connolly, 'The Great Famine and Irish Politics', in Póirtéir, pp. 36–9.

4 Putrefying Vegetation and 'Queen's Pay'

1. P.M. Austin-Bourke, *Visitation of God? The Potato and the Great Irish Famine* (Dublin, 1993) p. 174.
2. Ibid.
3. Mary Daly, 'The Leaf that Launched a Thousand Ships' in *Natural History* (January 1995) p. 29.
4. Father Mathew to Trevelyan, 7 August 1847, quoted in Charles Trevelyan, *The Irish Crisis* (London, 1848).
5. *The Nation*, 19 September 1846.
6. *The [Belfast] Vindicator*, 31 October 1846.
7. The divisions between the traditional aristocratic 'Foxite' Whigs and the liberal free trade radicals is explored in Peter Mandler, *Aristocratic Government in the Age of Reform; Whigs and Liberals 1830–52* (Oxford, 1990).
8. F.D. Munsell, 'Charles Trevelyan and Peelite Irish Famine Policy, 1845–46', *Societas. A Review of Social History*, (1971) pp. 299–315.
9. Labouchere, Dublin Castle to Russell, Russell Papers, 2 January 1847.
10. Robert Peel to Russell, Russell Papers, PROL 30 22 5A, 27 June 1846; for examples of correspondence between Clarendon and Peel, see Parker, *Peel*, pp. 514–18.
11. Quoted in J. O'Rourke, *The History of the Great Irish Famine of 1847 with Notices of earlier Irish Famines* (Dublin, 1902, 3rd edn), p. 149.
12. Donal Kerr, *A Nation of Beggars?* (Oxford, 1994) argues that Russell was concerned to introduce a 'golden age' to Ireland, but owing to a variety of circumstances was never able to achieve this.
13. O'Connell to Russell, Public Record Office, London, Russell Papers, 30 22 5B, 12 August 1846.
14. Ibid., Russell to O'Connell, 14 August 1846.
15. *The Tablet*, 2 January 1847.
16. S.J. Connolly, 'The Great Famine and Irish Politics' in Cathal Póirtéir, *The Great Irish Famine* (Cork, 1995) p. 42.
17. A. Bannerman to Russell, PROL, Russell Papers, 30 22 5B, 25 July 1846.
18. Clarendon to Russell, Clarendon Letter Books, Bodleian Library, 1 July 1847, 17 July 1847.

19. Poulett Scrope to Russell, Russell Papers, 30 22 5A, 23 June 1847.
20. Ibid., Russell to Clarendon, 29 June 1847.
21. Russell to Clarendon, Clarendon Papers, Bodleian Library, 2 August 1847.
22. Clarendon to Russell, Clarendon Papers,10 August 1847.
23. Russell to Clarendon, 24 February 1849, quoted in Mandler, p. 252.
24. Since 1843, Poor Law taxation had made landlords whose estates were subdivided responsible for paying a larger share of taxes.
25. *Fourteenth Annual Report of the Board of Public Works* (London, 1846) 9 December 1846.
26. Trevelyan, *Irish Crisis*, (London, 1848) *passim*.
27. William Henry Smith, *A Twelve Months' Residence in Ireland during the Famine and the Public Works, 1846 and 1847, with suggestions to meet the coming crisis* (London, 1848) pp. 51–2.
28. *Fifteenth Annual Report of Board of Public Works* (London, 1847).
29. Smith, pp. 55–6.
30. *The Tablet*, 2 January 1847; Smith, p. 67.
31. Smith, p. 62.
32. Report from Father John Aylward in Clough who asked government to send £1000 to area as public works inadequate, *The Tablet*, 2 January 1847.
33. J.A. Flood, 'The Forster Family and the Irish Famine', *Quaker History*, vol. 84 (Fall 1995) no. 2, p.122.
34. *The Nation*, 7 November 1846.
35. *The Tablet*, 2 January 1847.
36. Smith, pp. 59–60.
37. Christine Kinealy, *This Great Calamity, The Irish Famine 1845–52* (Dublin, 1994), p. 96
38. Cathʼl Póirtéir, *Famine Echoes. A Folk History of the Great Irish Famine* (Dublin, 1995) pp. 163–5.
39. For more on regional variations, see Christine Kinealy, 'Analysis of the Variation of Employment on the Public Works in 1846', in *This Great Calamity*, pp. 363–5.
40. *The Nation*, 27 March 1847.
41. In a number of areas, however, the public works did create a network of roads, some of which are still used today, for example in west Cork. I am grateful to Patrick Hickey for drawing my attention to this point.
42. *Illustrated London News*, 30 January 1847.
43. Póirtéir, pp. 159–61.
44. *Annual Report of Board of Works*, 1847.
45. Ó Gráda, p. 112.
46. *Account of the Number of Cattle exported from Ireland to Great Britain from 1846–49*, 1850, 423, lii.
47. *The Times*, December 1846–February 1847.
48. Isaac Butt, *A Voice for Ireland. The Famine in the Land* (Dublin, 1847).
49. *The Times*, 12 March 1847. Death from starvation was less common than death from famine-related diseases.
50. Austin-Bourke, p. 168.
51. The Bills of Entry have survived and contain information on the cargo of individual ships entered the main ports. I am very grateful to Hugh

Flinn for providing finance for research to be undertaken in this important yet underused source.

52. *Herald* (New York) 5 July 1847.
53. Bills of Entry for Liverpool for 1847, Merseyside Maritime Museum Archive.
54. Kinealy, *This Great Calamity*, pp. 65–7.
55. Póirtéir, pp. 59, 84.
56. Ibid., pp. 85–99.
57. Stephen Campbell, *The Great Irish Famine. Words and Images from the Famine Museum Strokestown park, County Roscommon* (Roscommon, 1994) pp. 46–8.
58. *The Tablet*, 2 January 1847; Póirtéir, p. 77.
59. Póirtéir, p. 71.
60. *Report of the Society of Friends on Distress in Ireland*, National Library of Ireland, Ms. Ir. 9410859.
61. Trevelyan to Routh, Chief Secretary's Office Papers, national Archives, Dublin, 0.1957, 12 January 1847.
62. Bessborough, Dublin Castle to Russell, Russell Papers, 30 22 16A, 23 January 1847.
63. Ibid.
64. Clarendon to Russell, Clarendon Papers, Bodleian Library, Book 1, 12 July 1847.
65. Charles Nelson, *The Role of the Botanic Gardens* (Dublin, 1995) pp. 3 1; M. Dergman, 'The Potato Blight in the Netherlands 1845–47', *International Review of Social History*, 1967, vol. 1 part 3, p. 429.
66. Austin-Bourke, p. 141.
67. Cabinet Memorandum, 1 November 1845, *Peel's Memoirs*, pp. 145–6.
68. *Northern Whig*, 27 September 1845.
69. Lord-Lieutenant to Peel, 20 October 1845, *Peel's Memoirs*, p. 129; ibid., Lord-Lieutenant to Peel, 8 November 1845, pp.169–70; ibid., extract from meeting presided over by Duke of Leinster, asking for ports to be opened, 31 October 1845, p. 149.
70. Ibid., Peel to Sir James Graham, 22 October 1845, p. 131.
71. *Dublin Evening Post*, 8 November 1845.
72. W. Torrens, *The Life of Sir James Graham*, vol. 2 (London, 1863) pp. 413–14; Parker, *Peel*, pp. 533, 534.
73. Austin-Bourke, p. 145.
74. Roger Price, 'Poor Relief and Social Crisis in Mid-Nineteenth France', *European Studies Review* (October 1983) p. 440.
75. Nelson, p. 419.
76. Ibid., pp. 391–2.
77. Ibid., p. 392.
78. Ibid., pp. 395–7.
79. Ibid., pp. 399–400.
80. Ibid., p. 413.
81. Ibid., pp. 414–16.
82. M. Anderson, *Population Change in Western Europe, 1750–1850* (London, 1989).
83. Price, pp. 440–5.

84. Ibid., pp. 436–7.
85. Ibid., p. 441.
86. Ibid., pp. 439–40.
87. Ibid., p. 447.
88. T. M. Devine, *The Great Highland Famine. Hunger, Emigration and the Scottish Highlands in the Nineteenth Century* (Edinburgh, 1988) p. v.
89. Ibid., pp. 34–5.
90. D.E. Gladstone, 'The Reform and Administration of Relief in Scotland, 1790–1850, with special reference to Stirlingshire', unpublished M Litt dissertation (University of Stirlingshire, 1973).
91. Routh to Trevelyan, 29 October 1846, *Correspondence Explanatory of the Measures Undertaken by Her Majesty's Government for the relief of Distress arising from the Failure of the Potato Crop in Ireland*, 1846 [735] xxxvii, p. 207.
92. Devine, pp. 101–2.
93. Quoted ibid., p. 84.
94. Ibid., p.91.
95. Ibid., p. 94.
96. Ibid., p. 39.
97. Ibid., p. 44.

5 'Black '47'

1. *Freeman's Journal*, 1 January 1847.
2. Laurence Geary, 'Epidemic Diseases of the Great Famine', *History Ireland*, vol. 4, no. 1 (Spring 1996) pp. 27–30.
3. Recollection of Richard Delaney, Wexford, in Cathal Póirtéir, *Famine Echoes*, (Dublin, 1995) p. 102.
4. Editorial in *Roscommon Gazette*, reported in *Banner of Ulster*, 12 January 1847.
5. *Freeman's Journal*, 1 January 1847.
6. Lord Dufferin and the Hon. G. F. Boyle, *Narrative of a Journey from Oxford to Skibbereen during the Year of the Irish Famine* (first published Oxford, 1847; reprinted Cork, 1996), p. 21.
7. *The [Belfast] Vindicator*, 20 January 1847.
8. *Freeman's Journal*, 1 January 1847.
9. *The Times*, 6 March 1847.
10. These figures are based on estimates as official eviction data were not kept until 1849. For more see James Donnelly, 'Landlords and Tenants', in W.E. Vaughan (ed.), *A New History of Ireland* (Oxford, 1989) pp. 13–26.
11. Christine Kinealy, 'The Poor Law during the Great Famine: An Administration in Crisis' in E. Margaret Crawford (ed.), *Famine: The Irish Experience 900–1900* (Edinburgh, 1989) pp. 157–75.
12. For more on the workings of the Poor Law, see Christine Kinealy, *This Great Calamity. The Irish Famine 1845–52* (Dublin, 1994) pp. 106–35.
13. Patrick Hickey, 'The Famine in the Skibbereen Union' in Cathal Póirtéir, *The Great Irish Famine* (Cork, 1995), pp. 187–9.

14. The average time lapse between public works being asked for and receiving Treasury sanction was 6–8 weeks. *Return of Number and Description of Works applied for, recommended and sanctioned in each District of Ireland in the year 1846*, PP 1847 (764) 1.
15. Quoted in Hickey, 'The Famine in Skibbereen', p. 187.
16. Ibid., pp. 188–9.
17. Ibid., p. 188.
18. *The Times*, 7 January 1847.
19. Dufferin and Boyle, 1 March 1847, p. 5.
20. *Banner of Ulster*, 12 January 1847.
21. *Banner of Ulster*, 5 February 1847.
22. Gerard MacAtasney, 'The Famine in North Armagh', in T. Parkhill and C. Kinealy (eds), *The Famine in Ulster* (Belfast, 1996).
23. *Northern Whig*, 12 January 1847; Kinealy, *This Great Calamity*, pp. 87–8.
24. Quoted in Gerard MacAtasney, 'Challenging an Orthodoxy: The Famine in Lurgan 1845–47', unpublished. MA thesis (Queen's University, Belfast 1995) p. 40.
25. *Londonderry Sentinel*, 6 February 1847.
26. For more on this debate, see T. McCavery, 'The Famine in County Down', in T. Parkhill and C. Kinealy (eds), *The Great Famine in Ulster* (Belfast, 1996).
27. Diary of Elizabeth Smith, 12 January 1847 in David Thomson with Moyra McGusty (eds), *The Irish Journals of Elizabeth Smith 1840–1850* (Oxford 1980) p. 113.
28. Ibid., pp. 113, 125.
29. Treasury to Relief Commissioners, 10 February 1847, Chief Secretary's Office, Registered Papers (National Archives, Dublin).
30. 10 & 11 Vic. c. 67. , 26 February 1847.
31. Queen's Speech at the Opening of Parliament, 19 January 1847.
32. Patrick Hickey, 'Famine, Mortality and Emigration' in P. O'Flanagan and C.G. Buttimore (eds), *Cork. History and Society* (Dublin, 1993) p. 879.
33. Poor Law Commissioners to George Grey, Home Secretary, forwarding correspondence on the subject of soup kitchens, Public Record Office (London) HO 45, 1706, December 1846.
34. Helen Morris, *Portrait of a Chef: the Life of Alexis Soyer* (Cambridge, 1938).
35. Alexis Soyer, *Charitable Cookery, or the Poor Man's Regenerator* (Dublin, 1847), this publication begins with an 'Address to the World in General, but to Ireland in Particular'.
36. Morris, p. 76.
37. The Lord Lieutenant, Lord Bessborough, was too ill to leave his carriage, but Soyer personally took his soup to the carriage to be consumed there.
38. *Dublin Evening Mail*, 7 April 1847.
39. Ibid.
40. Morris, pp. 78–9.
41. Ibid., p. 79.
42. *Roscommon and Leitrim Gazette*, 17 April 1847.

43. *Reports of the Temporary Relief Commissioners.*
44. Letter from Relief Commissioner to local Relief committees, 27 March 1847, quoted in *Dublin Evening Mail*, 5 April 1847 and *Roscommon and Leitrim Gazette*, 3 April 1847.
45. *The Times*, 24 March 1847.
46. *Roscommon and Leitrim Gazette*, 27 March 1847.
47. Treasury Minute, 10 March 1847, *First Report of the Relief Commissioners*, p. 36.
48. Galway Guardians to central Relief Commissioners, Public Record Office, London, HO 45 1942, 1 June 1847.
49. *Fourth Report of the Relief Commissioners*, PP 1847 [859] xvii, 19 July 1847.
50. Circular to the Inspecting Officers of each Union, 11 May 1847, *Appendix to Second Report of the Relief Commissioners*, PP [819] xvii, p. 18.
51. 'Rules and Regulations for Finance Committees under the Act 10 Vic. cap. 7, 10 March 1847, *Appendix to the First Report of the Relief Commissioners*, PP 1847 [799] xvii, p. 14.
52. Ibid., 'Regulations for the Relief Committees under the Act 10 Vic. cap. 7., 8 March 1847, p. 24.
53. Report of Board of Health to the Relief Commissioners, 10 March 1847, *Second Report of the Relief Commissioners*, pp. 6–7; ibid., 11 May 1847, p. 19.
54. Board of Health to Relief Commissioners, 21 June 1847, *Fourth Report of Relief Commissioners*, PP 1847 [859] xvii, p. 18.
55. *Roscommon and Leitrim Gazette*, 10 July 1847.
56. *Clare Journal*, 20 May 1847; *Roscommon and Leitrim Gazette*, 22 May 1847, 29 May 1847, 3 July 1847.
57. Ibid., 29 May 1847, 19 June 1847.
58. Appendix to First Report of Relief Commissioners, pp. 12–16.
59. *Roscommon and Leitrim Gazette*, 22 May 1847.
60. Based on numbers receiving relief from soup kitchens provided in Second, Third, Fourth, Fifth, Sixth and Seventh Reports of the Relief Commissioners. The population figures upon which these calculations were made were taken from the 1841 Census figures, which may be an underestimation.
61. For more on the regional diversity, see Kinealy, *This Great Calamity*, Appendix Three, pp. 366–71. Although few government soup kitchens were opened in the north-east of Ireland, some privately financed soup kitchens were opened.
62. Kinealy, *This Great Calamity*, pp. 126–9.
63. An Account of the Receipt and Expenditure of Monies Voted for the Relief of Distress in Ireland, 31 December 1847, *Supplementary Appendix to the Seventh Report of the Relief Commissioners*, PP 1847–48 [956] xxix, pp. 16–17.
64. Treasury Minute, 14 September 1847, *Seventh Report of the Relief Commissioners*, PP 1847–48 [876] xxix, p. 42.
65. *The Times*, 23 March 1847; *Dublin Evening Mail*, 5 April 1847.
66. Rules and Regulations for the Finance Committees, 10 March 1847, *First Report of the Relief Commissioners*, p. 14.

67. Circular to the Inspecting Officers of each Union, 15 July 1847, *Fourth Report of the Relief Commissioners*, p. 21.
68. Returns of mortality are rare, but a valuable exception is 'Marshall's return' for the Skibbereen area, quoted in Hickey, 'Famine, Mortality and Emigration', p. 881; see also, Appendix to Seventh report of Relief Commissioners, p. 11.
69. *Roscommon and Leitrim Gazette*, 12 June 1847.
70. *Dublin Evening Mail*, 7 April 1847.
71. Ibid., 9 April 1847.
72. For more on this, see Christine Kinealy, 'Potatoes, Providence and Philanthropy. The Role of Private Charity during the Famine', in Patrick O'Sullivan *The Meaning of the Famine* (Leicester, 1996). All amounts given relate to the value in the 1840s. To obtain a rough current equivalent, multiply the amounts by 50.
73. Letter by Home Secretary, reprinted in *The Tablet* 2 January 1847.
74. Trevelyan, pp. 84–8.
75. H.A. Crosby Forbes and Henry Lee, *Massachusetts Help to Ireland During the Great Famine* (Massachusetts, 1967).
76. Ibid., p. 3.
77. Gerard MacAtasney, 'Challenging an Orthodoxy: The Famine in Lurgan', unpublished. MA dissertation (Queen's University, Belfast, 1995) p. 40.
78. Quoted in Campbell, p. 206.
79. *Report of the Proceedings of the General Central Relief Committee for all Ireland.* (Dublin, 1848).
80. Ibid., p. 11.
81. Ibid., p. 7.
82. Minutes of British Relief Association, National Library of Ireland.
83. *Dictionary of National Biography*.
84. Memorandum by Lord John Russell, T.64/ 367 B (PROL) 30 April 1848, in which he stated that his government would continue to feed the schoolchildren.
85. Rob Goodbody, *A Suitable Channel. Quaker Relief in the Great Famine* (Dublin, 1995) p. 21.
86. Ibid., pp. 10–16.
87. James H. Tuke, *A Visit to Connaught in the Summer of 1847* (London, 1847).
88. Central Relief Committee of the Society of Friends, *Transactions of the Central Relief Committee of the Society of Friends during the Famine in Ireland in 1846 and 1847* (Dublin, 1852) Appendices.
89. Quoted in Jeanne A. Flood 'The Forster Family and the Irish Famine' in *Quaker History* vol. 84, No. 2 (Fall 1995) p. 120.
90. *Charleston Courier*, 8 February 1847, 11 February 1847.
91. Goodbody, p. 24.
92. James H. Tuke, *Report of Society of Friends on Distress in Ireland* (1847). Copy in National Library, Ireland.
93. Trevelyan to J. Pim, PROL T.64. 367. B/2 24 August 1848; Trevelyan to Pim, 2 June 1849, *Transactions*, p.452; ibid., Pim to Trevelyan, 5 June 1849, pp. 452–4.

94. Unpublished paper by Hugh Barbour, *Quakers and the Irish Famine*; Goodbody, p. 78.

95. John Francis Maguire, *Pontificate of Pius the Ninth* (London, 1870) pp. 45-6.

96. Donal A. Kerr, *A Nation of Beggars? Priests, People and Politics in Famine Ireland 1846-52* (Oxford, 1994) pp. 52–3.

97. This is apparent from the papers of Archbishop Murray of Dublin, through whom most of the donations were channelled, in the Dublin Diocesan Archive.

98. *The Tablet*, 2 January 1847; 9 January 1847, etc.

99. Kinealy, *This Great Calamity*, pp. 207–8.

100. *New York and the Irish Famine* (New York History Roundtable) (New York, 1994).

101. For more on these individual donations, see Kinealy *Potatoes, Providence, Philanthropy*.

102. *Arkansas Intelligencer*, 8 May 1847.

103. Ibid.

104. Cabinet Memorandum, 1 November 1845, Mahon, *Memoirs*, p. 145.

105. See Kinealy, *Potatoes, Providence and Philanthropy*.

106. *Freeman's Journal*, 2 July 1847.

107. Ibid.

108. *Royal Irish Art Union Monthly Journal*, 1 May 1847.

109. For more on Belfast during the Famine, see Kinealy, *This Great Calamity*, pp. 126–30, 165–7.

110. *Massachusetts Help to Ireland*, p. xxi.

111. Ibid., p. 9.

112. A vociferous critic of the British government was the Bishop of New York, John Hughes, who gave a lecture on the 'Antecedent Causes of the Irish Famine' in 1847, and in which he stated that 'bad government' was a major contributor (his complete text was published by Edward Dunigan in 1847 and is available in New York Public Library).

113. Quoted in *New York and the Irish Famine*, New York Roundtable, p. xxi.

114. *Arkansas Intelligencer*, 29 May 1847.

115. Speech at meeting in New Orleans by S. Prentiss reported in *Arkansas Gazette*, 20 February 1847.

116. *Arkansas Intelligencer*, 20 March 1847.

117. Ibid.

118. *Charleston Courier*, 8 February 1847.

119. Address to People by General Irish Relief Committee of New York, 12 February 1847.

120. *National Intelligencer*, 11 February 1847.

121. *Charleston Courier*, 17 February 1847, 2 April 1847.

122. *Cork Examiner*, 16 April 1847.

123. *Liverpool Mercury* , 10 April 1847.

124. *Massachusetts Help*, p. 49.

125. Ibid., p. 46.

126. *Cork Examiner*, 16 April 1847.

127. *Cork Advertiser*, 15 April 1847.

128. *Massachusetts Help*, pp. 51–3.

6 'The Expatriation of a People'

1. H.E. Maxwell, *The Life and Letters of George William Frederick, Fourth Earl of Clarendon*, 2 vols (London, 1913).
2. Clarendon to Henry Reeve, Clarendon Papers, Bodleian Library, 5 January 1847.
3. Clarendon to Russell, Irish Letterbooks, Bodleian Library, 8 August 1847.
3. Ibid., Clarendon to Russell, 5 July 1847.
5. Ibid., Clarendon to Wood, 12 July 1847.
6. Ibid., Clarendon to Wood, 15 July 1847.
7. Ibid., Clarendon to Wood, 2 August 1847.
8. Ibid., Clarendon to Wood, 21 July 1847.
9. *The Times*, 8 March 1847, 9 March 1847.
10. *The Times*, 12 October 1847.
11. Ibid.
12. An Act to make Further Provision for the Relief of the Destitute Poor in Ireland, 10 Vic, cap. 31 (8 June 1847).
13. Trevelyan to Wood, Hickleton Papers, 28 July 1847.
14. Twistleton to Trevelyan, Treasury Papers, (PROL) T. 64 369 B/1, 14 December 1847.
15. Wood to Clarendon, Hickleton Papers, 23 July 1847.
16. Ibid., Twistleton to Trevelyan, T.64 370 C/4, 27 February 1848.
17. Quoted in Canon John O'Rourke, *The Great Irish Famine*, (first published 1874; reprinted Dublin, 1989) p. 171.
18. Memorial by Lord Palmerston to Russell, 20 May 1848, in G.P. Gooch (ed.), *The Later Correspondence of Lord John Russell 1840–78* (London, 1925) p. 225.
19. Christine Kinealy, *This Great Calamity. The Irish Famine 1845–52* (Dublin, 1994) pp. 220–1.
20. O'Rourke, p. 171.
21. Ibid., pp. 222–7; *Copies of Correspondence upon which the Commissioners of the Poor Laws in Ireland took Legal Advice as to the Construction of the tenth Section of the Act 10 Vic. cap. 31; and of the Case submitted to them by Counsel; and of the Circular Letter of the Commissioners Issued Thereon*, PP 1847–48, liii, 519.
22. *The Tablet*, 1 January 1847.
23. For more on this see Kinealy, *This Great Calamity*, pp. 332–41.
24. Notice of Cardiff Guardians, Home Office Papers, (PROL) HO 100 257, 2 June 1849.
25. Sir James Graham to Lord Lieutenant, (PROL) HO 45 1080, box 1, 7 May 1846.
26. George Nicholls, *A History of the Irish Poor Law* (London, 1856) p. 357.
27. Trevelyan to Father Mathew, 14 August 1847, quoted in Cecil Woodham-Smith, *The Great Hunger* (New York, 1962) p. 303.
28. Christine Kinealy, 'The Role of the Poor Law during the Famine' in Cathal Póirtéir (ed.), *The Great Irish Famine* (Cork, 1994) p. 115.
29. Ibid., James S. Donnelly Jr, 'Mass Evictions and the Great Famine', p. 155.

30. Kinealy, *This Great Calamity*, p. 218.
31. Trevelyan to Twistleton, PROL, T.64. 370.B/1, 14 September 1848.
32. Quoted in Donnelly, p. 158.
33. W.S. Trench, *Realities of Irish Life* (London, 1868) pp. 56–72.
34. James S. Donnelly Jr, 'The Great Famine: its interpreters old and new', *History Ireland* (Autumn, 1993) pp. 27–33.
35. Stephen J. Campbell, *The Great Irish Famine. Words and Images from the Famine Museum, Strokestown Park, County Roscommon,* (Roscommon, 1994) pp. 40–1. Major Mahon also arranged for the emigration of his tenants. O'Rourke, p. 288.
36. James Hack Tuke, *A Visit to Connaught in the autumn of 1847; a letter addressed to the Central Relief Committee of the Society of Friends* (Dublin, 1847) pp. 24–6.
37. Ibid., p. 26.
38. Clarendon to George Grey, Clarendon Letter-Books, 3 July 1848.
39. *Hansard*, xcvii, cols 1007–9.
40. Russell to Clarendon, 15 November 1847, Maxwell, *Life and Letters of Fourth Earl of Clarendon*, p. 282.
41. *First Annual Report of Poor Law Commissioners for Ireland, 1849* (Dublin, 1849).
42. Kinealy, *This Great Calamity*, pp. 210–16.
43. *Second Annual Report of Poor Law Commissioners for Ireland for 1849* (Dublin, 1849).
44. Clarendon to Charles Wood, Clarendon Letter-Books, 15 July 1847.
45. The Vice-Guardians of Ballinrobe Union to the Commissioners, 13 December 1847, *State of Unions and Workhouses in Ireland, Fifth Series, 1848*, PP 1848, 919, p. 364.
46. Ibid., Captain Ommanney to Poor Law Commissioners, 4 January 1848, p. 520.
47. Ibid., the Knight of Kerry to Lieutenant-Colonel Clarke, 15 December 1847, p. 577.
48. Wood to Russell, Russell Papers (PROL) 2 May 1848.
49. Clarendon to Wood, Hickleton Papers, 21 July 1847.
50. Clarendon to Russell, Irish Letter-Books, 23 October 1847.
51. Twistleton to Tevelyan (PROL) T. 64. 366.A, 13 September1848, 15 November 1848, 21 January 1849.
52. Ibid., Twistleton to Trevelyan, 21 January 1849.
53. L. Curtin, *Apes and Angels: The Irishmen in Victorian Caricature* (Newton Abbot, 1971).
54. Margaret Crawford, 'The Great Irish Famine 1845–49: Image versus Reality', in Raymond Gillespie and Brian P. Kennedy (eds), *Ireland. Art into History* (Dublin, 1994) pp. 75–88.
55. See, for example, various correspondence in *The Times*, 15 October 1847, 19 October 1847, 20 October 1847.
56. *The Times*, 11 December 1847; *Hansard*, xcv, cols 675–84.
57. Peter Gray, '*Punch* and the Great Famine', *History Ireland* (Summer 1993) pp. 26–33.
58. *The Times*, 5 January 1847.

59. *The Tablet*, 2 January 1847.
60. *Nonconformist*, 13 January 1847.
61. *The Times*, 22 September 1847.
62. From *The Times*, quoted in *Freeman's Journal*, 4 January 1847.
63. J, Wolffe, *The Protestant Crusade in Great Britain* (Oxford, 1991) p. 174.
64. Eric Evans, 'Englishness and Britishness: National Identities, c.1790-1870', in Alexander Grant and Keith J. Stringer (eds), *Uniting the Kingdom? The Making of British History* (London, 1995) p. 237.
65. *Protestant Watchman*, 12 May 1848, quoted in John Killen, *The Famine Decade. Contemporary Accounts, 1841–1851* (Belfast, 1995) pp. 188–90.
66. *The Times* quoted in the *Northern Whig*, 15 February 1849.
67. *The Times*, 8 February 1849.

7   'A Policy of Extermination'

1. W. Bourke, Ballina Union, Russell Papers (PROL) 19 August 1848; ibid., Captain Hastings, Scariff, 19 August 1848.
2. Clarendon to Russell, Clarendon Letter-Books, 15 August 1848.
3. Poor Law Commissioners to Trevelyan, Chief Secretary's office, Registered Papers (NAD) 0.6624, 8 July 1848; Treasury to Poor Law Commissioners, Treasury Outletters, T. 64, 2414, 31 January 1849, 10 March 1849.
4. Twistleton to Trevelyan, T. 64. 367. B., 12 July 1848.
5. Monteagle to Clarendon, Monteagle Papers (NLI) 9 April 1849.
6. *Third Annual Report of Poor Law Commissioners*, 1850.
7. *The Times*, 21 June 1849.
8. Ibid.
9. Ibid.
10. *The Times*, 8 June 1849.
11. Resolutions of Committee of British Relief Association, 26 August 1847, *Papers relating to proceedings for Relief of Distress and state of Unions and Workhouses in Ireland*, 1847–48, 896, liv, pp. 2–3.
12. Memorandum by Lord John Russell, T.64. 367. B, 30 April 1848.
13. Private Report by Trevelyan, T.64.366. A. March 1849.
14. Ibid.
15. *Second and Third Annual Reports of Poor Law Commissioners*, 1849, 1850.
16. Clarendon to George Grey, Irish Letter-Books, 7 December 1847.
17. Clarendon to Trevelyan, Treasury Papers, T. 64/366 A., 27 December 1848.
18. Clarendon to Duke of Bedford, Clarendon Papers, 16 February 1849.
19. Clarendon to Russell, Irish Letter-Books, 12 February 1848.
20. Clarendon to Russell, Irish Letter-Books, 28 April 1849.
21. Christine Kinealy, *This Great Calamity. The Irish Famine 1845–52* (Dublin, 1994) pp. 250–4.
22. Poor Law Commissioner to Home Office, 30 April 1849, *Further papers relating to the Aid afforded to the Distressed Unions in the west of Ireland*, 1849, xlviii, p. 4.

23. *The Times*, 12 May 1849.
24. Ibid.
25. Cecil Woodham-Smith, *The Great Hunger* (New York, 1962) pp. 382–3.
26. Jonathan Pim to Trevelyan, 5 June 1849, *Transactions of the Society of Friends* (Dublin, 1852) pp. 452–4.
27. Lord Lansdowne to Russell, 9 August 1849, G.P. Gooch, (ed.), *The Later Correspondence of Lord John Russell 1840–1878* (London, 1925) p. 235.
28. Victoria to King Leopold, 9 August 1849, Arthur Christopher Benson and Viscount Escher (eds), *Letters of Queen Victoria: A Selection from Her Correspondence between the years 1837 and 1861* (London, 1907) vol. 2, p. 111.
29. Queen Victoria's Journal, 8 August 1849, quoted in Elizabeth Longford, *Victoria R.I.* (London, 1964) p. 191.
30. Quoted in Donal Kerr, *A Nation of Beggars?* (Oxford, 1994) p. 203.
31. Ibid.
32. Ibid.
33. I am grateful to the late eminent historian, T.P. O'Neill, for drawing my attention to this ditty.
34. Kerr, pp. 198–9.
35. Captain Kennedy to Poor Law Commissioners, 13 April 1848, *Copies of Correspondence between the Poor Law Commissioners of Ireland and their Inspector, relative to the statements contained in an extract from a book, entitles 'Gleanings from the west of Ireland* (1851), 218, xliv, p. 6.
36. *Report of Select Committee appointed to inquire into the administration of the Poor Law in the Kilrush union since 19 September 1848* 1850 [613] xi, p. xii.
37. Clarendon to Monteagle, Monteagle Papers (National Library of Ireland) 20 February 1849.
38. *Banner of Ulster*, 10 May 1849.
39. *Downpatrick Recorder*, 14 April 1849.
40. *Report of the Select Committee on the Poor Laws, Ireland, with minutes of evidence*, 1849 (403), xv, p. 3.
41. J. Grant, 'The Great Famine and the Poor Law in Ulster: The Rate-in-Aid Issue of 1849', *Irish Historical Studies* (1970), pp. 634–52.
42. *Newry Telegraph*, 6 March 1849, quoted in Gerard MacAtasney, 'The Famine in North Armagh' in T. Parkhill and C. Kinealy (eds), *The Famine in Ulster* (Belfast, 1996).
43. Evidence of Edward Senior, *Select Committee on Irish Poor Law*, 1849, xv, pp. 103–4.
44. *Hansard's Parliamentary Debates*, col. 62, 1 March 1849.
45. *Northern Whig*, 15 February 1849, 22 February 1849, 6 March 1849.
46. *Banner of Ulster*, 22 May 1849.
47. *Hansard's Parliamentary Debates*, cols 48–50, 1 March 1849.
48. *Banner of Ulster*, 10 May 1849.
49. Ibid., 1 June 1849.

50. G.P. Gooch (ed.), *The Later Correspondence of Lord John Russell 1840–78* (London, 1925) pp. 230–5.
51. For more on this, see Christine Kinealy, 'The Role of the Poor Law during the Famine' in Cathal Póirtéir, *The Great Irish Famine*, (Cork, 1995) p. 120.
52. Return of Accounts, *Rate-in-Aid (Ireland)*, 1852, xlvi, pp. 128–31.
53. Clarendon to Duke of Bedford, Clarendon Papers, 29 March 1849.
54. George Nicholls, *A History of the Irish Poor Law* (London, 1856) pp. 356–9.
55. Treasury Minute, 16 January 1849, *Papers relating to the Aid afforded to the Distressed Unions in the west of Ireland*, 1849, xlviii, pp. 3–4.
56. Poor Law Commissioners to Trevelyan, 7 March 1849, *Further Papers relating to the Aid afforded to the Distressed Unions in the west of Ireland*, xiviii, p. 14.
57. Evidence of Edward Twistleton, *Select Committee on the Irish Poor Law*, 1849, xvi, pp. 699–714.
58. Ibid., p. 717.
59. Clarendon to Russell, Clarendon Letterbooks, Bodleian Library, 12 March 1849.
60. David Fitzpatrick, 'Flight from Famine' in Póirtéir, pp. 175–6.
61. Kinealy, *This Great Calamity*, pp. 323–7.
62. Clarendon to George Lewis (Home Office), Clarendon Papers, 31 October 1851.
63. Kerby A. Miller, *Emigrants and Exiles: Ireland and the Irish Exodus to North America* (New York, 1985).
64. *The Times*, 5 January 1847.
65. *Liverpool Mail*, 6 November 1847.
66. *Liverpool Mercury*, 1 August 1848.
67. Trevelyan to Twistleton, T. 64. 370. B/1, 14 September 1848.
68. Quoted in Kerr, p. 297.
69. Cormac Ó'Gráda, *Ireland. Before and After the Famine* (Manchester, 1993) pp. 106–8.
70. Quoted in ibid., p. 104.
71. This accusation was made by Archbishop MacHale, amongst others, in *Freeman's Journal*, 8 August 1846.

Epilogue. 'The Famine Killed Everything'

1. The impact of the Famine on Irish society has been a matter of intensive debate, a number of historians seeing it as a watershed, others seeing post-Famine changes as a continuation of trends already evident in society. Examples of historians who favour the former interpretation include Joel Mokyr, *Why Ireland Starved: A Quantitative and Analytical History of the Irish Economy 1800–50* (London, 1983); Kevin O'Rourke, 'Did the Great Irish Famine Matter?' *The Journal of Economic History*, vol. li (March 1991); Christine Kinealy, *This Great Calamity. The Irish Famine 1845–52* (Dublin, 1994); historians sympathetic to the latter view include Raymond Crotty, *Irish Agricultural Production: Its Volume and Structure* (Cork, 1966); Mary E. Daly, *The Famine in Ireland* (Dundalk,

1986); Roy Foster, *Modern Ireland 1600–1972* (Harmondsworth, 1988).

2. There was geographical variation in the age of marriage after the Famine, with marriages in Connaught still taking place at an earlier age than in the rest of the country.

3. David W. Miller, 'Irish Catholicism and the Great Famine', *Journal of Social History*, ix (1975) pp. 81–98.

4. For example, Mary Carberg, *The Farm by Lough Gur* (London, 1937).

5. David Fitzpatrick, *Irish Emigration, 1801–1921* (Dundalk, 1984).

6. J.S. Donnelly Jr, 'The agricultural depression of 1859–64', *Irish Economic and Social History*, vol. iii (1976).

7. Cormac Ó Gráda, *Ireland Before and After the Famine. Explorations in Economic History, 1800–1925* (Manchester, 1988) pp. 128–30.

8. Tim P. O'Neill, 'The Persistence of Famine in Ireland' in Cathal Póirtéir, *The Great Irish Famine* (Cork, 1995) pp. 204–18.

9. Conor Cruise O'Brien, *Parnell and His Party*, quoted in 'The Forster Family and the Irish Famine' *Quaker History*, vol. 84 (Fall 1995) p. 124.

10. From *The Newtownards Independent*, 13 July 1872, quoted in T. McCavery, 'The Famine in County Down', in T. Parkhill and C. Kinealy (eds), *The Famine in Ulster* (Belfast, 1996).

11. Recollections of Máire Ní Grianna, Rannafast, the Rosses, County Donegal. Quoted in S. Deane (ed.) *The Field Day Anthology of Irish Writing* (Derry, 1991) pp. 203-4.

Index

wages: in France, 87; for public
works, 9, 72, 73–4, 76; for
relief officials, 104–5, 128
Waterford, County, 60
weather: cause of crop failure,
42–3, 45; and spread of potato
blight, 52, 67; winter
(1846–47), 75, 85
Wellington, Duke of, 27, 58, 96
Westport Poor Law Union, 104,
122
Wexford, 24
Whately, Richard, Archbishop of
Dublin, 5, 39, 146
Whig administration (Russell),
65, 68; criticisms of, 76, 82–3,
88, 138, 145; declares Famine
over (1847), 4, 116, 122, 132,
135; funds for emergency relief,
63, 98–9, 149; public works
policy, 66–7, 71–6, 92–3, 98;
rejects trade intervention, 66,
71, 76–7, 78–9; relief in form
of loans, 66, 72, 98, 125, 140;
Temporary Relief Act (1847),
98–9, 100, 104, 105–6, see also
Parliament, Westminster; Poor
Law; Treasury;; Trevelyan, Sir
Charles
Whig Party: commitment to free
trade, 33, 57, 66, 77; divisions
within, 65, 67–8, 131, 167n;

Irish support for, 27, 55, 69, see
also Whig administration
(Russell)
Whiteboys secret society
(Munster), 35
Wilde, Sir William, 42
William III, King, 18
Williams, T. Desmond (ed.), The
Great Famine (1956), 10, 14,
156n
women, 75, 146, 153
Wood, Sir Charles, Chancellor of
Exchequer, 60, 69, 120, 122,
136; ideological influence of,
68, 71, 121, 138, 165n, see also
Trevelyan, Sir Charles
Woodham-Smith, Cecil, The
Great Hunger (1962), 5–6, 10,
12, 156n
wool, 20, 31, 32
workhouses: in Ireland, 38–9, 40,
47–8, 63; overcrowding in, 93,
94–5, 122, 128, see also Boards
of Guardians

Young, Arthur, 29
Young Ireland movement, 6, 70;
uprising (1848), 13, 28–9, 118,
129, 132

Index by Auriol Griffith-Jones